I'll Tell You a Tale

I'll Tell You a Tale

by J. Frank Dobie

Selected and Arranged by the Author
and Isabel Gaddis

ILLUSTRATIONS BY BEN CARLTON MEAD

UNIVERSITY OF TEXAS PRESS, AUSTIN

International Standard Book Number 0-292-73821-8
Library of Congress Catalog Card Number 81-50221
Copyright 1931 by the Southwest Press
Copyright 1934, 1947, 1949, 1950, 1951, 1952 by the Curtis Pub-
    lishing Company
Copyright 1928, 1930, 1931, 1935, 1936, 1938, 1939, 1941, 1947,
    1949, 1950, 1951, 1952, 1955, © 1960 by J. Frank Dobie
Printed in the United States of America

Fourth University of Texas Printing, 1989
Reprinted by arrangement with Little, Brown and Company, Inc.

Requests for permission to reproduce material from this work
should be sent to Permissions, University of Texas Press, Box
7819, Austin, Texas 78713-7819.

Thanks are due the following for permission to quote from
copyrighted material:
    J. B. Lippincott Company for lines from "The Admiral's Ghost"
from COLLECTED POEMS, VOL. II, by Alfred Noyes. Copy-
right 1913, 1941 by Alfred Noyes. Published by J. B. Lippincott
Company.
    Rinehart & Company, Inc., for seven lines from "Mountain
Whippoorwill" from BALLADS AND POEMS 1915–1930 by
Stephen Vincent Benét. Copyright renewed, 1959, by Rosemary
Carr Benét.

♾ The paper used in this publication meets the minimum
requirements of American National Standard for Information
Sciences—Permanence of Paper for Printed Library Materials,
ANSI Z39.48-1984.

To the memory of my cherished friend

ROY BEDICHEK

a whole man of just proportions; a rare liver, in soli-
tude as well as with genial companions; ample
natured and rich in the stores of his ample
mind; always understanding, whether
agreeing or not; always enlarging
both his own views and those
of others. In talk he
called forth all my
powers, made
me laugh,
live more abundantly,
love life with more reason.

The Author's Intrusion

Rereading Hazlitt, Herodotus, Chaucer, Shakespeare, Boswell, Montaigne, and certain other emitters of luminosity never palls. Now and then I have dipped — only dipped — into myself with pleasure, but pursuit of that pleasure is certain to sharpen awareness of words not precise or harmonious, of clogged phrases, of sentences to be remodeled, of transpositions that would strengthen grace, of subject matter by hunks that had better be excised, and of interesting, delightful, winged things in my head that belong to the written composition. I am so grounded in respect for the English language as used by noble writers for more than five hundred years that I have never been contemporaneous with more than four or five writers whom I admire. My contemporaries have lacked amplitude, wit, Johnsonian horse sense, play of mind, and other virtues common to predecessors still waiting to be enjoyed. Most modern American writing in the "best seller" lists is so loosely — often sloppily, ignorantly, hideously — composed that it has no appeal for a craftsman disciplined to lucidity and the logic of grammar, bred to a style "familiar but by no means vulgar," and harmonized from infancy with the rhythms of nature.

However all this may be, Isabel Gaddis undertook, with my blessings, to select narratives from a dozen or so books for this "Dobie anthology." When she was very young, and I was not very old, she read — maybe even studied — Life and Literature of the Southwest (and West) under me at the University of Texas. She comes from the land of thorns, drouths, fine years, Mexicans, cow people, and the tempo of shadows under hot suns that I come from. In composing this book, my business would merely be to approve or disapprove of the selections: to sing out to one tale, "Come hider, my luve, to me," to bellow forth to another, "Depart ye hence into everlasting darkness, or at least go back where I originally put you." How easily one book at least would be made!

When I began reading the typewritten extracts from my own books, I found myself approving of nearly everything selected. I reminded myself of Stevenson's confessing in a letter to a friend that *Treasure Island* "seems the very story for me, if only somebody else had written it." But the practiced writer I am did not take long to down such an easygoing reader. I set myself to exercising the "art of omission" and otherwise having fun in improving both prose and tale-telling. Also, I could not agree with myself any more than with Isabel Gaddis on what is absolutely the best to put in the collection. All we can be positive of is that we like what is here.

The absurdity of that often-repeated epithet "a born storyteller" came to me with fresh force. No able storyteller, I am positive, ever used the epithet. Imagine Paderewski speaking of a "born piano player"; imagine "born cabinetmaker" coming trippingly from the tongue of Thomas Sheraton, or "born historian" from Gibbon.

> As yet a child, nor yet a fool to fame,
> I lisped in numbers, for the numbers came,

but Alexander Pope would have been the last to call himself a "born poet." I cannot call myself a "born reviser," for revision does not come by instinct; despised by romanticists, it comes only through will and cultivation. After exercising will power for a time on the skill of revising, I came to enjoy it.

Thirty-seven years have passed since I began trailing down tellers of folk tales, personal narratives and traveling anecdotes. A considerable number of those I found could not write at all; all were conscious of craftsmanship in narrating. A craftsman in any craft is always trying to "make something," is always after effects.

Newspaper reporters not infrequently label me "folklorist." I am not a scientific folklorist at all, for after I have heard a tale, I do all I can to improve it. "Do not let your characters talk as they do talk in parlors but as they might talk." If the characters in an orally told tale do not talk effectively, the business of any writer who adopts this tale is to make them talk better — with more savor, more expressively of both themselves and the land to which they belong. "Alas, the art so long to learn." I had happy times in the original weaving of these tales. Now, at this unanticipated chance to revise what was supposed to be the final edition, I have had happy times trying to improve them in spots.

The tales are laid in the Southwest and in Mexico. Most of the characters belong in speech, tempo, and ways to those lands. I have never considered myself a strict regionalist, that is, a county-minded provincial. The fact that Hester of *The Scarlet Letter* belongs to Puritan New England does not make Hawthorne regional any more than *The Two Gentlemen of Verona* makes Shakespeare regional. The Lady Known as Lou, the Man Who Was, the Brothers Karamazov, the Merry Wives of Windsor, the Last of the Troubadours, the Second Mrs. Tanqueray, and all other imagined characters from Adam (also Adam Bede) to Zuleika Dobson that have their feet on the earth belong to a particular area of it. Some of my tale-tellers, it seems to me, have more character than the figures in the tales they tell have. It is hard for anybody who writes a narrative on a longhorn steer, a mustang of the open ranges, Sam Bass from Indiana, the Lost Adams Diggings, a rattlesnake named Bill, and other subjects common to the western half of the United States not to be disposed of by the pigeonholers as merely a manufacturer of "Westerns." Taking my stand on the tales in this collection, I refuse to be tagged as "Western" or as regional. Whether I am or am not an artist others can say; I think I am — with many defects. I know I have tried to be.

Nobody now could capture these tales. Bob Lemmons, who turned mustang; José Beltrán, the mavericker who saw the phantom maverick bull; merry Tom Gilroy, and the fiddler sleeping in the hay in his livery stable — these and many another who told tales are gone forever, along with longhorn mavericks, with mustangs, with livery stables and the whole world of which they were a part. I hunted eagerly for storytellers, and I heard them gladly. They were mostly old-timers and I was mostly young, but my inheritance and the transporting power of imagination made me contemporary with them. Walt Whitman said, "I was at the Alamo." Only in the Walt Whitman way was I at the monte table when the Marqués de Aguayo excused himself and some hours later came back from the ride of vengeance on his young Angela and her lover.

As I read the tales over, it is not from any historical point of view that I primarily value them. I value them because they are — certainly the best are — of imagination all compact. Millions of people in the United States — from the President (of 1960) on down to the big money-makers he esteems so highly and the little flunkies to the money-makers — do not understand the evolution of society or the tides of history. I guess I'm among them. I'm sure I know more about the art of telling a tale, and I am not sure that a good tale isn't better for human beings than most of what passes for social science. I don't know; at the same time I am sure that *The Rime of the Ancient Mariner* has done mankind more good than all the discourses on omniscience that Samuel Taylor Coleridge ever uttered. Sometimes I wish I had never tried to do anything else but tell tales — sometimes only.

> I'll tell you a tale tonight
> That a seaman told to me
> With eyes that gleamed in the lanthorn light
> And a voice as low as the sea.

And now, listening "like a three years' child," we are in the land of the blessed.

Contents

CONTENTS

The

Longhorn Breed

Sancho's Return

I N the mesquite and whitebrush country southward from San Antonio, Kerr had a little ranch on Esperanza Creek. He owned several cow ponies and maybe forty cows and their offspring. His *pastor* (shepherd) dog, a mongrel, guarded a small flock of goats, bringing them about sundown to a brush corral near the house, where Kerr's wife barred them inside. Three or four acres of land, fenced in with brush and poles, grew corn, frijoles, watermelons and calabazas — except when a drouth was on. A hand-dug well equipped with pulley wheel, rope and bucket furnished water for the establishment.

Kerr's wife was a partridge-built Mexican named María. They had no children. She was clean, thrifty, cheerful, always making pets of animals. She usually milked three or four cows and made the soft cheese called *asadero* out of goat's milk.

Late in the winter of 1877, Kerr while riding along San Miguel Creek found one of his cows dead in a boghole. Beside the cow was a scrawny, mud-plastered, black-and-white paint bull calf less than a week old. It was too weak to trot; perhaps other cattle had saved it from the coyotes. Kerr pitched his rope over its head, drew it up across the saddle in front of him, carried it home, and turned it over to María.

She had raised many dogie calves, also colts captured from mustang mares. The first thing she did now was to pour milk from a bottle down the orphan's throat. With warm water she washed the caked mud off its body. But hand-raising a calf is no end of trouble. The next day Kerr rode around until he found a thrifty cow with a calf not over a week or ten days old. He drove them to the pen. The cow was black, splotched white, with a white line down her back. The hog-nosed skunk has a beautiful white line down its back also. María at once named the cow Zorrilla (skunk). By tying her head up close to a post and hobbling her hind legs, Kerr and María forced her to let the orphan suckle. She did not give a cup of milk at this first suck-ing. Her calf was kept in the pen next day, and the poor thing bawled herself hoarse. That evening a few drops of her milk were sprinkled on the orphan to give him the smell of the cow's own calf. Zorrilla was not deceived. María began feeding her some prickly pear with the thorns singed off. After being tied up twice daily for a month, she adopted the orphan as a twin to her own offspring.

Now she was one of the household cows. Spring weeds, es-pecially the tallow weed, came up plentifully, and the *guajillo* brush put out in full leaf. When Zorrilla came in about sun-down and her two calves bolted through an open gate for her bag, it was a cheering sight to see them wiggle their tails while they guzzled milk.

The dogie was a vigorous little brute, and before long he was getting more milk than Zorrilla's own calf. María called him Sancho, or "Pet." She was especially fond of Sancho, and he grew to be especially fond of her.

She would give him the shucks wrapped around tamales to hold them together while they are being steam-boiled. Then she began treating him to whole tamales, which are made of ground corn rolled around a core of chopped-up meat. Sancho seemed to like the meat as well as the corn. As everybody who has eaten them knows, true Mexican tamales are well seasoned with pepper. Sancho seemed to like the seasoning.

In southern Texas the little *chiltipiquin* peppers, red when ripe, grow wild in low, shaded places. Cattle never eat them, leaving them for the wild turkeys, mockingbirds and blue quail to pick off. In the early fall wild turkeys used to gorge on them so avidly that their flesh became too peppery for most people to eat. The tamale diet gave Sancho not only a taste but a passion for the little red peppers growing under trees and bushes along Esperanza Creek; in fact, he became a kind of *chiltipiquin* addict. He would hunt for the peppers.

Furthermore, the tamales gave him a tooth for corn in the ear. The summer after he became a yearling he began breaking through the brush fence that enclosed Kerr's corn patch. A forked stick had to be tied around his neck to prevent his getting through the fence. He had been branded and turned into a steer, but he was as strong as any young bull. Like many other pets, he was something of a nuisance. When he could not steal corn or was not humored with tamales, he was enormously contented with grass, mixed in summertime with the sweet mesquite beans. Now and then María gave him a lump of the brown *piloncillo* sugar, from Mexico, that all the border country used.

Every night Sancho came to the ranch pen to sleep. His bed ground was near a certain mesquite tree just outside the gate. He spent hours every summer day in the shade of this mesquite. When it rained and other cattle drifted off, hunting fresh pasturage, Sancho stayed at home and drank at the well. He was strictly domestic.

In the spring of 1880 Sancho was three years old and past, white of horn and as blocky in shape as any long-legged Texas steer ever grew. Kerr's ranch lay in a vast unfenced range grazed by the Shiner brothers, with headquarters on the Frio River. That spring they had a contract to deliver three herds of steers, each to number twenty-five hundred head, in Wyoming. Kerr was helping the Shiners gather cattle, and, along with various other ranchers, sold them what steers he had.

Sancho was included. One day late in March the Shiner men road-branded him **7 Z** and put him in the first herd headed north. The other herds were to follow two or three days apart.

It was late afternoon before the herd got its final "trimming" and was "shaped up" for the long drive. It was watered and eased out on a prairie slope to bed down. But Sancho had no disposition to lie down — there. He wanted to go back to that mesquite just outside the pen gate at the Kerr place on the Esperanza where he had without variation slept every night since he had been weaned. Perhaps his appetite called for an evening tamale. He stood and roamed about on the south side of the herd. A dozen times during the night the men on guard had to drive him back. As reliefs were changed, word passed to keep an eye on that paint steer on the lower side.

When the herd started on next morning, Sancho was at the tail end of it, often stopping and looking back. It took constant attention from one of the drag drivers to keep him moving. By the time the second night arrived, every hand in the outfit knew Sancho by name and sight — the stubbornest and gentlest steer of the lot. About dark one of them pitched a loop over his horns and staked him to a bush. This saved bothering with his persistent efforts to walk off.

Daily when the herd was halted to graze, spreading out like a fan, the other steers eating their way northward, Sancho invariably pointed himself south. In his lazy way he grabbed many a mouthful of grass while the herd was moving. Finally, in some brush up on the Llano, after ten days of trailing, he dodged into freedom. The next day one of the point men with the second Shiner herd saw a big paint steer walking south, rode out, read the **7 Z** road brand on his left side, rounded him in, and set him traveling north again. Sancho became the chief drag animal of this herd. Somewhere north of the Colorado there was a run one night, and when morning came Sancho was missing. The other steers had held together; probably Sancho had not run at all. But he was picked up again, by the third Shiner herd coming on behind.

He took his accustomed place in the drag and continued to require special driving. He picked up in weight. He chewed his cud peacefully and slept soundly, but whenever he looked southward, which was often, he raised his head as if memory and expectation were stirring. The boys were all personally acquainted with him, and every night one of them would stake him. He never lunged against the rope as a wild cow brute would.

One day the cattle balked and milled at a bank-full river. "Rope old Sancho and lead him in," the boss ordered, "and we'll point the other cattle after him." Sancho led like a horse. The herd followed. As soon as he was released, he dropped back to the rear. After this, however, he was always led to the front when there was high water to cross.

The rains came right that spring, and grass came early. By

the time the slow-traveling Shiner herds got into No Man's Land, beyond Red River, they were putting on tallow every day and the sand-hill plums were turning ripe. Pausing now and then to pick a little of the fruit, Sancho's driver saw the pet steer following his example. Learning to eat *chiltipiquíns* on the Esperanza had made him experimental in foods.

Meantime the cattle were trailing, trailing, every day and Sunday too, in the direction of the North Star. For five hundred miles across Texas, counting the windings to find water and keep out of breaks, they had come. After getting into the Indian Territory, they snailed on across the Wichita, the South Canadian, the North Canadian, and the Cimarron. On into Kansas they trailed and across the Arkansas, around Dodge City, cowboy capital of the world, out of Kansas into Nebraska, over the wide, wide Platte, past the roaring cow town of Ogallala, up the North Platte, under the Black Hills, and then against the Big Horn Mountains. For two thousand miles, making ten or twelve miles a day, the Shiner herds trailed. They "walked with the grass." Slow, slow, they moved. "Oh, it was a long and lonesome go" — as slow as the long-drawn-out notes of "The Texas Lullaby," as slow as the night herder's song on a slow-walking horse:

> It's a whoop and a yea, get along, little dogies,
>   For camps is far away.
> It's a whoop and a yea and a-driving the dogies,
>   For Wyoming may be your new home.

When, finally, after listening for months, day and night, to the slow song of their motion, the "dogies" reached their "new home," Sancho was still halting every now and then to sniff southward for a whiff of the Mexican Gulf. The farther he got away from home, the less he seemed to like the change. He had never felt frost in September before. The Mexican peppers on the Esperanza were red ripe now.

The Wyoming outfit received the cattle. Then for a week the Texas men helped brand **C R** on their long sides before turning them loose on the new range. When Sancho's time came to be branded in the chute, one of the Texans yelled out, "There goes my pet. Stamp that **C R** brand on him good and deep." Another drag man said, "The line riders had better learn his tracks and watch for them."

And now the Shiner men turned south, taking back with them their saddle horses and chuck wagons — and leaving Sancho behind. They made good time, but a blue norther was flapping their slickers when they turned the *remuda* loose on the Frio River. After the "Cowboys' Christmas Ball" most of them settled down for a few weeks of winter sleep. They could rub tobacco juice in their eyes during the summer when they needed something in addition to night rides and runs to keep them awake.

Spring comes early down on the Esperanza. The mesquites were all in new leaf with that green so fresh and tender that the color seems to emanate into the sky. Bluebonnets, pale pink Mexican primroses and red phlox would soon sprinkle every open flat and draw. The prickly pear was ready to be studded with waxy blossoms and the whitebrush to be heavy with its own perfume. The windmill grass — "rooster's foot," as the vaqueros call it — was crowding the tallow weed out in places. It was time for the spring cow hunts and the putting up of herds for the annual drive north. The Shiners were at work.

"We were close to Kerr's cabin on Esperanza Creek," John Rigby told me, "when I looked across a pear flat and saw something that made me rub my eyes. I was riding with Joe Shiner, and we both stopped our horses."

"Do you see what I see?" John Rigby asked.

"Yes, but before I say, I'm going to read the brand," Joe Shiner answered.

They rode over. "You can hang me for a horse thief," John Rigby used to tell, "if it wasn't that Sancho paint steer, four year old now, the Shiner **7 Z** road brand and the Wyoming **C R** range brand both showing on him as plain as boxcar letters."

The men rode on down to Kerr's.

"Yes," Kerr said, "old Sancho got in about six weeks ago. His hoofs were worn mighty nigh down to the hair, but he wasn't lame. I thought María was going out of her senses, she was so glad to see him. She actually hugged him and she cried and then she begun feeding him hot tamales. She's made a batch of them nearly every day since, just to pet that steer. When she's not feeding him tamales, she's giving him *piloncillo*."

Sancho was slicking off and seemed mighty contented. He was coming up every night and sleeping at the gate, María said. She was nervous over the prospect of losing her pet, but Joe Shiner said that if that steer loved his home enough to walk back to it all the way from Wyoming, he wasn't going to drive him off again, even if he was putting up another herd for the C R owners.

As far as I can find out, old Sancho lived right there on the Esperanza, now and then getting a tamale, tickling his palate with chili peppers in season, and generally staying fat on mesquite grass, until he died a natural death. He was one of the walking Texas longhorns.

Bill Blocker's Lead Steer

BILL BLOCKER was nineteen years old when he quit school against parental will, borrowed money on his own hook, and in partnership with two older men put up a trail herd. He went along as a hand with the understanding that he was to have no say-so in directing affairs. This was in 1870, and Abilene, Kansas, was the destination.

On the Pedernales River, two days' drive from where they made up their herd, they struck a bunch of wild cattle containing an **A P B** (Blocker) steer that young Bill immediately decided he had to take along. He would pay his father for it when he got back from Kansas. The steer was a big bay with black spots, lithe, in fine condition. But it was not his value as a mere bovine that drew young Blocker. "He looked so proud and free," Blocker used to tell long afterwards, "that he reminded me of the way I felt. I wanted him for company." Accordingly he roped the steer, ran the Backwards Seven road brand on him, and turned him loose in the herd.

Before the day was over the big bay was in the lead. Blocker's place was on the northeast corner, the right (or right-hand) point. Somehow the bay seemed also to sense something in the free-riding young point man that was kin to his nature. Within ten days this steer, which ran with the wildest bunch in the roughs of his home range, which would still have stampeded at the drop of a hat, and which carried himself so "proud and free," was walking up with Blocker's horse, never quite even with him, but with his noble head so near that the rider could put out his left hand and grasp the tip of the right horn. Blocker liked to ride along resting his hand on the powerful horn, and the steer seemed to like to have the hand there. He walked in rhythm with the horse. Blocker called him "Pardner."

No matter where he was after the cattle had watered or had grazed a while, when the yell arose to hit the trail and string out, Pardner would strike a long walk — sometimes a trot — and pass or go around everything until he was at the point. Plainly he enjoyed the feeling of power and self-assurance that leadership gives and felt himself a kind of peer to the high-headed leader on horseback.

When the outfit got near Red River, they learned that it was on a rampage. Herds were being held out from it, waiting for the water to go down. Several attempts to swim over had failed. Most of the trail bosses considered it useless to try further. Two or three rainy days went by and still the expanse of waters raged. Holding an idle herd is tedious business. Bill Blocker said to his partners, "If you men will let me take charge of this herd, I'll cross." There were responses of half-admiration, half-irony. The herd was turned over to the kid — the kid who was to have "no say-so" in bossing it.

His first order was to drive it back, south of the river, three or four miles. Then he swung it around and soon it was strung out in customary formation, headed towards faraway Abilene. By the time the steers hit Red River some of them should be thirsty enough to wade in. Bill Blocker rode at his customary position of pointer on the northeast corner. The proud and free bay steer stepped up with him in the customary manner, and hand rested on horn.

At the brink of the water neither hesitated. Centaur and steer plunged in together and were soon swimming, the herd coming on like mules strung out behind their bell mare. Other herds had prepared to follow, should the first take the water all right, and now they came on, each on the trail of the other.

That was a rainy year. At the Salt Fork of the Arkansas, the herd got into a mill, out in the middle of deep water. While Blocker was trying to break the mill and save the cattle from drowning each other, a plunging steer pawed his exhausted horse under. Weighed down with boots and leggins, he was making a desperate but losing struggle when the bay leader cut out of the mill and came by him, headed for the north bank. Blocker grabbed his tail and was towed out, the herd following.

After this the proud and free pair seemed to keep step with each other more constantly than before. However, had the man tried to approach the steer afoot, a chasm between them would have opened wider than the Mississippi. It was a great pity to deliver the bay leader along with the herd at Abilene. But what else could be done?

There was a last grasp of hand on horn, and then, "*Adiós,* Pardner, I hope you break loose and come back to Texas." But Pardner never got back.

Tablecloth – Outlaw

AFTER the ranges were all claimed and fenced, the outlaws that escaped ropes and bullets were comparatively few. The story of one escaper should fill any lover of freedom with glee.

His mother was a keen-horned, dun Spanish cow driven up from the south to the far-spread Shoe Sole Ranch bordering the Snake River in Idaho. Despite panthers and wolves that prowled the broken country she chose to range in, she always raised a calf, and she became a marked animal. One year her calf — a bull — escaped branding. She kept it in solitude, and when it was a yearling she charged a man trying to throw her into the roundup and hooked his horse in the hip. But the yearling was branded and castrated. Upon being turned loose, he butted down one brander and sent the others tearing out. His mother smelled with solicitude the blood and burned hair on his body, and as soon as she was let out, took him back to the "tall timbers."

He had a name now — Tablecloth, from his checkered blue, yellow and white color. The next year he was not in the roundup. He still ranged alone with his mother. The pair were seen occasionally, but by fleetness and constant alertness, and by taking cunning advantage of cedar-studded roughs, they escaped roundup after roundup until the cow was no longer seen. In the prime of life now, Tablecloth kept in fine condition and kept his figure too. He often led younger steers into wildness, but they could be cut off and rounded in while he vanished.

When he was ten years old, three punchers, with special orders to get Tablecloth, sighted him farther off from the canyon cedars than they had ever seen him. They hazed him, along with his little bunch, into a herd being trimmed for the market.

Tablecloth became one among two thousand grown steers bound for the shipping pens. He walked up with the leaders. The first night on the trail, watchful guards observed that he remained standing while the other cattle bedded down. While the Dipper swung around the North Star and one relief after the other circled the cattle, he roamed about, horning sleepers out of his way in a most domineering manner, until the Morning Star began to pale. Perhaps he was accustomed to little sleep. He was full of the pride and energy of life.

About the middle of the next night, storm clouds blew up and the herd arose on restless feet. All hands were called out. They prevented either a break or a drift, but when daylight came Tablecloth was gone. Tracks showed that he had left in a lope. The herd moved on.

Two years later, organized riders made a special hunt. One man sighted Tablecloth, fired his six-shooter as a signal, and fell in behind him up an open arroyo. The hoofs of both steer and horse were making a fine clatter, and maybe the puncher was gaining a little, when he saw an enormous bear rise up on his hind legs just ahead of Tablecloth, to investigate. Tablecloth never swerved an inch. He hit the bear, bowled him over, and tore on. He had to cross some open ground, and here two punchers "twined" him about the same time. They snubbed him to a tree until the lead ox could be brought.

Tablecloth tried his best to gore the yoke mate, but he was necked up too close for horn action. After getting to the beef herd, he was kept necked. At night he made life miserable for the gentle ox, constantly shifting around, never for a minute ceasing to look for a way to escape. In him the instinct for freedom seemed to be as strong as the instinct for breathing. But he was on his way to a packing plant, and the boss had promised treats to the whole outfit if they could shut the gates behind the outlaw in the shipping pens.

They had traveled for three days with Tablecloth necked to the lead ox, and he was still secure. On the night of the third day he actually lay down like the other cattle and was apparently asleep when in the silent darkness a coyote let out a sudden, piercing yell at the edge of the herd. Instantly two thousand big steers were pounding the ground. Riding to circle them, a puncher heard a moaning as if from an animal in great agony. He paused and saw Tablecloth standing on one side of a tree and the lead ox down on the other, choking to death. He had no time for anything but to cut the necking rope from the gentle animal's throat. Tablecloth was long gone before the ox could get to his feet. The stampede was not serious enough to delay the herd's arrival at the shipping pens. Once more the cattle train pulled away from them without Tablecloth.

Three years went by. The famous outlaw was still free. He had ridded himself of the necking rope and looked to be in the prime of condition. After returning from marketing the last fall shipment, the boss proposed that certain men take their Winchesters and bring in Tablecloth's hide and carcass. He thought he was offering an opportunity for big sport. He was surprised at the opposition that rolled up.

Hadn't Tablecloth fairly won life and liberty? For fifteen years now the whole Shoe Sole outfit had been after him — and he was still free. He was getting old. He had never really tried to kill a man. He had simply outplayed his opponents. He could not be called mean. Among his kind he was rarer than a cowman out of debt, as outstanding as Bugger Red among riders of pitching horses. By God, he deserved to live among the cedarbrakes and canyons he loved so well — and the boss agreed. Tablecloth continued to enjoy his liberty for several years. Then, like his mother, he was no longer seen. No man ever came across his skull.

Stampede on the Cimarron

I T was a June night of the year 1884, on the Cimarron. The air was hot, stifling, absolutely still. It had been thus all day. Now the sky became overcast, and dull sheet lightning began to blink along the horizon to the west. Two men rode around twenty-five hundred big steers, as snaky and sinewy as ever came out of the chaparral down by the Rio Grande. About two hundred yards away was camp, though the fire of cow chips had died and not a spark revealed the nine sleeping forms on pallets spread in haphazard pattern out from the chuck wagon.

Near each sleeping man stood a horse — his night horse, the clearest-footed and surest-sighted of his mounts — saddled and tied. Somewhere out in the darkness the horse wrangler kept drowsy guard over the remuda.

The cattle and the night were so quiet that the two herders stopped now and then on their rounds to listen. They could not help expecting something. The air grew warmer and more stifling, as the lightning flashes approached and dim thunder began to rumble up. The men could still skylight the cattle.

Presently a dun steer that had been in the lead of the herd

from the beginning and had been named Old Buck awoke, lifted his head slowly, rose to his knees, and looked around. Apparently he did not trust the looks of things, but, being long experienced in life, he wasn't startled, and he said nothing. He got on his feet, raising his nose to smell, and gazed towards the approaching storm. The two men on guard sang as gently as they could the songs they had sung over and over to soothe the cattle down and prevent any sudden sound from breaking in and frightening them.

But Old Buck had no idea of going back to bed. He seemed to be expecting something — something as sudden as a telegram used to be. Another steer got up, stood still, expectant; then others and others arose until the whole herd was on its feet, motionless. The songs grew louder now, unrelenting, pleading.

The night grew blacker, the lightning brighter, the humidity of the air heavier. And then, almost at once, on every tip of the five thousand horns of the waiting steers, appeared a ball of dull phosphorescent light — the fox fire, St. Elmo's fire, will-o'-the-wisp of the folklore of the world. In the intervals of utter blackness the two guards on the lone prairie could see nothing but those eerie balls pulsing on the tips of long curved horns. But the guards were not thinking of ghosts or remembering ghost stories now. Their voices rose high in the wild but cow-quieting notes of "The Texas Lullaby," which is not made of words and can't be conveyed by musical notation. It is made of syllables and tones conveyable only by voices trained in darkness and deep thickets. The notes come long, low and trembly. The wailers of "The Texas Lullaby" did not yell or shoot; as men who savvied the cow, they would not scare the as yet still cattle.

The ghostly balls of fire on horns must have looked as strange to the steers as to the men. The steers began to move at a walk, their motion becoming circular, the riders around them preventing any decided movement away from the bed ground. At first the walk was slow; soon it became faster. And then out of blackness came a great flash of zigzag lightning forking down over the seething mass of animals, so close that darting tongues of flame seemed almost to lick their backs. At the same time a mighty clap, a roar, a crash of thunder shook heaven and earth, reverberating and doubling.

Its answer was the thunder of ten thousand pounding hoofs that popped and clicked, while horn clacked against horn. The stampede started with the swiftness of the lightning's leap.

All hands in camp had mounted at the first salvo from the skies; they reached the herd in time to join the pursuit. The gigantic thunderbolt had knocked out the sluice gates of the sky. The water poured down in sheets and barrels. It rained blue snakes, pitchforks and bobtailed heifer yearlings all at once. One minute it was darker than the dead end of a crooked tunnel a mile deep under a mountain. Then the prairie was a sea of blue and yellow light dazzling to all eyes.

No matter. Hang with the cattle. Trust your horse. Follow those balls of fire tossing in the void of blackness, too dim to illumine even the horn tips they play upon, sometimes darting across to dance with each other, again fading out altogether. Now, truly, they may be the *ignis fatuus* that lures followers to Black Death. When the lightning won't light, run by ear. When the lightning blinds and the thunder drowns all other sound, keep on riding hell for leather. To get around them and circle the leaders, you must run wilder and madder than the horror-lashed cattle themselves.

It would probably have been better had the two night herders not been recruited. The object was to swing the leaders around into the tail end of the herd, thus turning it into a mill. A single man *who knew how* could do this better than a bedlam of riders. Then gradually the whole mass would be wound into a self-stopping ball, the momentum dying down like that of a spent top.

One of the two night herders with this stampede on the Cimarron was Robert T. Hill, who in later years became a mining and oil geologist renowned over the United States and Mexico. "Before long," he wrote, "I found myself and another rider chasing a small bunch of cattle, close upon their heels. Never has thunder sounded to me so loud as on that run nor have lightning crashes come so rapidly and so near.

"At a crash that seemed to be the climax my horse stopped dead in his tracks, almost throwing me over the saddle horn. The lightning showed that he was planted hardly a foot from the edge of a steep-cliffed chasm. A little off to one side, the horse of John Gifford, the other rider, was sinking on his knees, John himself slumping limp in the saddle. Just beyond him lay Old Buck, the mighty lead steer, killed by the bolt of lightning that had knocked John Gifford unconscious. The rest of our bunch of cattle were down under the cliff, some of them dead, some squirming."

When morning came, clear and calm, not a man was anywhere near camp. That did not matter so far as breakfast was concerned, for all provisions had been drenched and the cook could not begin to start a fire with the soaking-wet cow chips. The twenty-five hundred steers that had been trailed and guarded a thousand miles from southern Texas for the market at Dodge City were scattered to the four winds. Before noon, though, men by ones and twos began driving in bunches from different directions. Hours later the last man was in. Meantime the wrangler was supplying fresh mounts, and the boss, with all hands except three on herd, was combing the country in a long lope. The men could eat later on and sleep when there was nothing else to do.

The Man Who Hung Hisse'f

T H E N he hung hisse'f so he wouldn't stompede no more cattle." That is the way a quiet little old man, a certain Chaucerian shyness and gentleness in him and very religious, though not a conscientious objector to either war or capital punishment, named Alonzo Mitchell, of Lampasas, Texas, told it.

"That year, 1875," he said, "we were taking up a mixed herd to Wichita, Kansas. It was mixed sure enough — cows, bulls, steers, but no calves or yearlings. Lots of times a man couldn't tell from the looks of one of those cows that she was going to have a calf before daylight. She was wiry and ga'nt and could run, jumping bushes like a deer, even when about to bring a calf. Some of our cows begun having calves before we got across the Brazos River, and they kept on having calves all the way up. Generally they'd drop 'em on the bed ground at night. The next morning we'd shoot the newborns in the head with six-shooters and go on. A calf just dropped is too wobbly on its legs to walk up with any herd. We had an ox wagon, with the bed calked for crossing rivers, but it didn't have room for hauling the calves, and 'calf wagons' hadn't then come into use. The calves were not worth much of anything. We had to take the cows along or lose them. The shooting was just an act of mercy.

"Some trail bosses would rope the cows at night and hobble them, so's to keep them from going back to hunt their calves. I don't remember that our cows gave us much trouble. They seemed to know their calves were dead. Sometimes one would have a calf while trailing along. She'd drop back into the drag, and then we'd let her stop until she was fully delivered, shoot the calf, and drive her on.

"When we got into North Texas, a woman came to the bed ground before daylight one morning driving a wagon. She asked if we had any little calves. We said maybe so. Then she said she'd like to have them if we were going to get rid of them anyway. She got three or four and put them in her wagon. The next morning, ten or twelve miles north of that camp, she was on hand again, this time with a boy to help. She must've been raising quite a bunch of dogies. We learned she was picking up calves from all the cow herds passing her way. She had better luck than the Kansas nester who got to a steer herd after dark to await the morning crop of calves. The boss told him he could have them if he'd take a turn at standing guard. Somehow his 'trick' lasted from the first shift till it got light enough for him to see the animals in the herd. Then he rode away without even coming to camps for coffee.

"In our herd were steers that stood seventeen hands high and were as fat as mud. But we never killed any of our stuff on the trail. There was lots of talk about 'trail fever,' 'traveling fever' and the like — later recognized as tick fever — and we were afraid to eat the meat of trail cattle. Some outfits butchered range cattle they sighted along the trail, but we didn't believe in that sort of business.

"Our leaders were a pair of prairie steers we named Broad and Crump. Broad was a brown with wide-spreading horns that twisted straight out; Crump was a white with horn tips that crumpled in. When they walked, their heads would sway, their horns weighed so much, but they'd walk side by side, right up at the lead, day after day, with their heads swinging in such harmony that their horns never clicked or interfered with each other. The way they got timed to each other was remarkable, and we boys used to talk about it often. When they were grazing in high grass, heads hidden, we could see their horns bobbing and balancing.

"When there was a stompede — and we had several on this trip — no matter which way the herd ran or which part of it got off first, Broad and Crump would soon be in the lead. If a man racing along towards the point got a glimpse of them by a flash of lightning or skylighted them, he'd yell across to any hand on the other side to give way, for he knew that with Broad and Crump leading, he could turn the runaways and put the herd into a mill.

"Chain lightning caused more stompedes than anything else, and next came lobo wolves — the smell of them. After we got up into the Indian Territory, we could depend upon nearly all the storms coming from the northwest. Men and cattle alike generally got warnings out of the sky, but the storm nearly always broke with great suddenness and fury.

"The cowboys would holler to the cattle and sing and pray. Yes, they'd pray to God loud, making all sorts of promises. Then next morning at breakfast they'd laugh, cursing and poking fun at themselves and each other.

" 'Don't you ever pray in a storm?' they'd ask me.

" 'No.'

" 'Well,' each man said to me at one time or another, 'I pray when I get scared. I don't see how anybody keeps from it.'

" 'I'll tell you,' I said more'n once, 'why I don't pray. When I was twenty-one years old I turned myself over to my Heavenly Father. I pray to him regularly, and under his care I'm no more scared when it lightnings than when it don't.'

"On one trip up the trail we got next to a herd that was stompeding every night almost, the owner said. I told him he must be packing his cattle too close on the bed ground. If cattle were bedded down so close together that a steer switching his tail hit another in the face, there was mighty apt to be a stompede. The critter hit would jump up with a beller, and then the whole herd would be off like a flash in the pan. Well, this man asked me to bed his cattle for him. I had an awful time getting his men to spread out and let the cattle take natural room and positions, just as they'd take if left to themselves. 'Good gracious,' the man kept saying, 'how much more room do they need?' And 'We're going to have an awful big territory to ride around,' he'd say. I told him the men on guard had to keep riding anyhow and it didn't make any more work to ride around five acres than one.

"After the cattle got their positions, there was a full steer-length between many a one of them and the next animal. There wasn't a bobble that night. The trail boss was satisfied. From then on he gave his stuff plenty of room and had no trouble above the ordinary.

"Up in the Indian Nation somewhere, south of a creek that I can't remember the name of, a man who was loose-herding a small bunch of cattle eased up to our herd one evening and told us we'd better expect trouble. Every herd that crossed that creek, he said, was stompeding. According to him, a jayhawker was waylaying the place, and, after the cattle ran and split up, was cutting off little bunches and driving them up a side canyon, where he'd hold them until the owners got out of the country and then turn them over to a gang of fellow thieves. We even found out where the jayhawker was holing up.

"This creek had a reputation up and down the trail, but the cause of the stompedes had been a mystery. The trail down to the crossing was steep and thickly timbered on both sides, with lots of underbrush, all cut by gullies. The average herd did not have a man riding in front of it, the two point men guiding the leaders and holding them down if they got to walking too fast.

"My brother Bob Mitchell was boss, and when we started down to the creek bottom, he took his place on the right point. He didn't show hisse'f, but as the lead cattle strung along, Broad and Crump right in front and doing their duty, he rode so's to get a look ahead. D'reckly he saw something black down in the bottom flop like two big wings. He pulled his sixshooter and shot, and a man left on his horse in a hurry. Bob just got one glimpse of him in the brush. We got across all right.

"The stompeder left his paraphernalia right where he was in the habit of using it. It consisted of a kind of scarecrow with adjustable wings that could be moved up and down. When the lead animals of a herd suddenly saw this thing working at close quarters, of course they'd tear out, those following down the hill breaking off from the narrow trail-opening and scattering from hell to breakfast.

"We made camp that night on the prairie. On the edge of it next to the creek were a lot of oak trees. A funny thing. Next morning the man that had been stompeding the herds was hanging from a limb of one of them trees — considerably off to one side of the trail so's not to scare any cattle. Right by him was hanging his scarecrow machine. He hung hisse'f so he wouldn't stompede no more cattle. That's what they said."

The Maverick Branded MURDER

IN 1890 most of the trans-Pecos country was still unfenced, and in the timbered and brushed roughs plenty of longhorn blood still ran wild. On January 28 of that year the small cattle owners operating around the Leoncita waterholes in northern Brewster County — a county as large as some states, taking in the Big Bend National Park — held a roundup to brand what calves had escaped the fall work. Between two and three thousand cattle were thrown together in the herd.

The chief operators in this part of the country were Dubois and Wentworth. They did not approve of such early work and were taking no part in it, but one of their riders named Fine Gilleland showed up to represent their interests.

Among the "little men" was Henry Harrison Powe, a Mississippian who had left college to fight in the Confederate Army and was one-armed as a result. He had come to Texas during the hardhanded Reconstruction days. Not many miles from the roundup grounds he had buried the body — eleven bullet holes in it — of a murdered nephew. He was considered an honest man, not at all contentious, but ready to stand up for his rights. His brand was **H H P** — his initials.

In the roundup, among other unbranded animals, was a brindle yearling bull. It was not following any cow, but the roundup boss and another range man informed Powe that the bull belonged to a certain **H H P** cow. They had seen him with the cow and knew both animals well by flesh marks. "Are you positive?" Powe asked. They said they would swear to the brindle's identity. Then Powe rode into the herd and brought the brindle out, heading him into a small cut of cows and calves being held by his own son.

Very soon after this, Fine Gilleland galloped up to the cut. "Does that brindle bull have a mother here?" he asked the boy sharply.

"No," the boy replied, "but the boss told my dad it belongs to an **H H P** cow."

"He'll play hell taking it unless he produces the cow," Gilleland retorted. Then, without another word, he separated the brindle and ran him back to the main herd.

Powe saw the bull coming, followed by Gilleland. He rode out and the two men passed some words not heard by others. Then Powe turned back into the roundup and started to cut the brindle out again. Gilleland made straight for him. Halted in the middle of the herd, the two men had some more words. They were very brief. Powe was unarmed. He rode to the far side of the herd and borrowed a six-shooter out of a friend's saddle pocket.

Back into the herd Powe now rode, found the brindle bull and started him for the **H H P** cut, following him out. Midway between the cut and the big herd, Fine Gilleland met them. He roped at the bull but missed. Powe pulled his six-shooter and shot at the bull but missed. By this time, Gilleland was off his horse shooting at Powe to kill. He killed.

Gilleland now remounted and left the roundup in a run. In

all probability he was honest in claiming the brindle maverick for his employers. Perhaps he shot in the flush of anger. Perhaps he hoped to make a reputation. There was a strong tendency on the range for little owners to "feed off" any big outfit in their country. The big spreads sometimes hired men to be hard.

The Powe boy rode immediately to Alpine to notify rangers of the killing. Meanwhile men remaining with the roundup branded-out the calves and yearlings, the **H H P** stock included.

When the brindle bull was dragged up to the branding fire, there was a short discussion. He was thrown on his right side. Then a man with a running iron burned deep into the shaggy, winter hair on his left side the letters **M U R D E R.** The letters ran across the ribs from shoulder to flank.

"Turn him over," the man said. The bull was turned over. Then with a fresh iron the man branded on the right side, **JAN 28 90.** The bull was not castrated or earmarked.

A few days later two rangers killed Gilleland in the mountains. What happened to the brindle maverick, with that brand that no one would claim, is not so definitely settled. R. W. Powe, son of the murdered man, whose account of the matter has been followed in this narrative, says that the murder bull was eventually driven out of the country with a trail herd bound for Montana.

Whether he was or not, stories long circulated in the trans-Pecos country about "the maverick branded **M U R D E R**": How for years he wandered a lone outcast on the range, never seen with other cattle, and, for that matter, seldom seen at all. How he turned prematurely gray, the hair over the scabs of his bizarre brand showing a coarse red. How cowboys in the bunkhouse at the Dubois and Wentworth ranch one night saw the bull's head come through an open window; he was looking, they imagined, for the man responsible for that brand of horror traced on his own side. Some brands grow in size with the growth of animals; generally they do not. According to the stories, the **MURDER** brand grew until the elongated letters stood out in enormous dimensions, making one think of the pitiless Scarlet Letter that blazoned on Hester Prynne's breast.

The Murder Maverick became a "ghost steer." A cowboy might see him, usually about dusk; and then he "just wasn't there." There were some who did not want to see him. Eugene Cunningham, Barry Scobee and perhaps other writers have woven "the murder steer" into Wild West stories for the pulp magazines. The gray Confederate coat with slit sleeve worn by the murdered Powe of one arm is in the little college museum at Alpine, under the mountains where the roundup was held, January 28, 1890. That brindle bull hide with the outlandish brand on it really would be a museum piece.

The Bull Who Was Not

JOSÉ BELTRÁN was the most astute of all trappers of wild cattle on the vast O'Connor ranch back in the days when cattle and horses ran wild by the thousands and a man could see as many as a hundred deer together, stringing out in a run, one after the other, "like mules." He began trapping for *ladino* cattle not long after windmills began pumping water on the ranch. At the Mexican Waterhole a big pen made of slick wire doubled around high posts closely set together in the ground enclosed well, windmill and troughs. Nothing could jump that fence or knock it down. At one corner a gate opened into a small, equally strong holding pen. The big pen served as a trap for wild cattle. The gate from the pasture into it was always left open so that cattle could enter and drink at will. A strand of slick wire led from the free end of the gate to the platform on the windmill tower, about thirty feet above ground. The trapper sat on the platform and watched. When animals came in that he wanted to catch, he pulled the wire, thus closing the gate.

José Beltrán was little and black and bowlegged and *muy alerto,* with eyes that gleamed and peered everywhere. When telling a story he could not sit. He stood, knelt, bent over on all fours, squatted, lay down, jumped up, looked out yonder, beholding whatever it was he was telling a story about; he imitated the sound of hoofbeats, the bark of a coyote, the bleat of a calf, the snort of a doe that has heard but cannot see. I found myself jumping up and down, looking, listening, waiting with him.

"*Bueno,* when Don Patricio Lambert told me to go to the Mexican Waterhole, he sent another vaquero also. We hide our horses way off, way off, out of the wind. We do not walk through the gate. No, we climb over wires at a place next to granjeno where cattle cannot come. We leave no smell.

"It is hot summer. We take off our clothes and bury them in sand. The body of a man, just in his own skin, does not give out scent like the clothes he sweats in. We rub dirt and cow dung all over our bodies and in our hair. Now we do not stink like a man at all. We go to the windmill tower. There is a bucket. I take water in it out of the trough and pour water on our tracks. We touch nothing except the rungs on the ladder. We climb to the platform under the wheel of the windmill. There is no wind. It does not turn. All is silence.

"On top we take off our shoes, so a step will not make one sound. We sit down. I face the gate, and the other vaquero he watches too. The wire is ready to pull. The moon is bright like day. We wait and wait. There is nothing. I see a coyote that wants some water. He makes no sound lapping at the trough. We wait and wait. I hear maybe so one armadillo in the sticks, outside the pen. Now it is close to the middle of night. I hear one little, very weak cry; maybe it is from a *ratón,* maybe little rabbit. Nothing is coming tonight, I think. After midnight the wild cattle do not come to water, until about five o'clock in the morning.

"My *compañero* and I do not speak all this time, except with a finger and *ssh,* like that. I am nearly asleep. Then I hear away off in the brush one bull. *Bru-uh-uh,* he says, not loud, low down in himself. *Shh.*

"Good, I think. He is on a trail to water; he brings wild cows, maybe steers too, with him. In the summer the bulls do not stay by themselves as in the cold time. He makes that talk again, *bru-uh-uh,* low, deep down, quiet, like the far stars. He is closer, but he comes slow. He wait, wait. Then in that bright moonlight I see him at the gate. He is black, black, *puro negro.* He stops and smells the ground. He smells the gate posts. I am looking for the other cattle. He turns away from the gate as if he expects something, somebody. He smells all the planks of the gate from one end to the other. He stands a long time, long time at the gate opening, looking. But he does not look up. That is the way with cattle and deer.

"The other vaquero and I wait with him — wait, wait. Then, all alone, he comes in. He walks straight to the trough. I can hear him drinking, *hillkk, hillkk.* He drinks until he is full. He belches — that way. I am looking for the other cattle. Still they do not come. I can see the unmarked ears on the black bull. He is maverick. Now he starts for the gate.

"I pull the wire. I hear the gate slam. Then I hear *psh-hh-hh.* I tell this vaquero to go to the gate at the little pen in the corner and when I scare the bull through it, to shut it. I go easy to the fence and climb over and go on the outside to the big gate in front of the bull. I will scare the bull and make him run to the corner and go into the little pen. He will fight with me if I am inside with him. But outside I can play with him.

"The bull is not at the gate. I look and look. I go all around that pen, looking through the wire, looking in the bright moonlight. The pen is not too big; no brush grows in it, just one huisache and six mesquites, all trees. The other vaquero he looks too. No black bull is in the pen. It is empty, as it was when we came. No, do not deceive yourself into thinking any bull could jump that fence, that gate.

"Listen. This bull is not one bull. He is *el diablo*. I do not wish to stay at the Mexican Waterhole longer that night. Maybe so it is the Devil's Waterhole. We put on our clothes and ride to the ranch. Nobody ever saw that maverick black bull again. Nobody had seen him before that night. What does this seem to you?"

Bulls at a Waterhole on the Ramireña

I N wintertime the bulls kept apart, some individuals staying utterly alone, others ranging together in small bunches, looking upon each other with lackluster eye, hardly looking at cows at all, not one quickened by the faintest intimation of the virility latent in his bullhood. But by the time the grass was up high enough to afford whole mouthfuls, even the draggiest old bull had the feeling that the sun rose for his particular benefit, while the "shelliest" old cow shed her poverty-bedraggled hair and came into ambitions that made her forget the misery of suckling a calf on weak weed-tips in front of a February norther.

A seasonable spring was becoming summer in some year before 1890. Any ranch in the southern half of Texas might be taken as the setting, but to please my own memories I shall particularize one — of modest dimensions — on Ramireña Creek in Live Oak County, about the season when wild turkeys begin chasing grasshoppers through the green of grass and weeds and mustang grapes are getting big and hard enough for bullets.

A brindle bull, six or seven years old, at the apex of his prowess, had been hanging around the Ramirez Waterhole for hours. His powerful neck showed a great bulge just behind the head.

He had a big dewlap accenting his primitive origin. He had drunk but was by no means waterlogged, for he belonged to a breed that knew what it was to drink only once every three days and then walk directly for hours back to grass. Overeating or overdrinking would never allow those powerfully muscled legs and lithe flanks.

Five or six other bulls were among the cattle, perhaps a hundred and fifty head, resting in the vicinity. But Brindle paid little attention to them. They knew their places and they regarded him as impersonally as did the cows, heifers, calves and steers. A bull does not cut out a bunch of cows, herd them together and claim them for his own, as a stallion claims mares, fighting all other stallions away. His promiscuity demands no loyalty in either himself or the cows. He is free of the jealousy that goes with loyalty. He has no cohesive following. The dominion of a champion fighter of the range was territorial, the other bulls in that territory recognizing his prowess but being free to go their own ways with any cows that showed them favor.

A majority of the cattle this day at the Ramirez Waterhole were lying down or standing in the shade, out of sight of Brindle, chewing their cuds. Yet all, by the way they turned their heads and now and then ceased their cud-chewing to listen, indicated an interest in him — the acknowledged bull of their woods. The woods consisted of prairie land running into and islanded with thorny thickets and of noble live oaks overtopping mesquites, hackberries, *granjeno, brazil* and other growth along the creek bottom.

Brindle had been calling plenty of attention to himself. He seemed mad through and through, though it was not in his nature to vent his rage — a rage sullen and reserved — on just any member of society that got in his way. Utterly oblivious for the time of the world animate and inanimate, male and female, around him, he went on nursing his wrath to keep it warm against some contester worthy of his mettle that might emerge from beyond the rim of his acknowledged domain.

Having taken a position on a rise of open ground perhaps a hundred yards up from the waterhole, he had for a long while been pawing dirt from an old bull-scrape in the soft soil — a sink about like a buffalo wallow. He lifted the dirt with his forefeet so that it went high up in the air and fell in part upon his own back. While pawing, he often stopped to hook one of his horns — the "master horn," as Spanish bullfighters call it — into the ground, goring down to a clayish damp that stuck to the tip. He even hooked both horns in, one at a time, and, kneeling, rubbed his shoulders, throat and dewlap against the bank of the wallow. At times the uplifted dirt from his flexible ankles came down in clumps and dust on tossing horns. The powerful lungs in his body, free from choking fat, bellowed out streams of breath that sprayed particles of earth away from his nostrils. Now, earth daubing his horns, matting his shaggy frontlet, and covering his back from head to tail, he was a spectacle.

But pawing and dirt-hooking were nothing compared to his vocal goings-on. When he came in to water, he was talking to himself, his truculent head swaying with the rhythm of his walk and the weight of his thick horns. Hoarse and deep, like thunder on the horizon, his mumbling talk went *uh-uh-uh-uh*, four deliberate notes, the last a low-descending jerk, in four steps. This was his war march. Often he stayed the throaty *uh-uh-uh-uh*-ing and halted to raise his head in a loud, high, defiant challenge that might be described as a basso scream, combining a bellow from the uttermost profundities with a shriek high and foreign. Beside the waterhole a fat two-year-old calico-colored heifer craved his attention, but only by a few curls and astounding twists of his upward-pointing nose after he smelled of her did he seem aware of her existence. His mind was on other things.

Thus, now, pawing up dirt, lunging his horn in as if to rip out the guts of the earth, bawling, bellowing, muttering, shattering the air, Brindle was sending his threats, his oaths of revenge, his challenge to earth, and to hell too, over the hills, against the echoing caliche cliffs on the far side of the Ramireña, and up a little canyon that emptied into the creek just above the waterhole. As his fury waxed, he now and then let out in quick succession a series of far-carrying bawls, agonizing — yet fascinating — to human senses, for they seemed to be tearing the very lungs out of the bawler.

Then at what seemed the zenith of this ecstasy of rage he heard something that infuriated the bottommost reserve of passion.

He shook his head and jarred the water.

What he heard was an answer to his prayer, a response to his invitation, a defiance of his boasted power, a mockery of his challenge. The sounds were coming from the prairie divide between Ramireña and Lagarto creeks, the eager-for-battle maker of them having been lured from his trail to another watering. He could not be seen yet, but he was drawing nearer. *Uh-uh-uh-uh*, and then mighty throatings, growling a deep and hollow roar.

At length he came into view, a glossy dunnish-brown merging into black — the *golondrino* (swallow) color — white speckles and splotches on his rump and a washed-out copper line down his back. His thick horns, like Brindle's, were set forward for tossing a lobo wolf into the air or ripping any kind of belly open as effectively as that scimitar-curved Mexican knife called *saca tripas* (gets the guts).

It was a belief that the bulls kept their horns sharpened for bloody work by rubbing them against trees and brush and whetting them in the ground. A hundred yards off, the *golondrino* bull stopped and went to pawing dirt, answering bellow for bellow. He not only gored the earth but thrust his horns into the tough stems of a *cenizo* bush and, jerking and twisting his head from side to side, broke the bush to stubble. He came nearer, but the preliminaries were long-drawn-out, each warrior practicing his thrusts, each seeming to wait for the other to take upon himself the war-guilt of the first assault, yet neither wearing himself out with exercise. This bullying was more than sound and fury; back of it lay immense reserve.

Brindle emerged from his wallow. Then he and Golondrino began to circle one another, each fronting his antagonist and maneuvering for an opening. They halted perhaps four yards apart. Meanwhile the other cattle had congregated, keeping well out of the way, and with sympathetic bawlings were adding to the atmosphere. Yet more cattle, attracted like boys to a dogfight, came stringing in at a trot from far away. The big steers, which often seem to imagine themselves bulls and which no bull ever notices, were especially interested. "Like a steer, I can try," the old saying goes.

Now the time for talk by the champions was over. The object of each was to get a side entrance for a horn, but each was a master of defense. At the simultaneous lunge that brought them together, the impact of skull against skull and of horn against horn made an air-shattering report like that when the iron coupling of one freight car is rammed into that of another. Then, heads locked, the bulls stood planted in the soil, neither giving way to the other. Shoulder muscles stood out like bronze studies; massive neck thews rose almost to the height of humps on Brahman bulls; backs curved tensely, the downward sweep of line as beautiful in its grace and strength as any curve of nature that art ever revealed. One bull and then the other tried a quick side step to unbalance his opponent and get in a side thrust, but neither could win the advantage. With horns that were both weapon and shield, they parried strokes in such rapidity that the clashes could hardly have been counted. A turkey gobbler that had showed up with several mates went to gobbling in his ridiculous way at each fresh impact of horns. The bulls backed and rushed again and again. The dust they raised went up into the air like a signal smoke. The ground they fought over was torn up as if giants with spikes and spades on their feet had wrestled there.

The shovings, the head-on lunges, the dodges, the impregnable stands went on and on. The heat of the strain brought slobber to mouths, and tongues lolled out. Eyes, bloodshot, bulged forth. Once Brindle's horn nicked a hole — hardly a wound — in Golondrino's brisket. The smell of blood was caught by an old blue steer among the surrounding cattle and the blood bellow went up and volumed in a discordant chorus. That blood call, that prairie funeral of primitives, moaning, murmuring, screaming — who can describe it? The cattle now thronging together and taking the stage away from the bulls were as uneasy and excited as ten thousand robins gathered to migrate from the cedarbrakes of the Colorado River to their summer homes on the Atlantic coast two thousand miles north. A coyote came to peer from behind a prickly pear bush up the ridge.

The sun swung low. The wild turkeys disappeared. The bulls backed off from each other and pawed the dust. Then with hearts still pumping against bursting lungs, they clashed again. Darkness came.

Cow Music

IN talking of bulls I have dwelt long on their wonderful utterances. No wild animal, or domestic either, that I know of has as many vocal tones as the longhorn. In comparison, the bulls and cows of highly bred varieties of cattle are voiceless. The cow of the longhorns has one *moo* for her newborn calf, another for it when it is older, one to tell it to come to her side and another to tell it to stay hidden in the tall grass. Moved by amatory feelings, she has a low audible breath of yearning. In anger she can run a gamut. If her calf has died or been otherwise taken from her, she seems to be turning her insides out into long, sharp, agonizing bawls. I have heard steers make similar sounds. They seemed to be in the utmost agony of expressing something so poignant to them that the utterance meant more than life, something that would willingly be paid for by death.

The bawling of thirsty cattle used to be all too familiar a sound on ranches before wells and tanks became plentiful and the gasoline engine was devised to pump water when the wind fails to blow. Day and night, day and night, it would go on around empty water troughs, the moans getting weaker in time, though the endurance of a cow brute in keeping up a continual bawling would make insignificant the record of any long-winded filibusterer holding the floor of Congress. Cattle walking a fence in futile anxiety to get back to a range they have been driven from make the same distressful, relentless sounds.

The mingled bawls and lowings, each of a different pitch and timbre, of a big herd of mixed cattle held forcibly while hungry and thirsty after a day of being ginned about, frantic heifers and headstrong old cows separated from their calves, calves in misery for their mothers, yearlings adding to the din in the same way that each of forty babies will go to crying if one opens up, steers bawling for their lost powers of masculinity or for the same reason that great arctic wolves bay at the midnight sun or from some urge that only God is aware of, bulls bellowing at the memory of past combats or maybe without memory at all — all make music to a cowman's ears, especially at a distance.

Bill Halsell was a cowman of the old Texas breed that held their horses against Comanches, their cattle against thieves, and, for a little while, their ranges against settlers. He fought his hardest fights, though, against blizzards and drouths. And now after the rise, the plateau, and the fall of fighting and holding, Bill Halsell lay a-dying in faraway California. His friend Charles A. Jones of the S M S Ranch went to the hospital to see him.

"I'm not long for this country, Charlie," the cowman on the bed said.

There was a pause. Then he added, "Before I leave there's one thing I'd like mighty well to experience again. I've been wishing for it for days. You couldn't guess what it is."

"No, but I imagine it has to do with ranching."

"Yes, I'm camping again away out yonder where it's quiet and roomy and the wind's blowing over mesquite grass. I'm listening one more time to an old Texas bull beller down the canyon. Don't talk to me about a lot of taller-faced angels singing hymns. Who that's ever rode a good horse and heard a genuine bull beller could want to be a god-damned angel, anyhow?"

Bill Halsell and the original Thomas O'Connor represented a breed of men and a breed of cattle both vanished from the earth except here and there in some kind of menagerie isolation. In 1836, about the time when the word "cow-boy" denoting border raiders after Mexican cattle came into use, Tom O'Connor had a ranch on which some of the lifted cows stopped. As the years passed, he accumulated sections of land by the score, and ten thousand cattle wore his T-H-C connected brand, ⊐C. Then, having galloped a little while with the years more swiftly than the weaver's shuttle, Tom O'Connor could no longer pull up into his saddle and ride free across the seas of grass on which his brand fattened and multiplied.

One night he told Pat Lambert, his boss, to take all hands out early next morning and bring in the biggest herd they could gather. To Pat Lambert, early morning always meant by four o'clock. After he and his hands had ridden out a few miles, they stopped to wait for daylight. They rode hard and they rode far, and about an hour before sundown they drove a vast herd of mixed cattle to the holding and cutting grounds not far from the O'Connor ranch house. Bulls were challenging, cows were bawling, stags were bellowing, calves were bleating. Heifers, yearlings, young steers and old mossy-horns, all ages of cattle of both sexes milled about, their blended voices rising above the dust raised by their hoofs.

While some of the hands held the herd and others changed horses, Pat Lambert went into the room where Tom O'Connor lay on his bed.

"We made a big drag, Mr. Tom," he said.

"I hear them," Tom O'Connor replied. His voice was thin.

"What you want me to do with them, Mr. Tom?"

"Nothing, Pat. Just hold them there. I'm a-dying, and I want to go out with their music in my ears."

Mustangs
and Mustangers

T H E R E were no horses in the Western Hemisphere when it was discovered, nor had there ever been any of the historic type. Horses brought over by the English, French and Dutch made history, and some of their descendants ran wild in Virginia, the Carolinas and elsewhere, but the mustangs of the West were, at the climax of their numbers and of their fame, straight Spanish. Arab blood flowed in veins of Barb and Andalusian horses brought over by Spaniards. The escapees from Spanish-owned caballadas *and their progeny that came to run as wild as any primitive horses were called* mesteños, *whence the word* mustang.

The "horse power" of the average mustang was not high by gasoline engine standards, but the ownerless mustang and the saddled Spanish, or Mexican, horse were blood brothers — and no better-bottomed horse ever carried a man over the rangelands. No one who conceives him as only a potential servant to man can apprehend the mustang. The true conceiver must be a true lover of freedom — one who yearns to extend freedom to all mankind.

Halted in animated expectancy or running in abandoned freedom, the mustang was the most beautiful, the most spirited and the most inspiriting creature ever to print foot on the grasses of America. When he stood trembling with fear before his captor, bruised from falls by the restrictive rope, made submissive by choking, clogs, cuts and starvation, he had lost what made him so beautiful and free. Illusion and reality had alike been destroyed. Only the spirited are beautiful. The antlered buck always appears nobler leaping the brush than he measures lifeless upon the ground. One out of every three mustangs captured in southwest Texas was expected to die before they were tamed. The process of breaking often broke the spirits of the other two.

The Pacing White Steed of the Prairies

E V E R Y section of the mustang world had its notability — the subject of campfire talk and the object of chases. Supreme above all superiors was the Pacing White Mustang. A superb stallion of one region in the beginning, he became the composite of all superb stallions. The loom of human imagination wove him into the symbol of all wild and beautiful and fleet horses. Riders everywhere over a continent of free grass came to know of him and many to dream of capturing him. His fame spread beyond the Atlantic. He passed from the mortality of the bounded and aging into the immortality of the legended.

The great horse went under varying names — the White Steed of the Prairies, the Pacing White Stallion, the White Mustang, the Ghost Horse of the Plains. His fire, grace, beauty, speed, endurance, and intelligence were exceeded only by his passion for liberty. He paced from the mesas of Mexico to the Badlands of the Dakotas and even beyond, from the Brazos bottoms of eastern Texas to parks in the Rocky Mountains.

According to some accounts, this "wind-drinker" was never caught. "He seemed to glide rather than work his legs, he went so smoothly. He did not seem to be trying to get away from his

pursuers, only to lead them on. He moved like a white shadow."
At one time, the mares in his bands might outnumber those of
half a dozen other bands. Again, if his freedom depended upon
his leaving every single follower behind, he racked on and on —
alone over the prairie grasses, "like a bird flying low," "like a
spirit horse" — as singular in his streaming whiteness as the
white whale Moby Dick, as the solitary white blackbird in a flock
of thousands, as the one white buffalo of unspeakable "medicine" in an earth-darkening migration of a million.

No one of the organized hunts after him ever won the reward
of dollars offered for his living body. In the fall of 1879, for example, an owner of fine race horses hired riders at Bonham, Texas,
rode with them up into the Indian Territory (now Oklahoma)
and there engaged a number of reservation Indians to close in on
the champion racer of the unfenced world.

"The hunters found the great Mustang all right. They laid
all kinds of traps for him and tried all kinds of dodges to run him
down or hem him in. But when he was crowded he would break
off from his *manada*, they said, and pace away like the wind. According to their report, he was not pure white but of a light
cream color with snow-white mane and tail. The Indians believed
him to be supernatural and called him the Ghost Horse of the
Prairies or the Winged Steed. When running at a distance he
showed nothing but a fast-flying snow-white mane and snow-
white tail that looked like wings skimming the ground. The boys
who got nearest to him said he had a piece of rawhide rope
around his neck. They thought he had been snared at some
watering and that the experience had helped to make him what
he was — the most alert and the wildest as well as the fleetest
animal in western America.

"Mustang hunters kept after him, and, according to report, he
changed his range from the Washita to the South Canadian.

Such a change showed wonderful cunning, for the ordinary mustang when chased would keep circling within certain limits until he was finally closed in. Some of the mustangers swore they would get the White Ghost of the Prairies even if they had to shoot him. Death from a rifle may have been his fate."

If "death from a rifle" was the uncatchable animal's "fate," he came to life somewhere else. According to one story, a vaquero not far from the Rio Grande happened to see him after he had paced for two hundred miles away from a band of professional mustangers. This was away back yonder, before the Civil War. The vaquero roped him, got help from two other men, fixed a clog on one of his forefeet, and staked him so that he could not choke himself to death. When night came, he was standing where they left him, not having taken a mouthful of grass. The next day they carried a sawed-off barrel, used as a trough, within the horse's reach and filled it with water. He did not notice it. For ten days and ten nights he remained there, grass all about him, water within reach of his muzzle, without taking one bite or one swallow. Then he lay down and died.

No matter what claims may have been advanced by reputed captors or what tales rumored, the White Steed of the Prairies never surrendered. He and his kind no longer graze and watch over the wild and free world that they once dominated, but the mystery of the Ghost Horse of the Plains is not likely to vanish.

Along in the '50s, as the story goes, a fiddling, yarning character called Kentuck reached Santa Fe and threw in with an Arkansas gambler operating under the name of Jake. They heard so much talk about the White Steed of the Prairies and Jake had such a run of good luck that he decided to take his partner and hunt down the horse. He bought pack mules, everything needed for a pack trip, and four New Mexican horses of speed and endurance.

"I don't know exactly whur to hunt," Jake said, "but we'll ride on the prairies till we find the hoss or till they are burned crisp by the fires of Jedgment Day." He had a kind of fever in his mind.

They rode east on the Santa Fe Trail, and then away north of the Arkansas River; they crisscrossed the endless carpet of short buffalo grass back southward until they were on the Staked Plains of the Canadian. They shot buffaloes and lived on hump. They dodged Indians and met no white man. Wherever wild horse sign led, they followed. They saw many bands and many stallions without bands, with now and then a white or gray among them, but not the Pacing White Stallion.

Summer passed into fall and northers brought the fluting sandhill cranes. Kentuck, who had not from the start had much heart in this wild-goose chase, yearned for bed and bed-warmer in Sante Fe. The longer Jake hunted and the more mustangs he saw, the hotter he grew on the quest.

"Go back if you want," he said with a fixed hardness to his partner. "Go and rot. I hev sworn to git what I come to git. If I don't git him, I'll keep on a-hunting till the Day of Jedgment." He knew that Kentuck would not break away from his domination.

The White Pacer and the Day of Judgment seemed linked in his mind, and nothing else in it came to the surface. As winter opened, he took it into his head that the White Stallion would appear pacing out of the southwest. Whether riding or camping, he seldom looked now in another direction.

One cold, misty day, visibility cut to only a few yards, their camp backed against a rise of ground to the north, near a lake, the men huddled and pottered about a feeble fire of wet buffalo chips. They existed only to hunt on. About sunset the skies cleared. For an hour not a word had been said. Now, while

Kentuck rustled for chips dry on the bottom side, Jake squatted in his serape, straining his eyes towards the southwest as if he expected to catch the movement of something no bigger than a curlew's head in the rim of grass blades. The glow of the sun had melted and a full moon was coming up in the clear sky when he yelled, "Yonder," and ran towards his staked horse.

"I supposed it was Indians and grabbed my rifle," Kentuck later told. "Then my eyes picked up the white horse. He stood there to the southwest, maybe a hundred yards off, head lifted, facing us, as motionless as a statue. In the white moonlight his proportions were all that the tales had given him. He did not move until Jake moved towards him. As I made for my horse, I saw that Jake was riding without saddle, though he had bridled his horse and held his reata. We kept our rawhide lariats well greased so that they would not get limp from water and stiffen when dry.

"The White Pacer paced east, against the moon, and against a breeze springing up. He seemed to glide rather than work his legs, he went so smoothly. He did not seem to be trying to get away, only to hold his distance. He moved like a white shadow, and the harder we rode, the more shadowy he looked."

After the run had winded his horse, Kentuck called out, "Jake, I don't like this. There's no sense to it. I'm remembering things we've both heard. Let's stop. We can't no more catch up with him than with our own shadows."

Jake had lost his hat. His long black hair was streaming back. His set features were those of a madman. He screamed out, "Stop if yer want. I've told yer I'm a-going to foller till the Day of Jedgment."

Not another word passed between the two. Kentuck did not stop. "Riding on and on out there in the middle of nowhere, not even a coyote breaking the silence, it didn't seem like this world," he said. Then he made out a long black line across the ground ahead. "It'll soon be settled now," he thought, "and we'll know whether the White Stallion can cross empty space like a ghost." Pulling back his horse, he yelled to Jake, "Watch out for the canyon — the bluff."

The word "Jedgment" came to his ears and he saw Jake using his coiled reata for a quirt. Then he disappeared over the bluff. Kentuck was watching him so intently that he did not see what became of the Pacing White Stallion.

Kentuck walked from his heaving horse to examine the canyon brink. He could hear nothing below. Downward in the moonlight he saw only jags of ground amid the stubby growth called *palo duro* (hard wood). He called, but there was no response. He hobbled his horse and about daylight found a buffalo trail leading down the turreted bluffs. Soon after sunup he came upon what was left of Jake and his horse, a full hundred feet below the jumping-off place. He did the best he could for a grave.

Black Devil

TALES about man-killing black stallions among the mustangs seem to be mostly Indian folklore. Some time before the Civil War, so one tale goes, a strong band of Shoshones came from the north to raid horses among the Comanches on the San Saba River. One night they awoke to the sounds of a great commotion among their horses. Rushing forth, they saw a monstrous black stallion gnawing the hobbles from the mares and turning them into his own *manada,* which stood to one side. The Indians shouted, but the marauder paid no attention. They shot their arrows, but the arrows glanced off the black skin of the target as harmlessly as if it were obsidian. Then a few of the boldest warriors rushed upon him. One swung his long reata and cast the loop over the stallion's head. Squealing with rage, the black made for the roper, seized him in his mouth, and, carrying him as easily as a coyote carries a cottontail rabbit, disappeared into the darkness, his mares fleeing before him.

The trail lay plain under the moon. The Shoshones followed to the rescue. At daylight they came into the rank grass of a dried-up lake. There they saw the stallion, amid his mares, eating the flesh of their comrade.

The next night Black Devil, as he came to be called, returned to the Shoshone camp and gnawed the hobbles off sixteen other mares. Better to lose another life at his jaws than be left afoot. The braves painted themselves for the warpath and with a medicine man at their head set out to recapture the stolen stock. But Black Devil protected his mares with such ferocity that the Shoshones were glad to get away with the loss of only one man, whom the stallion dragged from his horse and pawed to death. Again bows and arrows proved futile. Within a few nights the black beast had stolen every mare the Shoshones possessed. They left the San Saba for their own hunting grounds.

A few years went by, and in Reconstruction days a troop of Negro cavalry was ordered to Fort McKavett, on the San Saba. The depredations of the black stallion had ceased with the withdrawal of the Shoshones, but traditions of him lingered among the sparse inhabitants of the region. They were of a nature to appeal especially to Negro imagination, and "Ole Black Debble" was no joke to them.

One morning a trooper rode out alone on a mare that had been abandoned by the Apaches; at sunset he limped in afoot. Black Devil, he swore, had rushed upon him as he was rounding a hill, pulled him to the ground, and made away with the mare. Shortly afterwards two other troopers were attacked by a black stallion.

About this time two Scotsmen set up a ranch in the San Saba hills. They lived in a dugout and built a high rock wall around a little patch of ground, which they planted in corn. They were mustangers, and after the crop was gathered used the enclosure to hold wild horses. They had a well-bred stallion, and were putting picked mustang mares and fillies with him.

One night in their dugout the Scotsmen heard the shrieks that only stallions engaged in deadly combat make. Grabbing their six-shooters, they ran for the rock pen, and there in starlight they saw a powerful black horse fighting with their own stallion. The mares were ringed around the pair, and by the time the men got close enough to shoot without endangering their own horses, the black invader had thrown his antagonist to the ground and was chewing on him.

One of the men rushed back to the dugout for lariats. They had the far-famed Black Devil in their pen, and their one thought was to crease and tie him. Gun in hand, the first Scot crept nearer, his companion with lariat close behind. Black Devil knew the art of war. His mouth dripping blood, he lunged at his attackers. One of them fired, but the shot went wild and only tore into the horse's flank. Nevertheless, it saved the lives of the two men, for while they were madly scrambling over the fence, Black Devil stayed to bite at his wound.

But the halt was only momentary. He leaped the fence at one bound and plunged into the opening of the dugout. Though the dugout itself was roomy, the passage into it was narrow. As the powerful animal crashed downward, his hips and hindquarters caught between the solid uprights. One of the men cut his throat. They had to butcher him into pieces before they could clear the doorway. The mustang terror of the San Saba had come to an end.

Some settlers said that the stallion killed by the Scotsmen was not Black Devil, that Black Devil was purely a myth of the Shoshones, and that this was another horse. For a long time, at any rate, the Scotsmen used leather made from a black stallion's hide; one of them had a *cabestro* woven from his tail, and the other a girth twisted from his gleaming mane.

Blue Streak

I N the early part of this century Blue Streak lived in the arid mountains of Nevada, occasionally coming down to the sagebush mesas. In one angle of sunlight his color was an intensified *grullo* (crane-colored), indicating his Spanish ancestry; in another angle, blue-black, with sheen of grackle, except for white stockings and blazed face. His small hoofs were flint hard. All his flesh seemed to be deer-leg muscles, integrated by the finest steel springs. His neck had the curve of the bronze horses of Lysippus,* which once stood on Nero's arch in Rome and now animate the front of St. Mark's Cathedral in Venice. His back was saddle perfect.

One winter day Rube Terrill with two other ranchers jumped him and his small band of mares on a mesa against a mountain. They were riding grain-fed horses, and while they managed two or three times to head the bunch towards rocked-up blind canyons in which other mustangs had been trapped, Blue Streak jumped over and across natural impediments that might make mountain goats hesitate. He had trained his mares to jump in the

---

* Some authorities on art deny that these horses are by Lysippus.

same way. He led them back into mountain roughs by ways that no rider could follow.

It was three winters before Blue Streak was again seen on a mesa. That was a very hard winter, every bite of food in the high ground under ice and snow. Fully twenty men had tried first and last to capture Blue Streak. After several runs, Rube Terrill swore off trying to capture him as he had sworn off whiskey. Then about the first of March he and two of his men went to Cockalorum Spring to bring in some saddle horses. As they approached the spring without being seen and against the wind, they saw the horses drinking, just beyond a barbed-wire fence. Blue Streak was with them — without his mares. Perhaps in all the chasing he had become separated from them; perhaps they had been captured; perhaps in hunger and loneliness he had from mountain security seen the saddle horses and come down for company and grass. Anyhow, there he was.

Near the spring and on the edge of the meadow was a corral with walls eight feet high that had been used as a trap for wild horses when all the springs in the country but Cockalorum went dry. The wide gate was open. Rube Terrill dismounted, went through the barbed wire, grabbed up a handful of pebbles and with a yell threw them towards the horses. Blue Streak acted as if he had no knowledge of man on his own feet. He certainly was not so fearful of him as he would have been of a horseman. He ran with the *remuda* into the pen.

He accepted his Waterloo with dignity. His almost docile acceptance of the saddle was disappointing. Rube Terrill left him a stallion and gave him no chance to return to the wilds.

One day he rode him to Minersville. Everybody in the country now knew Blue Streak by description and reputation if not by sight.

"Give you five hundred for him," a man yelled out.

Excited by foreign noises, smells, people, houses, Blue Streak pranced on more magnificently while his owner yelled back, "Seven hundred fifty would not touch him."

"I guess a thousand would." The speaker was a mining magnate named Abner Temple from Salt Lake City.

He paid over the thousand and had a boxcar especially padded and bedded, supplied with grain and water and put under the care of a reliable man for transporting Blue Streak. The stallion never had shown viciousness and he traveled with an even temper.

Riding through Salt Lake City on Blue Streak, Abner Temple made the kind of sensation he had yearned for. He took pride in owning a horse that other men wanted. One night somebody tried to steal him. He put padlocks on every gate, door and window of his pen and stable. He had a blacksmith shoe Blue Streak.

Then one night the Temple household heard a tremendous pounding in the stable. By the time they arrived with a lantern, Blue Streak was gone. The wall looked as if it had been knocked out with sledgehammers. Abner Temple offered a thousand dollars for apprehension of the thief. When evidence failed to come in, he offered a thousand dollars for return of the horse and no questions asked. Newspapers ran articles describing Blue Streak and giving his history. There could not be in all Utah and Nevada another blue-black stallion with his blazed face, white stockings and spirit-lifting carriage.

Finally, Abner Temple received a letter from a farmer on the Utah-Nevada line. "Sur," he wrote, "I seen in the papper about your blue and black stallyern. day before yisterday I sighted an animal of that deskripshun he was in some willers. yisterday morning there was a big hole in my plank and picket fence where he had gone throe. $5 will cover damages and oblige."

Abner Temple now got the idea that Blue Streak was managing his own escape instead of being managed. He sent for the blacksmith who had shod him. They examined the torn-out planking of the stable wall and decided that marks on it were from powerfully driven horseshoes. Abner Temple set out by automobile for Nevada. He heard that a farmer driving a team at night over the approach to a canyon bridge had been startled by hoofbeats on the wooden floor and then, while trying to control his runaways, had seen a black streak going east.

Abner Temple took the train for Minersville and from there rode to Rube Terrill's ranch. Rube Terrill had not heard the news. The reward Abner Temple offered woke him and his riders up. After riding for ten days out from the Indian Creek country and sighting various mustangs, they came upon a dead sorrel stallion, terribly mauled and lacerated.

"Blue Streak took his mares," Rube Terrill said.

That afternoon through glasses he got a sure view of the blue-black priding it over seventeen mares. He was up in the roughs, at home in his citadel.

"Maybe he'll come down this winter," Rube Terrill reported to impatient Abner Temple.

"I want him now," the mining magnate said.

"It would take five outfits of mustangers to do any good at all in those mountains," Rube Terrill explained.

"How much would six outfits of mustangers cost?" Abner Temple had checkbook in hand.

It took Rube Terrill two weeks to get the mustangers organized. Up in the mountains they guarded all waterings over a big spread of country and learned that Blue Streak could go dry for five days at a time. They located horse trails through narrow defiles; they set snares; they learned that mustangs — the Blue

Streak kind of mustangs, at least — can climb around mountain passes. They decided to run the *manada* down by relays. They ran it until Blue Streak had only six mares left. Then they lost the bunch. They went back to their homes and regular work.

One day a message came to Rube Terrill from a Paiute Indian named Roki that the blue-black stallion was in the Wind River Mountains of Nevada, a hundred miles away. Roki said he would have him in a hair rope and would deliver him for "much money." The mustangers rode for the Wind River Mountains.

One mountain of this group rises from a gulched and tumbled plain like Gibraltar above the Mediterranean. It somewhat resembles the form of a lion with tail down. The only trail up it is along the tail — not difficult at all. Whoever goes up that trail must return the same way.

And now Blue Streak and the last of his mares were climbing it. Without relenting for one hour, the Paiutes had for days and nights been at their heels, witnessing leaps across chasms and clamberings up bluffs they had never expected any horse to make. The Rube Terrill mustangers arrived at the lion-shaped mountain just in time to witness, in broken glimpses, the ascent of pursued and pursuers.

Blue Streak was in the lead, followed by four mares. Behind them rode Roki and three other Paiutes. There could be no wild rushing up the steep, narrow lion's tail of rock, defined by sheer bluff on either side. The lion's back is broader, the sheer bluffs deeper. Blue Streak led on over the back and the roughly narrowed neck to the jut of the lion's head. This head has one ear, maybe a hundred yards long, hardly twenty feet wide at the point. Now the Paiutes were at the base of the ear, the mares and the stallion out on the short, narrow projection.

As the Indians paused for their horses to breathe, they took down their ropes. Head high and breathing in whistles, the blue-black faced them, came forward a few steps as if intending to rush upon them. They swung their loops. He whirled and hurled himself through the huddled mares, rushed on, and, without pausing for an instant, leaped into space. The mares quickly followed to the granitic jags hundreds of feet below.

Alacrán

T H E relator of this true history of a horse was in some ways the most interesting *hombre de campo* — man of the outdoors, master of all the ways and lore of mountains and plains — that I have ever known. He was Don Alberto Guajardo, of Coahuila, Mexico, on the frontiers of which he lived his whole life. He knew more about medicinal plants than a dozen *curanderas* (herbwomen), and used to export bales of them, dried, to Czechoslovakia and Italy. At his home in Piedras Negras he employed Indian weavers to make blankets — and I would not trade two of them that warm me every winter for any sold in stores. He was expert at bleating up both jaguars and deer, generally does — and in the old Indian way he was, when out for meat, no respecter of sex or season. Born about 1855, he fought Indians in boyhood and became a general in one of the Mexican revolutions. He claimed to have had a bullet wound properly treated by minnows while, after one of his battles, he lay in shallow water of the Rio Grande. He was a ranchero by breeding, and after he moved to town his mind ranged habitually among horses on grass.

Meagerly schooled, he had in youth taught himself to read

Latin, French and English; he spoke English only haltingly. He asserted that the main contributors to his education had been an ancient Lipan Indian and two or three Kickapoos with whom he grew up. The sense of wonder at the instincts of animals never left him. He personified the dignity of natural men. He was helpless amid machine-geared society. I loved and respected him.

About the time the Civil War was ending in the United States, vaqueros mustanging on the plains of Coahuila some fifty miles south of Eagle Pass, Texas, captured a dappled-gray, two-year-old stallion. He was led farther south by his owner, castrated, and kept from escaping by a hair rope that tied a front foot to the limb of a mesquite tree. He was very strong for his age and proved to be a fierce pitcher. He tried to bite anyone coming near him, and his owner tossed from a distance what hay or fodder he fed him. This owner disliked him and sold him at a bargain to Don Miguel Guajardo, father of the boy Alberto.

Tied up short to a hayrack, the young horse tried to bite and kick his new owner whenever he brought hay and corn. Don Miguel scolded him and calmly let him go hungry until he accepted food as a favor. Soon he was caressing and currying him and bathing him at the waterhole. He put a saddle on him, without drawing the cinch tight, and left it all day. Next he tied a piece of rawhide to his tail and left it there until the horse ceased to fear it and to twist and kick at it. The hairs growing out of the end of his tail were sparse, and when he raised it, it resembled the tail of a scorpion. Thus he received a name — Alacrán, or Scorpion.

Soon Alacrán was a different horse from the starved, abused animal that Don Miguel bought. Fat and sleek, as alert and ready as a wild gobbler, he carried himself haughtily. After saddling him one day, Don Miguel told a vaquero to mount him. A few jumps and Alacrán was riderless. Don Miguel tied a bundle of hay on either side of the saddle and left him until he was accustomed to the burden. The next day he mounted the horse himself, rode him gently, and began teaching him to rein. Thereafter, no one else tried to ride him; he became Don Miguel's most trusted mount.

About this time cotton was bringing boom prices. Many wagons of it were freighted out of northern Mexico to Eagle Pass, thence to San Antonio and on to a Gulf port to be shipped to England. When Alacrán was five years old, his owner rode him to conduct a train of cotton wagons. On the route a cow-buyer headed for the Rio Grande joined the train. Danger from bandits and Indians made company desirable. One afternoon the freighters camped on a creek north of the Río Sabinas — in the very range where Alacrán had been captured as a mustang. Don Miguel staked him on the prairie by digging a hole in the ground with his knife, tying a double-knot in the end of the *cabestro,* putting the knot well down in the hole, and packing the earth back on top of it. A well-buried knot can be pulled up vertically, but it cannot be pulled up by a horse setting back or running on his rope.

The cow-buyer had come to admire Alacrán so much that during the evening he offered two hundred pesos for him — a very high price at the time — and was refused. That night during a rainstorm Alacrán broke the rope, near his neck, and left. When daylight came, though visibility was very poor on account of low heavy clouds, Don Miguel climbed on top of a load of cotton to look. In the distance he made out a moving object that he took to be Alacrán. He shelled corn into a *morral* (a fiber nose bag), wrapped himself in his blue cape, and started off afoot.

"You had better ride one of the mules, Don Miguel," advised a driver. "Your horse is far off and the grass is very wet."

"If I ride, Alacrán will mistrust me," Don Miguel replied. "This is his country. He remembers how riders raced and caught him here."

Don Miguel walked on through the thick, wet grass and in time neared the grazing runaway. At sight of the man, Alacrán snorted and turned as if to flee. Don Miguel stopped, rattled the corn in the *morral,* and called the horse's name loudly in accustomed tones. The mustang snorted, took two steps forward, snorted again, then walked to put his nose in the *morral,* not without a final puff. Don Miguel unloosed his pistol belt and used it to lead Alacrán.

As he walked into camp, the cow-buyer said, "Don Miguel, yesterday I offered you two hundred pesos for that horse. Today I offer you three hundred."

"I do not wish to sell the horse at any price," Don Miguel replied, "but I shall have need of the money in San Antonio. I accept your offer. Before I deliver the horse to you, however, I must tell you something of his peculiarities, even defects."

"Nothing you could tell would alter my estimate of the horse," the cow-buyer quickly interposed. "I too am a man of the camps. Let us count the money. The horse is mine."

The silver pesos were counted out of the owner's saddlebags. Despite the buyer's indifference to information, Don Miguel gave him these warnings: "Before mounting Alacrán you will do well to look him in the eyes: if they are inflamed and red, pacify him and wait until the wild look subsides before stepping into the stirrup. You had better uncoil the rope attached to Alacrán's neck and hold it in your hand before dismounting. He always knows whether or not he is loose. Until he becomes used to you, you had better hobble as well as stake him at night. I present you with this pair of hobbles."

The buyer rode on north, ahead of the wagon train, leaving

the horse he had been riding to be delivered at the Rio Grande. It was known that he carried five hundred silver pesos, wrapped in paper, in his saddlebags.

Over the rain-soaked ground the wagons made slow progress. While the train was nooning next day, the cow-buyer dragged into camp afoot. He had been out all night and was famished. After reviving on coffee, frijoles and tortillas, he lit a cigarette and made explanation.

"Yesterday about dark," he said, "I rode up to the camp of a goatherder who was cooking supper in front of a well-thatched shed. He gladly gave me permission to spend the night. Like a fool, I started to dismount without taking down the rope as you advised. Just as my right foot was out of the stirrup, a dog rushed up barking. Alacrán reared back, throwing me to the ground, and ran off — with saddle and the five hundred pesos. The last I saw of him he was coming down the road in this direction. I have hunted for him all morning without seeing him or even his tracks. Don Miguel, will you help me find him?"

"I will help you hunt for him," replied Don Miguel, "but I cannot assure you of success. A frightened horse carrying a saddle stampedes all the *manadas* he meets. As they run, he runs after them. Was the saddle cinched tight or loose?"

"Tight," the cow-buyer replied. "There is no danger of his getting rid of it."

"It is not that," observed Don Miguel. "If the saddle is tight, the horse will not travel far without stopping. How far from here did Alacrán break away?"

"About three leagues."

The two men saddled horses and rode forth immediately. The cow-buyer wanted to search the country on both sides of the road. Don Miguel said, "If I am to help you, you must follow me. We will ride up the road until we strike Alacrán's tracks turning out of it. Then I will trail him."

They found where Alacrán had turned out of the road not a great distance south of the goatherder's camp.

"Was he sweaty when he broke away?" Don Miguel asked.

"The heavy ground had made sweat drip from him," the cow-buyer replied.

"Good!" exclaimed Don Miguel. "That means less travel."

After the general course of the runaway was evident, Don Miguel rode in wide circles, scanning in all directions. About sundown he spied Alacrán at the foot of a range of low hills. The two rode in a roundabout way so as to approach without being seen. When they were fairly near, Don Miguel dismounted, wrapped himself in his blue cape, told the other man to remain out of sight, and started walking. He could see mud on the saddle, from the horse's having rolled on it. On account of the stinging sweat on his back and the pinching girth, Alacrán was switching his tail nervously. He was in the act of lying down to roll again when Don Miguel called his name. He pitched his head up, whinnied for pleasure, and ran to his old friend, rubbing his neck against him.

Don Miguel loosed the cinch, took the rope down from the saddle horn, and led him to where the cow-buyer was waiting. "I have left the saddle for you to remove," he said.

The cow-buyer appeared to be more concerned over his silver than over his horse. Examining the saddlebags, he found only eighty or ninety pesos left. "Somebody has robbed me," he cried.

"Impossible," said Don Miguel. "No human being on earth but myself could have approached this horse near enough to touch the saddle without either roping or shooting him. Any robber who got his hands on the silver would have taken all. It is my belief that Alacrán while wallowing broke the wrappings about the pesos and spilled them on the ground.

"Listen, my friend. To show this intelligent horse that you understand him and to win his gratitude, remove the saddle and blanket at once and then with handfuls of dry grass rub the caked mud and sweat from his sensitive skin. Later, when we arrive in camp, we will bathe him and he can rest refreshed."

It was now too late to hunt for the pesos. That night Alacrán was washed and well fed. In the morning Don Miguel mounted him and, followed by the cow-buyer, rode to the spot where he had left the wagon road. Alacrán seemed disinclined to follow his old tracks, but Don Miguel knew that he, like many other range horses, was expert at trailing himself, either forward or backward. As he was gently made to understand what was desired, he began to step in the very tracks he had made two nights and one day preceding.

"Watch for wallowing places," advised Don Miguel.

For hours the trailers rode at a walk. Frequently Alacrán put his nose to the well-turfed ground to smell. In many places the grass pressed down by his hoofs had sprung back erect, leaving no visible trail. The trailers wound in and out and around. About midday they came to a spot where Alacrán had lain down but had not wallowed to any extent. An hour later they came to a waterhole where he had drunk and then wallowed energetically. Pesos were shining in the sand. By dusk most of the missing money had been recovered from a half dozen or so wallowing places. Then Alacrán forsook the trail he had so patiently followed and made for camp. He had done his duty. It was unsaddling time.

That night the cow-buyer, whose education in the management of an intelligent horse had been specifically advanced, insisted, without success, on Don Miguel's accepting half of the recovered money. When he rode off the next morning, he was more than owner of Alacrán; he was his understanding friend and partner.

Mustang Gray

T H E most successful snares — though men who made mustanging a business seldom wasted time on them — were set at trail passages through brush or woods. If wild horses were rushed at such a place, some might run their heads into loops cunningly suspended from branches. Unless the rope was tied to a limb that would give, a snared horse was likely to choke himself to death before the snarer arrived. Twelve snares set in the Nueces River country in 1869 caught three mustangs out of thirty. One broke his neck; one broke the rope and got away; only one was captured alive. It was hard to hide a noose so that an undisturbed mustang would not detect it.

Better in theory than in practice was a man's climbing a tree under which he had tied a mare, fixing himself for free casting of a reata, and dropping the loop over the head of an interested stallion. It was snaring from a tree that gave Mustang Gray his name.

Mayberry B. Gray of South Carolina — called Mabry by the Texians whom he joined when nineteen years old — fought in the battle of San Jacinto, led raiders after Mexican cattle and horses, captained a company of rangers in the Mexican War, shortly thereafter died in the arms of a señorita on the Rio Grande, and then for many years had his life prolonged in a song carried by trail drivers all the way to Montana.

> There was a gallant Texian,
>   They called him Mustang Gray,
> When quite a youth, he left his home,
>   Went ranging far away.
>
> He ne'er would sleep within a tent,
>   No comforts would he know,
> But like a brave old Texian,
>   A-ranging he would go.

Not long after coming to Texas, he was a-ranging after buffalo, far away from the settlements, when his horse fell, throwing him to the ground. He held to the reins, but the charge of a buffalo mortally shot so frightened the horse that he jerked away and ran out of sight. After trailing him for a long time and finding his tracks mingled with those of wild horses, Gray came back to the slain buffalo for a meal. He took some of the meat to a pond nearby, built a fire, and cooked it.

Tracks and freshly topped mounds of horse droppings told him that mustangs were watering here. If he but had a rope, he might catch one. He climbed a tree over the main horse trail for a look. Before long he saw a band of mustangs galloping to water. Some of them, including a heavy-set stallion, passed beneath him. The smell from a man, or any other animal, in a tree does not generally float groundward.

After the mustangs had watered and left, Gray came down from the tree with a plan. If he attempted to walk back to the settlements, he would certainly suffer from thirst. Walking was against his principles, anyhow. He went to the dead buffalo, skinned it, and pegged the hide out to dry. Hot sun and dry wind did their work quickly. He trimmed the hide into an oval and, beginning on the outside, cut a thong, maybe two fingers wide, around and around, until it was about thirty-five feet long. He wet it, tied one end to a bush, twisted it into a rope, worked it, greasing it with buffalo tallow, to make it pliable. The whole process occupied him for about three days. In the end he had a reata strong enough to hold a buffalo bull. He made, also, a hackamore, or halter. Meantime he kept out of sight and smell of the mustangs and lived well on buffalo ribs.

Animals have regular hours for watering, and when the time approached on the fourth day for the mustangs to come to the pond, Gray was ready for them. Having tied one end of the reata to a low, stout branch, he took the other up the tree to an open space immediately over the trail and made it into a loop. He knew that he would have but one throw at one mustang. He wanted the heavy-set stallion. He did not miss.

The stallion jerked himself flat, but got up. For hours he plunged, ran, jerked, snorted, but gradually as the man talked to him in low tones and moved gently, he calmed down. It was the next day before he tremblingly allowed a hand on his neck and then the hackamore on his head. Gray was six feet and one inch tall and as active as a wild bull. He leaped on the mustang's back and leaped free when the mustang hit the end of the reata, without, however, jerking himself down. The taming process went on until Gray was sufficiently master to untie the reata from the tree and secure it to the hackamore. He was determined to take his rifle, but the only way he could manage was to strap it to his own back. That made mounting difficult, but by using his bandanna as a blind he got the stallion to stand until he was firmly seated. Then, headed towards the settlements, he pulled the bandanna free. For many miles the prairie was open. The mustang ran until he was completely exhausted. That evening

Gray watered him and hobbled him short. The next morning
he had comparatively little trouble keeping him under control.
Riding bareback, he came to the camp of men who knew him.
They dubbed him Mustang Gray, a name still attached to a
place as well as to legend and song.

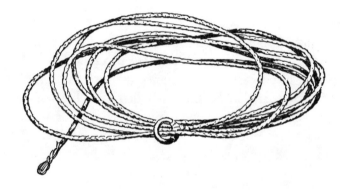

The Mustanger Who Turned Mustang

T H E most original mustanger I ever met, either in person or through hearsay, was an ex-slave named Bob Lemmons. He was not a pure-blooded Negro. The mixture probably came from Southern chivalry, but he had an Indian look. He was eighty-four years old when I talked with him in 1931 on his little ranch out from Carrizo Springs, west of the Nueces, in southwest Texas. He had grown up with the mustangs; until he was mature he had known no other life than that of range and trail; after people and fences came, he lived alone in the brush.

"I acted like I was a mustang," he said. "I made the mustangs think I was one of them. Maybe in them days I was. After I stayed with a bunch long enough they'd foller me instid of me having to foller them. Show them you're the boss. That's the secret."

Bob Lemmons always mustanged alone. It was never his aim to "dry out" a band — starve it for water — or to tire it down. He rode a horse with a good bottom, but he seldom struck a run. After starting a bunch he made no effort to keep up with it; he followed tracks. He trailed one bunch for five days without seeing it. In a country of wild horses he knew how many were in the bunch he was after, and he could distinguish the tracks made by two or three of these animals from all other tracks. About the second day, droppings from traveling horses will be dry in contrast to the moister and softer droppings of horses undisturbed on their range. Bob Lemmons looked for and "read" all kinds of "sign."

After he began following a *manada*, he changed neither horse nor clothing until he led it into a pen. Any help until he was ready to pen would have been a hindrance. A rider from ranch headquarters who wanted to tell him where to find a supply of provisions was not allowed to approach nearer than a hundred yards. The provisions were in a *morral* hung on a tree. When Bob Lemmons rode up to it, he took out the contents and put them in his own *morral*, to the smell of which the wild horses had grown accustomed. His bedding was a Mexican blanket that served also as slicker.

Within a week the band he was after would usually allow him to direct their course. His purpose was to get them to accept him as their leader. Towards the end of the second week he was supplanting the stallion as commander. At this stage he would begin working them away from the range over which they had been circling, for on strange ground they would surrender more readily than at home.

By long and patient observation, he had come to know not only wild horse habits but preferences as to water, grass, travel ways and bed ground. When he led them to a watering, he considered direction of wind and the lay of the ground so that they would feel safe from attack by panther or some other way-layer. He let them see him smelling for danger. Sometimes, to show his power, he would not allow them to drink. When he was ready, he would ride into the water with them.

He would not allow them to come too near his horse, though they were curious and eager to associate with him more closely. If the stallion had a chance, he might fight the horse or run him off. At night he unsaddled in front of the mustangs and picketed his horse at his head. When the mustangs saw him afoot, they kept their distance, though when mounted he could move very near, even among, them.

He was a light sleeper. Many a night he was awakened by a nicker, telling him that stallion or mare wanted to leave and was calling the other mustangs to come along. Certain mares, after they were fairly mastered, would not want to leave. They had given, in the manner of females, their allegiance and were not willing to turn from the horseback leader. When he was awakened by a restless nicker, he would saddle, round up the *manada* in the manner of a stallion, and leave with it.

If he saw a man riding a long way off, he would gaze at him with a demonstration of alertness and distrust — just as if he were a wild horse — and then lead in flight. If his band came to a wagon road, he would snort his suspicion and run away. Fresh panther sign made him as wary as a mare that had lost her colt to a panther. Once when he saw where a "leopard cat" (ocelot) had killed a colt, he led the stampede. If he saw an unusual piece of brush or a chunk of wood in a trail through a thicket, he made his horse "climb the mesquites" getting around it.

If for any reason he left his mustangs, he would upon returning come with the wind so that they would smell him and not be alarmed. Thus day and night, for week following week, across prairies and through thickets, huddled in rain, spread out on the ground in sunshine, listening in starlight to the encircling coyote concerts, lingering for the grazers as unhurried as the shadow of a circling buzzard, this lone man in primeval silence and space lived with the mustangs and, except in not eating grass and in having the long, long thoughts that only a human being can have, lived as one of them.

He was not invariably successful. One band that he started out of the Anacacho Hills, near Spofford, never submitted to his direction. After veering around considerably, these mustangs coursed southeast until they came into the great Randado horse ranch, about a hundred and eighty miles by direct line from the starting point. When he got among the *manadas* of the Randado, he gave up the chase, for it was not ethical to disturb them. He figured that either the stallion or the lead mare had been raised on this ranch, though neither bore a brand. The conduct of these horses occupied his mind for years. He concluded that some smell from his *morral* made them averse to him.

Another *manada* he started was led by a big bay stallion that was branded, as were three of the mares. He could not get close enough to them to make out the brands, but after they left their range and began coursing southeast, they allowed him to keep fairly near. On the third day of this direct traveling they crossed several wagon roads and Bob Lemmons glimpsed a few ranch houses and "lots of people" — perhaps a dozen. The bay stallion did not shy from these signs of man. He coursed straight and finally led his mares into a corral behind a ranch house. A man came out and asked Bob Lemmons what he meant by driving those horses. They were his, in his brand, though he had not seen them for three years. His supposition was that Indians or other horse thieves had driven them away and lost them up the Nueces, where the stallion had added wild mares to his bunch. The ranch where Bob Lemmons now found himself was in Live Oak County. He rode home with a note from the rancher to his employer explaining why he was not bringing in the band of mustangs.

Habitually, after he got a band under control, he led them homeward, taking plenty of time. One day he would see a rider on the lookout. Giving the mustangs to understand that they were to remain behind, he would ride to within shouting distance. Then he would stop and ask what day of the week it was. He would set the day and hour for penning, provided the wind was right. The ranch hands would know what to do at the pens. On the appointed day Bob Lemmons would increase his speed gradually as he led the mustangs towards the opening between the wings of the pen. When their position was right for the waylaying ranch hands to crowd them from the rear, he would break into a dead run, the wild horses at his heels. After he entered the gate, he would dash across the big round corral and be let out at a small gate kept in readiness by a man placed there for the purpose. This man and one or two others would suddenly appear before the now terrorized horses, waving blankets and shouting in order to get them milling and prevent their dashing into the fence. Meanwhile the wide entrance to the pen had been strongly barred. After the horses had milled until they were tired, ropers would enter and catch and clog them.

There are men whom bees will not sting. There are men whom a fierce yard dog will not bark at, much less bite. What in the nature, smell, movements, other qualities of certain individuals makes horses untamable by others submit to them? There have been some horse-whisperers who were not fakes. Back in the days of open range and long trails, when *remuda* men for months at a stretch guarded, grazed, watered and moved over an unpeopled world with the saddle horses of isolated cow outfits, one now and then led instead of driving his *remuda*. The horses would follow him like mules magnetized by a bell mare. I myself have known of only two such *remuderos*: one was a Mexican and one a Negro — primitives with primitive instincts not worn slick by the machinery of society. No Indian medicine man, mounted on a white horse, bleating like a buffalo calf, maneuvering at precise distances and gaits, and employing other ruses, showed more primordial skill — magic, some have called it — in leading a herd of buffaloes by moonlight to the *pis kun*, or slaughter pen, than Bob Lemmons sustained until he actually became the leader of a band of wild horses that, as fresh as they had been when he first sighted them, followed him into a pen — a pen that would take away their freedom forever.

The Headless Horseman of the Mustangs

A B O U T the middle of the last century, not long after the Mexican War ended, a rider without any head was reported to be ranging in the great mustang country along the Nueces River in southwest Texas. Several borderers who saw him said that he carried his head, under a Mexican sombrero, tied to the horn of his saddle. Some added a "band of gold bullion" to the sombrero. About his shoulders fluttered a brush-torn serape over a buckskin jacket, and his legs were encased in rawhide leggins, such as were then made and worn by most vaqueros, flesh side turned out. He bestrode a heavy black mustang stallion as wild as anything that ever raced over prairie or plunged through chaparral thicket.

At no particular time or place were mustang and rider to be seen. In the bright sunshine of morning some hunter might glimpse them climbing the rough breaks far up the Nueces Canyon, and then in the dusk of evening a lone rancher on the Leona forty miles away might see the bleached buckskin and rawhide of the strange rider on the black stallion tearing across prickly pear flats. Neither horse nor horseman seemed ever to tire, and it was observed that the rider never bent or turned in the saddle but sat as rigid as if he were made of wood and had been spiked to the animal's back.

The creature carrying the awful thing was shunned by all other mustangs. Sometimes he could be located by a stampede of wild horses away from his presence. He never stayed long in one locality, as horses usually range, but roved far and wide. Indeed, he seemed a thing possessed, fleeing wildly at sight of any human being.

Indians, ever superstitious and ever horse-hunting, saw the mustang with the headless rider on his back and tried to keep clear of his range. Mexican vaqueros and *pastores* (sheep or goat herders) were just as scared. A glimpse that some of the troops stationed at Fort Inge on the Leona River got of the rider resulted in a much-expanded tale. According to tradition, Mayne Reid, who had been with the American army at the capture of Mexico City, was for a brief time thereafter stationed at Fort Inge. He was an eager listener to camp tales about mustangs, buffalo hunters, scalp hunters, and other frontier types. In *The Headless Horseman: A Strange Tale of Texas* (London, 1886), a romance immensely popular for a generation, he added to the legend.

"No one," he wrote, "denied that the thing had been seen. The only question was how to account for a spectacle so peculiar as to give the lie to all known laws of creation. At least half a dozen theories were started. . . . Some called it an 'Indian dodge'; others, a 'lay figure.' Still others said that it was a real rider so disguised as to have his head under the serape that enshrouded his shoulders, with perhaps a pair of eye-holes through which he could see to guide his horse. Again, the headless horseman was Lucifer himself."

Perhaps the "lay figure" cited by Mayne Reid is explained by the following. Patrick Burke, who was born in 1834 on the Texas coast about an hour after his mother landed with other settlers from Ireland, became a noted rancher east of the Nueces River. He said that in early days mustangers he ranged with would, if they could, catch a strong stallion and tie a scarecrow, a kind of imitation man, on him and then let him loose. He would tear away, and after a while make for his own band of mares, trailing it like a bloodhound. As soon as any mustangs saw the scarecrow, they would stampede. Their frightened running would set other mustangs running. Sometimes thousands would be running over the prairies at the same time, all going in the same direction, band after band joining together. Their hoofs pounding on the earth sounded like the terrific roar of a cyclone. After the mustangs had run themselves down, the mustangers could guide them into pens with long wings that had been built to hold them.

One theory not mentioned by Mayne Reid was that the phantom horseman of his tale was the *patrón* — the ghostly guard — of the lost mine of the long-abandoned Candelaria Mission on the Nueces, to protect it against profane prospectors.

No one ever got very close to the black mustang, but a few frontiersmen who took long shots at the headless rider declared that their bullets passed through him as easily as through a paper target. They were less superstitious than Indians, Mexicans, or soldiers, but even some of them developed a feeling of awe. Finally, a half dozen or so united to capture the mustang and put an end to the mystery.

They ambushed him at Bull Head watering on the Nueces and shot him down. On his back they found a dried-up Mexican carcass perforated with bullets. It was lashed to horse and saddle so tightly that the rope had to be cut to unfasten it, and a skull with a frayed sombrero bound around it was tied to the horn of the saddle.

But the mystery was only half solved. How had a vaquero's body come to be fastened on a mustang and his head lashed to the saddle? In time Bigfoot Wallace and Creed Taylor answered the questions, but a full explanation carries us back years before the mystery began.

On the night of December 4, 1835, a little while before the besieging Texans heard that deathless cry, "Who will go with old Ben Milam into San Antonio?" a deserter from the Mexican stronghold slipped into their ranks. He was a lieutenant named Vidal. He brought valuable information, and during their capture of San Antonio he convinced the Texans of his friendship. One who noted the Mexican's lithe body, deft movements, and alert eye was Creed Taylor.

After the battle of San Jacinto settled the fight between Mexico and Texas, and the fighters turned to occupations of peace, Vidal took up horse stealing. It was a risky business, for at that time one man could take another's life with less risk than his horses. At first Vidal's reputation as a patriot cloaked his operations. By the time his real character became known, he was commander-in-chief of a chain of horse thieves operating on both sides of the Rio Grande and sneaking stolen stock clear into Louisiana and Mississippi. They were cunning enough to throw suspicion for their operations on the ever horse-raiding Comanches.

In the summer of 1850 Vidal and three picked confederates gathered up a considerable bunch of horses on the San Antonio River and headed southwest towards Mexico. The raid was well timed, for most of the sparse settlers were away to the north chasing a band of Comanches who had swooped down on the Guadalupe settlements a few days before.

But not all were away. Contrary to custom, Creed Taylor was not after the Indians — and some of his horses were among those stolen. Creed Taylor was a Texian among Texians. He had killed Mexicans with Bowie and Milam, fought the Indians as a ranger under Jack Hays, and scouted for old Rough-and-Ready in the Mexican War. He was yet to be involved in the lethal Taylor-Sutton feud. He was not the kind of man to let any thief gallop off with his horses.

A Mexican rancher named Flores who chanced also to be at home had likewise lost horses. Both he and Creed Taylor suspected Vidal as they struck out on the trail of the thieves. The farther they trailed, the surer they became that they were following Vidal. They found cattle carrying arrows that had been shot into them. "Vidal's trick to make greenhorns smell Indians," Creed Taylor said, and went on.

At the Frio the trailers met Bigfoot Wallace — always ready to "up" any "copperbelly" who needed upping. With joy he joined the hunt.

At the Nueces, the trail of the horses veered up the river. Two days later, close to dusk, about twelve miles from Fort Inge on the Leona, the trailers, unseen, sighted the stolen *caballada* and the camp of thieves. The Mexicans, who had been pushing ahead hard, now seemed to consider themselves secure from pursuers. The smoke from their campfire was rising thick and high; only one man was on herd; no sentinel was out scouting for sign. The Texans lay low and waited.

Night came on. There was no moon but the stars were bright. When the Evening Star was well up, Creed Taylor crept forward to reconnoiter. He avoided passing too near the stolen horses and kept the wind on them. He was more afraid of their giving the alarm than he was of the man on herd, who occasionally moved around at a sleepy walk. The camp was on the edge of a mesquite and prickly pear thicket. Crawling up to it, Creed Taylor made out three sleeping forms. One of them, he was sure, was Vidal's. Then he stole back to his waiting confederates. Their work must be done before the man on herd awakened his relief.

Each of the three Texans had a six-shooter and a rifle. They made their plans. Flores was to give Creed Taylor and Bigfoot Wallace ample time to crawl to the sleeping thieves. In ambush, he was to wait until the thief on herd passed near him, and then to shoot. The sound of his shot would be the signal for the other two men.

They had reached the camp, each had picked his man, and, cocked six-shooters in hand, they were awaiting the signal shot when it rang out, followed by the yell of a struck man. In an instant the sleeping Mexicans were on their feet. Two revolvers flashed, and two horse thieves went back to sleep — forever. The third broke for the thicket, but two bullets stopped him. As it turned out, Flores's target was only wounded and got away in the brush, but he did not take any horses with him.

At daylight the bodies of the dead men were inspected. There was no question as to the identity of Vidal's. He was a little man. Bigfoot Wallace, always daring and eccentric, now made one of his original proposals. In the recaptured *caballada* was a black mustang stallion that had been herd-broken but that had never felt a cinch under his belly. Bigfoot proposed that he be roped, saddled, and mounted with Vidal's body. Perhaps Bigfoot jested. He thought it a good joke, once, when in a brush with Indians he picked out the biggest one for his own, saying he "needed a pair of leggins," and, after killing him, actually pulled the leggins off and wore them. Perhaps Bigfoot wanted to give warning to other horse thieves. At any rate, his pro-posal was considered good.

The black mustang was roped, tied up, blindfolded with a red bandanna, saddled with Vidal's saddle. Then the Texans cut off Vidal's head and, with chin-strap and thongs, fastened the horse thief's sombrero firmly to it. Next, making deft use of buck-skin, they laced the sombreroed head to the horn of the saddle. It was a Mexican saddle, rawhide-rigged, with a wide, flat horn.

They dressed Vidal's headless body in full regalia — leggins, spurs, serape — and with more care than an *arriero* in the Sierra Madre takes in packing a mule with silver bars, fixed it in the saddle. They tied the dead man's feet in the stirrups and dou-ble-fastened the stirrups to each other under the mustang's belly so that they could not fly up.

During all these operations the black mustang was shivering

and snorting, for nothing terrifies a horse more than the smell of foreign blood. Finally, the blind was removed from the stallion's eyes and, without bridle or halter, he was set loose. In after years Bigfoot used to declare that he had seen many pitching horses, but that he had never seen any other animal act like that black stallion with a dead Mexican on his back. After he had pitched in every direction, snorted, squealed, pawed the air, reared up and fallen backwards, rolled and then stood quivering, the thing was still on his back. For maybe five minutes he stood with feet spread out, sides heaving, nostrils dilating, his whole body quivering. Then, with a wild and terrified squeal, he broke away into a run that, as we have seen, scared up a legend not yet dead.

Creed Taylor, Bigfoot Wallace and Flores drove the captured horses back to the ranches on the San Antonio River. They agreed to keep still for a while.

Running with the Wild Mares

T H E Papago Indian reservation — Papaguería, as it is called — encloses two and a half million acres of desert and mountain in southern Arizona against the international boundary line. Before the line was fenced, Papago stock used to drift far down the Altar Valley in Sonora. There were many wild horses, and no better or wilder horsemen ever rode than some of the Papagos.

Noted among them were two brothers named Siliaco and Sandiego. Their story came to me in Tucson, in April, 1951, from their tribesman Juan Xavier, a magnificent man in stature, in silence and in reserve, a great mystery in his eyes and in the contours of his face. After the poet E. E. Cummings came to know him while spending a season in Tucson, he painted a picture for him as a parting present. Juan Xavier wanted to respond with something personal also, something out of himself. He decided to give Mr. Cummings a story of his land and his people. His American wife, whom he had married while aiding her in anthropological work, wrote down the story as he told it for the friendship gift. With oral additions, he let me have a copy to read. He could not allow me to use it, however, without consent from the friend to whom he had presented it. A letter finally overtook Mr. Cummings in Rome. With his permission as well as that of Juan Xavier, I tell it.

Siliaco and Sandiego lived in the village of Tecolote (which means Owl) near the Sonora line. Sometimes they went down into the mountains and camped by a little lake where many men in the night had heard the wild horses coming in from the desert to drink and had heard strange noises among them. These brothers grew tall, slim and strong, but about the time they came to full manhood "their minds turned in a curious way."

They came to believe that they themselves were horses. Sandiego was married, but he and his brother deserted the village, separating themselves from all other people. They threw away their clothes and ran naked with the wild horses. Now and then people from a distance caught sight of them. A stallion would be seen leading his *manada* to a waterhole, mares and colts strung out behind him, behind them some wild burros, and then, last of all, Siliaco and Sandiego. They would be running, galloping, trotting like horses, throwing up their heads to sniff the wind, looking about for danger, and then bending over and drinking on all fours like horses. They could not live on grass. They must have eaten mesquite beans, cholla buds and the fruit from cholla and other cactus in season, but this diet would not sustain them the year round. Nobody really knew how they lived, but it was believed that the mares gave them milk.

Certainly the wild mares and stallions were not afraid of them, though at sight or smell of any other human beings they fled. Perhaps the wild horses understood by the smell of the naked boys that they had the natures, even the minds, of horses. Sometimes one brother would be with one band of horses and the other with another band, and then again they would come together, shifting about as the wild horses shifted.

The Papagos are a swift-running people; their young men are trained to foot-racing. Siliaco and Sandiego grew lither and swifter and more enduring than any others. They kept up with the wild horses wherever they ran.

Once Siliaco was caught and kept in a tamed condition for a little while. This is the way they tell it. Papago riders had gone down into Sonora to help in the Mexican roundups and to bring back any of their own cattle that had drifted to those ranges. While they were down there, a Mexican vaquero riding alone on the desert saw a palo verde tree covered heavily with wild gourd vines. The vines appeared to be so dense that he rode nearer to observe them, and as he approached the tree he saw something stir in the shade.

What animal could this be? he thought. Then a naked man with long hair jumped out and went running off at an astonishing speed. The vaquero thought it must be one of the Papagos who lived with the horses. He felt the wish to catch him, and there on the open desert he spurred after him. After a long chase he got within roping distance. He swung his loop and threw it. As the rope tightened around the wild man's middle, he behaved like a wild horse or steer that is roped. He plunged and twisted and tried to free himself, but was jerked down and had to submit.

The vaquero saw that the man was Siliaco. He began gentling him down with quiet talk, and after Siliaco became quiet he told him to come with him to camp for food and tobacco. Siliaco seemed to return in mind to human ways. He said he would come. He got up on the horse behind the vaquero, and thus they rode to camp.

Vaqueros there, both Mexican and Papago, saw them approaching. One Mexican yelled out, "Who is riding there naked behind you?"

The vaquero yelled back, "It is Siliaco."

All had heard about him, this Indian who ran with the wild horses. They gathered about him to see and wonder, but they were quiet and acted gently towards his disturbed mind. They gave him cigarettes and good beans and tortillas, fresh-cooked meat and hot sugared coffee. They gave him shirt and pantaloons to cover his body. As night came on, he sat with the other men around the fire, quiet and warm and fed and clothed, and listened to the talk and singing. His mind seemed again to be that of a man and not of a wild horse.

He stayed there in camp until the roundup was finished. Then he went with his captor and some other vaqueros to the Mexican village of El Plomo. Here the people treated him kindly and with respect. One night, somebody saw him walking away. Eyes were always on him, for, after all, the people knew that he was not like other men. A man followed him, keeping out of sight, to see what he would do. After Siliaco had walked a good distance into the desert, he stopped and stood for a long while, looking at the stars. He seemed to be listening. Maybe he heard something in the wind like the sound of hoofs. Presently he jerked off his clothes, threw them aside, and ran on into the desert and the darkness. He never came back. Later he was seen again with the wild horses. Then after a time had passed he was not seen. The only evidence of what might have become of him was the bones of a man found by a hunter in the mountains of Sonora.

Sandiego had no children when he ran away. Perhaps it was remembrance of his wife that brought him back. Anyway, he came back to the village of Tecolote and to the house and woman he had left. His mind cleared and his ways were steady.

He was respected by the people, not for any special power, but because as a normal man he went on leading a good life. He had two sons. One joined the Mormon church and the other became a good cattleman. In his old age these sons saw that he was well dressed and well fed; they were good to him in all ways.

He never spoke of his life with the wild horses, but he would never ride a horse or work one to wagon or plow. He always walked wherever he was going, though he would get into another man's wagon if a ride were offered him. He could travel in a sort of trotting walk all day, sometimes breaking into a run. His swiftness and endurance as a runner lasted into old age. He was proud of this power. If sometimes, lying hidden in stillness far out alone, he watched wild horses trotting like foxes down to water from the mesa, or grazing in alertness, never for a moment easy with the security felt by creatures subject to man, or running until even their dust disappeared, he never followed. He laid out a race course near his village and ran over it with other racers, and he ran over the mountains to his own solitudes until he died at the age of eighty. That was about the time also that the last of the wild horses disappeared from Papaguería.

The Saga of the Saddle

A H O R S E'S *performance under the saddle tells what he is. The stories that follow are, in a way, the finality on the mustang breed. They belong to the times when "a man on foot was no man at all," when a man's "best friend" was his horse, and a horseman unhorsed was sin pies — without feet. They express or imply the cooperation between carrier and the carried, flesh conforming to flesh, spirit blending with spirit, intelligence recognizing intelligence.*

Little Aubry's Ride

F O R sustained endurance, speed and distance, I rank a ride made by François Xavier Aubry as supreme in the whole riding tradition of the West. "Little Aubry," they called him. He was only five feet and two inches tall, weighed hardly more than a hundred pounds. Every ounce of his body was distilled energy. He was quiet and modest; he loved fame and adventure. He led wherever he went.

A French-Canadian by birth (in 1824), he came to St. Louis at eighteen and went to clerking in a big store of general merchandise. He heard talk of bull trains and pack outfits. He sold goods consigned to Independence, the jumping-off place for the West, up the Missouri River. The stuff in his body was not compounded of clerkly tameness. He bought goods on credit from his employers, went to Independence, and joined one of the freight trains setting out for Santa Fe. He prospered as a trader and soon had extensive interests.

The year of his great rides was 1848. It generally took from three to four weeks to ride the eight hundred miles between Santa Fe and Independence. The schedule of the military mail was thirty days; ox wagons required from two to three months.

Early in January, Aubry arrived in Independence after having been on the road only fourteen days. Five men who started with him had dropped out. Mexican robbers, Indians and a blizzard had delayed him; he had killed three mules and covered the last three hundred miles in three days. The *Daily Missouri Republican* (published in St. Louis) declared the ride "unprecedented in Prairie life."

For Aubry it was a warming-up exercise. As soon as the first weeds of spring were greening for oxen to graze upon, he loaded his wagons for Santa Fe. By the time they reached their destination the whole country was on a boom; the United States had defeated Mexico in a war of conquest and taken from her an immense territory that included New Mexico. Aubry sold his goods at 100 per cent profit and determined to return to Missouri and bring out a second cargo the same season. This procedure was "unprecedented." The freight outfits in Santa Fe could not get back in time to haul for him, but there were always oxen and bull whackers on the Missouri.

He announced that he would make the ride in eight days — and bets ran high. Before he had gone three hundred miles, six men who set out with him had fallen behind. The remainder of the trip Aubry performed alone. He killed three horses and two mules. Indians took his baggage, his food, even letters he was carrying; but he contrived to slip away from them. He walked forty miles, went three days without a bite to eat, slept — off his horse — only four or five hours on the whole route, though he cat-napped now and then while riding, riding, riding. It took him eight days and ten hours to make the trip; but, counting out the time lost to Indians and on the walk they made him take, his actual traveling time was about seven days.

When Aubry got back to Santa Fe in late summer, the plaza was buzzing over his record. "I can do better," he said. "I'll bet a thousand dollars that I can make the ride within six days." The money was covered. Aubry at once began making preparations. He sent men ahead to have horses in readiness at Fort Mann on the Arkansas, Council Grove and another point or two. Over certain stretches of the route he would drive extra mounts, California style. It was to be a lone ride over an empty land.

Before dawn on September 12 he left Santa Fe in a swinging gallop, and he ate only six meals on the ground, stopped only once to sleep — for two hours — before he reined up his final horse, heaving and atremble, at Independence on the Missouri. On the way he had killed six horses and broken down six others, several of them purchased from wagon trains encountered on the road. He ate a little while riding, and after the first day and night out tied himself to the saddle so that he could doze without danger of falling off. So long as he kept steady in the saddle, a good horse would keep the gait. It was the rainy season of the year; for a whole day and night rain fell on him continuously, and high winds were blowing most of the time. Streams were swimming deep.

Picture Little Aubry as he makes his ride! In the yellow morning sun and under the slant rays of autumn noon he races down the mountains past the village of San Miguel, where he changes horses, and on to another change at the Rio Gallinas, now the site of Las Vegas. For hours and miles and for miles and hours, in twilight and then in darkness, he listens to hoofbeats. In the dead of the night he comes to the camp of a Mexican pack train; the boss knows him and lets him have a *grullo* that has never been tired. The Morning Star is still shining when, nearing Point of Rocks, he gives the long-drawn-out "coyote yell" of the West and the man whom he sent out a week ago stirs the coals around a pot of coffee and draws in the stake rope of a fresh mount.

The mount is a "yellow mare" — without doubt a Spanish dun — named Dolly. One deduces that all the mounts Aubry sent out from Sante Fe were native New Mexican horses — Spanish blooded.

"I'd kill every horse on the Santa Fe Trail before I'd lose that thousand dollar bet," he says to his man, "but it's not the money I care about. I'm riding to prove that I can get more out of a horse and last longer myself than any other man in the West."

The man by the fire of buffalo chips does not have time to answer. The saddle has been changed, Aubry has gulped down a quart of simmering coffee and sprung onto Dolly's back with a roasted buffalo rib in his hand.

"*Adiós!*"

He rides on. The high, dry country recedes behind him and a chill autumn drizzle hides the sun. He cannot see Rabbit Ear Mounds, but he knows where they mark an edge of the wide, flat plains. At Rabbit Ear Creek he passes Alexander Majors's wagon train "at a full gallop without asking a single question as to the danger of Indians ahead." At roaring Willow Bar he takes off the bridle for a blow and a drink.

But where are the relay horses that were to be here, over one hundred miles from Point of Rocks? Indians? A dead man's scalped head answers. Beautiful Dolly must go on. On, on, until she has carried Little Aubry one hundred and fifty, two hundred miles in twenty-six hours. So far as I know, this is the world's record for one horse in one day and night, plus two hours, of galloping.

The yellow mare bears him lightly across the Cimarron of the quicksands, and somewhere beyond he delivers her for safekeeping to a generous-natured wagon master who knows him and gives him the best horse he can pick from his train. Hidden in timber above the ford on the Arkansas, three fresh horses await him. He mounts one and cracks his whip over the other two. The old church at Santa Fe is still less than four hundred miles behind. He is not quite halfway to Independence. He cannot spare horseflesh now. He wears the first of the relays down in ten miles, the second in about the same distance; the third unexpectedly drags his feet. In a minute Aubry has unsaddled, hidden his saddle and blanket in the grass, and, silver-plated bridle in hand, is trotting on east afoot. For twenty-four miles he does not see a human soul. Then he walks into Fort Mann, where he finds one of his own freight trains and has to spend a long while tending to business. Here he lies down for two hours and sleeps while a certain horse is being brought in.

Refreshed now, he skims the ground past Coon Creek and past Pawnee Rock, where so many good men have bit the dust. To detail all the changes of horses would betray Aubry's swiftness. At Council Grove he pauses long enough for coffee to boil, ties himself on a fresh horse, rides on. It is a hundred and fifty miles to Independence yet. He hardly notices the beautiful trees and hills to which the plains have given way; he does not hear the cawing of the crows in the valleys. It takes a full twenty-four hours, most of it in rain, to make that last lap. At Big John Springs, by paying heavy boot, he swaps with a trapper for one of the best mounts on the journey.

At ten o'clock on the night of September 17 he halts in front of the Noland House, called also the Merchant's Hotel. It is bright with lights. Men rush out from the bar and "lift" him from his saddle. It is "caked with blood." The few words he breathes out are in a thin whisper. He has won his bet. He bolts ham, eggs and coffee and tells the proprietor to wake him in three hours. The proprietor waits six hours before rousing him. He bounds up "rather wrathy" at the misjudged kindness. "I like to take my food and rest in broken doses," he says. He is up in time, however, to catch a steamboat just leaving the dock for St. Louis.

The next summer in Santa Fe, Captain R. B. Marcy met Aubry at a supper being paid as a debt to the great rider. At Marcy's request Aubry wrote down and signed a short account of his ride. "I made the trip," he said, "travelling time only counted, in 4 days and 12 hours, though the time spent between Santa Fe and Independence was 5 days and 16 hours. I made a portion of the trip at the rate of 250 miles to the 24 hours; made 200 miles on my yellow mare in 26 hours."

In 1852 the California gold boom drew Aubry on west, pioneering a new route across deserts and mountains. He rode the yellow mare out of Santa Fe, followed by ten big wagons loaded with goods, a herd of thirty-five hundred sheep, and over a hundred surplus mules and horses. When he got back to Santa Fe the next year he gathered up fourteen thousand sheep to drive to the booming market, and other men followed his trail with three times that many. He kept diaries of these trips. On August 3, 1853, west of the Little Colorado River in Arizona, he recorded: "Indians shooting arrows around us all day wounded some of our mules and my famous mare Dolly, who has so often rescued me from danger by her speed and capacity for endurance." There is "no suffering like the suffering from thirst," he added. On August 16, held back by weaker men, all living on half rations of horse meat, he himself having been wounded eight times, he entered these words: "I have the misfortune to know that the flesh we are eating is that of my inestimable mare Dolly who has so often saved me from death at the hands of Indians. She gave out on account of her wound."

A year later a newspaper bully in Santa Fe stabbed Little Aubry to death, aged thirty. The newest and fastest steamboat on the Missouri River had just been christened the *F. X. Aubry.*

Between her smokestacks she had the carved figure of a light rider on a yellow mare. This was fame. Later the Santa Fe Railroad followed, between Albuquerque, New Mexico, and Bakersfield, California, the routes he had pioneered and recommended. Long ago the *F. X. Aubry* with her emblem of horse and horseman was turned to dust and rust. Nevertheless, so long as a few people know the length of a mile measured by the legs of horses and men and multiplied by hundreds, Aubry will live. No riding legend of Tartar, Scythian, or Cossack calls up his superior.

Chester Evans and Prince

CHESTER EVANS was seventy-eight years old and was running the weekly newspaper at Lebo on the plains of western Kansas when he told me the main story of his life. This was in 1940.

Sixty-six years before that, back in Iowa, he had bought for eighteen dollars the colt he named Prince. The colt's mother was a Sioux mare of unmixed Spanish blood; his sire was a French-Canadian stallion, with a touch of Spanish. Chester was only a colt himself, his mother dead, his father always busy at his printing office. They lived in a boardinghouse. Prince and Chester grew up together, keeping steady company with each other. The colt would come at the boy's call and follow him wherever permitted. He delighted in carrots and lumps of sugar. He was a strawberry roan with blazed face and white stockings on front feet.

Chester wanted to be a cowboy. After he nearly died from lung fever in the winter of '77-'78 and continued to be frail, his father said he might go west to the Smoky Hill Pool northwest of Dodge City. An uncle worked on this range. Riding Prince, the boy set out with a man driving a team of big sorrel horses to a wagon. While they were still hundreds of miles from Dodge City, and the country was getting wilder all the time, one of the sorrels took colic and died. The owner sold the other to a government horse buyer, and Chester went with him. He was delivering a bunch of horses to Fort Riley. From there Chester trailed a troop of cavalry to Dodge City. Herds of longhorns were coming up from Texas. The town was alive with young men who wore spurs that rang. Within a few days the uncle came in and took Chester out to the Smoky Hill Pool headquarters, seventy miles away on Cheyenne Creek.

Now four years old, Prince weighed around a thousand pounds. He had an extra heavy mane and tail, and he carried his neck arched and his tail curved. Chester was sixteen years old and went at once to riding the line. "I'm not saying how good I was," he said, "but in time Prince got to be as good a roping horse as a cowboy ever swung a loop from, and, without a finger touching the bridle reins, he could cut out any cow that dodged and doubled in a herd."

That fall, word came from the south that Chief Dull Knife was stirring up the Cheyennes in the Indian Territory. Two years before they had been herded down there from their Montana range. On the morning of September 27, 1878, the valley of Cheyenne Creek looked to be full of Indians. Somebody had to notify Fort Monument on Smoky Hill River eighteen miles away. Because Chester was light weight — and had the best horse around — he was selected to make the dash.

He led Prince up the canyon a way, mounted, and hit the flat a-running. Fifteen Cheyennes dashed to cut him off. Prince ran several miles before they got in shooting distance. Then an arrow stuck in his shoulder. Chester pulled it out and the blood spurted so that he held his thumb in the wound. Next Chester got an arrow in his right leg. To pull it out he had to shift his hand from Prince's shoulder, and then he noticed that the blood had stopped flowing. When he yanked on the shaft, it came free but left the arrowhead in his leg. Three more arrows clipped him, and Prince got one in the rump. A sergeant at the fort, there being no doctor, cut out the arrows. Prince never liked Indians after this experience. He could smell them as far as he could smell water. Twenty years after this run, some Oklahoma Indians stopped at a blacksmith shop in Lebo half a mile away from the little pasture in which Prince grazed. He snorted like a buck deer that's heard something he can't wind and he pawed the ground like a challenging bull.

In the spring of 1880 Chester was hunting antelope about twelve miles south of the ranch when the wind changed in both direction and intensity and he found himself facing a raging prairie fire. He did not have a match with which to start a back fire. Prince seemed to understand that he must run for the lives of both. When they reached a big buffalo wallow with about a foot of water in it, Chester thought of trying to save himself there. But what of Prince? Instantly the decision was made: "If one of us has to die, we will die together." Prince spurted up his speed, but the fire was gaining. It was racing literally faster than the wind, for the heat brought the cooler air rushing to the blazing waves. By the time boy and horse reached a plowed fire guard, the cinders were falling thick on them and the air was stifling. That fire guard saved them.

The next spring it rained. In turning a steer, Prince fell on the slick grass. He got up, but his rider could not stand. His leg was broken. The two were alone. In the words of Chester Evans, "I called Prince and he was at my side. I hate to think of the pain and the struggles to get into the saddle. Prince seemed to try to help me. He took me nine miles to the ranch. Nobody was there except the hired girl. I lay down on the floor and braced my good leg against the door jamb while she pulled on the other. She couldn't pull it into place, and I told her to tie the bridle reins around my foot and to set back on them. She did, twisting around a lot, and the break finally slipped into place. We splintered it. She left me on a pallet, got on Prince and rode him to Wakeeney, forty-four miles away, for the nearest doctor. All he did when he got to the ranch was to put on more and better splints. The leg healed first rate."

A year later Chester rode Prince to a ranch south of Amarillo in Texas and helped trail a herd of cows back to Kansas. On range and trail he rode other horses, but Prince remained to him "the only horse I ever really knew. I could camp anywhere with him and he would never leave me. With his keen senses he was a sentinel for game, wild cattle and horses by day and for anything prowling by night. He would grab the neck of some bunch-quitter — a horse trying to leave the *remuda* — and bring him to his milk."

You can look at the map of Kansas north and west of Dodge City and see that not many people live there to this day. Fewer by far were in the country when the big blizzard of '87 hit. That was the winter Charlie Russell painted "The Last of the Five Thousand" and struck the trail for fame.

Before daylight on the morning of January 7, Chester's uncle woke him and told him to ride for the doctor at Wakeeney. His wife was about to give birth. He bade Chester tell the doctor to come at once but said to put Prince in the livery stable and let him rest four hours before starting back. It was dusk when Chester headed for home, and the wind was rising. Prince seemed as eager as ever. Before long the mist had turned to snow and sleet and the wind cut like knives.

"I guess I made a mistake in not turning directions over entirely to Prince," Chester Evans related. "I kept quartering the wind when I should have headed into it. It was more west than north. There was no real road, and the snow blotted out all trace of whatever trail there was. A man, like any other animal, has an instinct to turn his back to a blizzard. Then he will veer and try to course against the wind, only to dodge it later. Daylight came and I didn't know where we were. If Prince knew he couldn't tell. I got down and he put his muzzle close to me and seemed to say we had better keep going. That day wore on. We didn't strike even a lobo track. All cattle had drifted south. A lot of them were already dead. It was slow, slow work breaking through the drifts of snow. Sometimes I got rid of the freezing numbness by walking. At the deepest drifts I would help break through.

"There were times when we couldn't see anything for the driving snow. There was no shelter, just plains of snow and ice, on and on, no canyons, no breaks. Dark came early. I knew Prince was hungry. Several times that night while I was stumbling along I tried to sit in the snow. Each time Prince would nuzzle me, and if the nuzzling didn't stir me he would paw me — not hard, just enough to make me move. He never would have left me.

"The second day came and some time that morning Prince brought me to a standstill at the Steele ranch on Beaver Creek. It was away south of the home ranch. We had missed the head of Cheyenne Creek to the east. The creek would have told me where we were. We got something to eat. The blizzard had broken. Mr. Steele got on his horse and rode home with me. The doctor had arrived in time to help bring a baby boy into the world. Prince did not seem any worse off for the experience, but it was several days before I was able to leave the house. Thirty-eight men died in western Kansas in that blizzard. The Smoky

Hill Pool started into the winter with six thousand head of cattle. The next spring we gathered a hundred and eighty-one."

After this breakup in the ranch business, Chester Evans and Prince moved to Lebo. The only person in town who thought the young man better looking than his horse was the girl he married. When the Cherokee Strip was opened for settlement in 1889 and thousands of people lined up to wait for the pistol shot that was to start the race for land, Evans rode Prince. He staked out his quarter section, lived on it two years, and then hitched Prince and "a five-year-old Know-Nothing" to a spring wagon and headed for California. Before long he and his family, in which he included Prince, were in a boxcar rolling back to Lebo to settle down for good.

In telling this story of his horse, Chester Evans seemed to have no thought of any other person and of himself only in association with Prince. At the very end his voice choked so that he had to pause for words.

"I bought a little pasture," he said, "joining the townsite and built a good shed on it to shelter my friend. He would bring the milk cows in from the pasture of an evening. I would hitch him to a spring wagon and turn him loose and he would go to the feed store, where somebody would load the wagon, and then he would bring the load back to the barn. He enjoyed grazing and enjoyed being with me, especially when I talked to him. My children and their playmates learned to ride on him.

"The center pole of this shed I built was set on a flat rock. The feedbox was attached to it. As the years went by, Prince's teeth wore down until they were of little service. He took to pawing while he ate. This pawing, without my giving proper attention to the matter, loosened the dirt around and under the big rock. One day in the fall of 1912 a telephone lineman hurried to my office with word that Prince was trapped under the fallen shed. The rock had settled to one side, causing the center pole to slip. Prince was pinned to the ground by timbers across his back. He had attracted the lineman's attention by whinnying to him. We raised the timbers and Prince tried to get up but could not make it. He seemed paralyzed in the hindquarters. We got a board under him, helped raise him, and supported him to the spring.

"Here he took a good drink and stepped off a little distance and lay down on a nice bed of bluegrass. I stayed with him all that day and all that night. Two or three times he kind of lipped my hand like he used to do on the range. Maybe he was remembering back. I don't know. The next morning I went to breakfast. When I came back to him, he was dead. He was thirty-eight years old. He had been my constant companion and my friend during his whole life. No man could have had a more congenial companion or a truer friend."

The Marqués de Aguayo's Vengeance

THIS Marqués de Aguayo owned lands stretching from the interior of Texas to Zacatecas, and he made a ride that is still the wonder of all this country of riding tradition. Folk living on the haciendas to which he once held title sometimes yet see him in the night desperately spurring — so they who want to be credulous say. As I myself rode and slept among such witnesses, the Marqués became far more of a reality to me than he appeared when I read the excellently documented book of facts written to refute the legend. But this legend belongs; I tell it as generations of vaqueros, drivers of wood-laden burros, and old women of the *metate* have blended it to make it their own *Cid* of spur and blood.

To begin, as the old ballad about the Marqués begins — for there is a ballad — "the ancient parchments tell not, nor do the chronicles point out with exactitude, the year or the day of this strange event." But it was three hundred years ago or so — say, around 1650. Of the various subdivisions of land called *estancias* that the Marqués owned, his favorite — even above Las Cinco Llagas — was La Villa de los Patos. Here in mature but vigorous years he brought his young and beautiful wife Angela. Here also came as visitor and ward a comely nephew, Don Félix. The Marqués was often away for long periods, sometimes riding great distances both by day and night, overseeing his far-flung enterprises, making war on savage marauders, and not infrequently halting to carouse and gamble.

One day, upon returning to Los Patos from a prolonged absence, he discovered something that made him as jealous as Othello. It was his nature to act swiftly, and now he was fury-bent. He had many horses that were as fleet on the mountain trails as they were sure-footed. He had many peons who obeyed without question. In those days it was the custom to travel with a *caballada* of horses for changes on the route. The Marqués ordered five peons, besides his *mozo* of the stirrup, to prepare to ride with him and twelve picked horses for his *caballada*. As soon as men and horses were ready, which was promptly after his order was issued, he set out for Mazapil, a combined mining camp and hacienda that was also one of his possessions.

Mazapil as the crow flies lies some twenty leagues — around fifty miles — south of Los Patos across a mountain-wrinkled basin. As the trails twist, the distance must be at least sixty miles. The country between the two points is without water or trees. About four leagues out from Los Patos the Marqués ordered one of his servants to halt with two horses and to remain there until he should return. Four leagues farther on he left another peon with two horses, and at like intervals over the entire distance he arranged *postas*. He rode into Mazapil accompanied only by the personal *mozo*.

At Mazapil he had friends. It was not long after dark before, with plenty of brandy of Parras — where the cellars of the Marqués de Aguayo yet age the juice of grapes — they had begun a game of monte. Soon the Marqués took occasion to withdraw.

"Con permiso," he said, and stepped out. His comrades went on drinking and gambling, deeply absorbed.

As he had ordered, he found his horse saddled and ready, *mozo* by the stirrup. He was setting out on a journey to which he wished no witnesses. Accordingly he seized the peon by the throat and quickly choked him to death, in silence and without marks. It took but a few minutes to put the body out of the way. The place for it had been prepared, for this "Croesus of Mexico," it must be remembered, owned and ordered everything. Then he rode.

He rode for honor, for death, for vengeance. There is no way to tell how fast he rode; he rode without regard for horseflesh. In an incredibly brief time he was at the place where he had posted his last relay of horses. As he dismounted, his horse spread his legs out stiff, swayed, and then fell over dead. In a minute's time the saddle was changed, and, leaving the peon to hold the other fresh horse against his return, the Marqués was again on the road, alone. Thus killing every horse he rode but managing with fine precision to reach a *posta* before the mount succumbed, he sped on to La Villa de Los Patos — and to the room of his young wife Angela.

As he expected, Don Félix was with her. Anger did not prevent finesse. He stabbed the woman before either she or her lover knew that he was there. Then, overpowering the nephew, he forced him to stab himself. He left the knife in his hand so that the double murder would have the appearance of having been done by the betrayer of the bed. In the patio the Marqués found a watchful house servant. The dead do not bear witness. The Marqués was leaving no witnesses.

While getting a fresh mount from his stables, he met another servant; this man also he killed. Then back towards Mazapil he rode. He returned, if possible, more swiftly than he had come.

Only now, as he changed mounts at the *postas*, he killed one by one the witnesses of his nighttime ride.

Just how many hours it took him to make the round trip the story does not say. It was dark when with a polite *"con permiso"* he excused himself from his comrades and set out. It was still dark and the game of monte was still going on when he reentered the room at Mazapil and took his place.

When, the next day, news came of the deaths at Los Patos, the Marqués appeared to be stricken with grief. He ordered a royal funeral and made provision for countless Masses. But despite the care with which he had removed all witnesses, despite the arrangement he had made of the dead lovers, and despite his own high position — or perhaps because of it, for the higher in station a man stands the higher up do enemies rise — he was suspected and brought to court. The only evidence was circumstantial, and the admitted fact that he was at Mazapil at both the beginning and the ending of the night on which the Marquesa and Don Félix met their death proved an alibi. That in the intervening hours he could have ridden to Los Patos and returned was considered humanly impossible. Some say that a little servant girl who had witnessed the killing of the Marquesa Angela appeared but was barred by law from testifying.

Investigations went on for many years. The viceroy of the king of Spain in Mexico City took a hand. At length a high judge — the *oidor* — from Guadalajara came to Los Patos, where, except for hirelings, the Marqués lived alone in the dark, gloomy house still pointed out as *la Casa de Cadena.** His plan was to draw out a confession. Yet if such a confession were

---

* The House of the Chain, so called because, according to tradition, it was a sanctuary for anyone who passed the chain stretched between the rock pillars at the entrance of the surrounding wall. The medieval principle of sanctuary, fostered by the church, was never much exercised in Mexico, I believe, although *casas de cadena* are not extremely rare.

brought into court, the Marqués would deny having made it. The *oidor* foresaw this and foresaw the necessity of having testimony to corroborate his own word. Having, as he thought, gained the confidence of the Marqués, he one dark evening hid a man under the table, which was heavily draped with a green cloth, in the salon where guests were usually received.

After a good dinner at which both *oidor* and Marqués fortified themselves well with wine, the two entered the salon. The candles but shadowly lighted it.

"Come, now, Señor Marqués," the *oidor* said in an easy way. "As you know, the court can do nothing with you. There is no testimony. Not as an official but as your friend and as a human being with intense curiosity, I burn to know how in one night you kept the game of monte going in Mazapil and at the same time that of daggers in Los Patos."

"I will tell you," the Marqués replied with a frankness that surprised his guest. "When a man who loves glory has achieved some remarkable thing, he itches for it to be known."

"Yes, yes," the *oidor* eagerly assented, "and your name, my Marqués, praised by the king of Spain in the Escorial beyond the ocean and trembled at by every savage Chichimec in Nueva Vizcaya, must be ever gathering to itself fresh renown."

"For that reason only, I talk now," the Marqués went on. He seemed absolutely careless. "Those who say that the dead have better memories than the living lack blood and are stuffed with pigeon livers."

But before beginning his story the Marqués pulled his chair up against the mantled table, on the side across from the *oidor*, who sat near the brazier of coals. He told all in detail — of the relays stationed, of the ride, of the swift dispatch of lovers and witnesses alike. Then he concluded: "It was a dishonor that only blood could wash out."

At the end of the story the high judge from Guadalajara arose and called out, "Witness, you have heard. Come forth. We have the confession."

But the witness under the mantled table did not speak or stir. The Marqués remained seated, at his ease.

"Witness of the court," the *oidor* called in a more commanding voice, "come forth. We have heard what we came to hear."

Still there was no stir or response. The Marqués had not moved from his relaxed position.

A third time the *oidor* spoke. He was impatient. "Why do you not respond?" he called.

Then the Marqués spoke. *"Porque los muertos no hablan."* Because the dead do not talk.

At these words he quietly pulled up the overhanging folds of the heavy green cloth. Huddled on the floor under the table lay the lifeless body of the secret witness. The Marqués had choked him with his sharp knees. The exercise of furious and constant riding, it is said, had given to Aguayo's legs and knees muscles that, even to a generation of men living on horseback, were astonishingly strong.

"You have authority," the Marqués added, looking at the *oidor*, "to hold inquests. Here is paper with pen and ink. You will write that this man, whose name I know not but who is known to you, died in my house on this night of apoplexy."

The *oidor* wrote and left. The processes of law never got further.

I Remember Buck

A L L the old-time range men of validity whom I have known remembered horses with affection and respect as a part of the best of themselves. After their knees begin to stiffen, most men realize that they have been disappointed in themselves, in other men, in achievement, in love, in whatever they expected out of life; but a man who has had a good horse in his life — a horse beyond the play world — will remember him as a certitude, like a calm mother, a lovely lake, or a gracious tree, amid all the flickering vanishments. I remember Buck.

He was raised on our ranch and was about half Spanish. He was a bright bay with a blaze in his face and stockings on his forefeet. He could hardly have weighed when fat over 850 pounds and was about fourteen hands high. A Mexican broke him when he was three years old, but I don't think he pitched much. From then on nobody but me rode him, even after I left for college. He had a fine barrel and chest and was very fast for short distances but did not have the endurance of some other horses, straight Spanish, in our remuda. What he lacked in toughness, he made up in intelligence, especially cow sense, loyalty, understanding, and generosity.

As a colt he had been bitten by a rattlesnake on the right fore ankle just above the hoof; a hard, hairless scab marked the place as long as he lived. He traveled through the world listening for the warning rattle. A kind of weed in the Southwest bears seed that when ripe rattle in their pods a good deal like the sound made by a rattlesnake. Many a time when my spur or stirrup set these seeds a-rattling Buck's suddenness in jumping all but left me seated in the air. I don't recall his smelling rattlesnakes, but he could smell afar off the rotten flesh of a yearling or any other cow brute afflicted with screw worms. He understood that I was hunting these animals in order to drive them to a pen and doctor them. In hot weather they take refuge in high weeds and thick brush. When he smelled one, he would point to it with his ears and turn towards it. A dog trained for hunting out wormy cases could not have been more helpful.

Once a sullen cow that had been roped raked him in the breast with the tip of a sharp horn. After that experience, he was wariness personified around anything roped, but he never, like some horses that have been hooked, shied away from an animal he was after. He knew and loved his business too well for that. He did not love it when at the rate of less than a mile an hour he was driving the thirsty, hot, tired, slobbering drag end of a herd, animals stopping behind every bush or without any bush, turning aside the moment they were free of a driver. When sufficiently exasperated, Buck would go for a halting cow with mouth open and grab her just forward of the tail bone if she did not move on. Work like this may be humiliating to a gallant young cowboy and an eager cow horse; it is never pictured as a part of the romance of the range, but it is very necessary. It helps a cowboy to graduate into a cowman. A too high-strung horse without cow sense, which includes cow patience, will go to pieces at it just as he will go to pieces in running cattle or in cutting a herd.

Buck had the rein to make the proverbial "turn on a two-bit piece and give back fifteen cents in change." One hot summer while we were gathering steers on leased grass about twelve miles from home, I galled his side with a tight cinch. I hated to keep on riding him with the galled side, but was obliged to on account of shortage in horses. As I saddled up in camp one day after dinner, I left the cinch so loose that a hand might have been laid between it and Buck's belly. We had to ride about a mile before going through a wire gap into the pasture where some snaky steers ran. As we rode along, a vaquero called my attention to the loose cinch.

"I will tighten it when we get to the gap," I said.

"*Cuidado* (have care) and don't forget," he said.

At the gap, which he got down to open, I saw him look at me. I decided to wait until we struck something before tightening the girth. Two minutes later my father yelled and we saw a little bunch of steers high-tailing it through scattered mesquites for a thicket along a creek beyond. I forgot all about the cinch. Buck was easily the fastest horse ridden by the four or five men in our "cow crowd." He left like a cry of joy to get around the steers.

As we headed them, they turned to the left at a sharp angle, and Buck turned at an angle considerably sharper. Sometimes he turned so quickly that the tapadero (toe-fender) of my stirrup raked the ground on the inside of the turn. This time when he doubled back, running full speed, the loose saddle naturally turned on him. As my left hip hit the ground I saw stars. One foot was still in the stirrup and the saddle was under Buck's belly. I suppose that I instinctively pulled on the reins, but I believe that Buck would have stopped had he not been bridled. His stop was instantaneous; he did not drag me on the ground at all. He had provocation to go on, too, for in coming over his side and back the spur on my right foot had raked him. He never needed spurs. I wore them on him just to be in fashion.

Sometimes in running through brush, Buck seemed to read my mind — or maybe I was reading his. He was better in the brush than I was. In brush work, man and horse must dodge, turn, go over bushes and pear and under limbs, absolutely in accord, rider yielding to the instinct and judgment of the horse as much as horse yields to his.

Buck did not have to be staked. If I left a drag rope on him, he would stay close to camp, at noon or through the night. He was no paragon. Many men have ridden and remembered hardier horses. He was not proud, but he carried himself in a trim manner. He did the best he could, willingly and generously, and he had a good heart. His chemistry mixed with mine. He was good company. I loved to hear him drink water, he was so hearty in swallowing, and then after he was full, to watch him lip the water's surface and drip big drops back into it.

Sometimes after we had watered and, passing on, come to good grass near shade, I'd unsaddle and turn him loose to graze. Then I'd lie down on the saddle and, while the blanket dried, listen to his energetic cropping and watch the buzzards sail and the Gulf clouds float. Buck would blow out his breath once in a while, presumably to clear his nostrils but also, it seemed, to express contentment. He never asked me to stop, unless to stale, and never, like some gentle saddle horses, interrupted his step to grab a mouthful of grass; but if I stopped with slackened rein to watch cattle, or maybe just to gaze over the flow of hills to the horizon, he'd reach down and begin cutting grass. He knew that was all right with me, though a person's seat on a grazing horse is not nearly so comfortable as on one with upright head. Occasionally I washed the sweat off his back and favored him in other ways, but nobody in our part of the country pampered cow horses with sugar or other delicacy.

All the rose-lipped maidens and all the light-foot lads with whom I ran in the riding days of boyhood and youth have receded until they have little meaning. They never had much in comparison with numerous people I have known since. Buck, however, always in association with the plot of earth over which I rode him, increases in meaning. To remember him is a joy and a tonic.

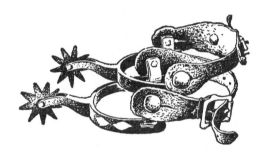

Characters
and Happenings
of Long Ago

Tom Gilroy's Fiddler

IN 1928 my uncle Jim Dobie began urging me to talk with his old friend Tom Gilroy. Uncle Jim was always wanting to do me a favor, and he wasn't going to have much more time to do favors to anybody. He and Tom Gilroy had first met in Kansas, about 1882, where they were selling horses trailed up from Texas. That was before Uncle Jim became a cowman — mostly a steer man. Tom Gilroy was on the Chisholm Trail with cattle in 1868, but he liked to talk most about his experiences with horses.

One winter on a horse-buying expedition in the state of Chihuahua he had made camps two days' ride west of Chihuahua City better than six thousand feet above sea level. By dark the air was ice cold. Some time after he fell asleep under a heavy Mexican blanket he felt it being slowly pulled off his body — very slowly, as slowly as an inchworm moves. He woke up, he said, more curious than frightened and let the pulling go on to see what would happen or who was making it happen. All he had to do to apprehend the puller was to breathe out loud to his *mozo* sleeping at his feet. The *mozo* grabbed the thief. He proved to be a Tarahumare Indian, naked as a jay bird except for a breech clout.

Tom Gilroy chunked up the fire for light as well as for warmth. When he saw the Indian and realized how much he needed the blanket, he became interested in him as a human being. The Tarahumare said he'd left Chihuahua City that morning — a good hundred miles away. His tribesmen are world-famous as runners. He had had a blanket but lost it betting on a cockfight in the city. "I always did like a good race horse," Tom Gilroy said, "and a good sport. I gave him my blanket and all the grub he could pack away in his belly. He was getting close to home."

Uncle Jim and I met Tom Gilroy at the entrance to the Gunter Hotel, on Houston Street in San Antonio, one November day. At that time the Gunter was headquarters for cow people from all over southwest Texas. The big lobby, bountifully provided with chairs and lounges, had not been cut into cubicles for rent. The lobby "well" stood open for three stories — before all that space was floored over for more rent. I'm trying to convey the idea that the original Gunter Hotel, built by a cowman, was an oh-linger-here place of amplitude in which people, especially cow people, had ample time. The hallway from the lobby out to Houston Street was ample and there was ample room in front of the galleried entrance in which to loiter and talk.

Tom Gilroy had been expecting me and it didn't take him any time to warm up. He was dumpy in build. His ruddy face shone with brightness and zest. He seemed made out of eagerness.

"Listen," he'd say, tugging at your coat or punching you in the ribs. You laughed; you couldn't keep from laughing. He was laughing all over from the inside, his features looking like a wet blanket half rolled up. He was not yet well started on his story, and the funniest part was still to come. "Listen," he'd cry, bursting to share his joy. He must check your laughter in order to be heard, and somehow he must control his own in order to get on. How in the devil he was going to do it he could not know nor you either; you were laughing so completely that you did not know anything — not even why you were laughing. "But listen," he cried, tugging at your coat like a famished bull calf at its mother's teats. "Listen. That ain't all."

Transferring Tom Gilroy's talk to print is like transferring a log cabin out of its wilderness setting and expecting it to appear natural on a concrete pedestal surrounded by fuming traffic. Now, Tom Gilroy's story:

One day I was in my livery stable at Sherman. This was in the 'seventies. A tramp-looking feller with something in a sack that I took to be a fiddle limped up. He appeared all wrung out. "Mister," he says, "I've come to Texas all the way from Illinois. I ain't got but fifty cents left, I'm dead tired, and I wish you'd let me sleep in your hay."

"Hell," I says, "you won't hurt the hay. Crawl in back yonder and sleep all you want to."

Well, he hadn't been in the hay more'n an hour when I heard a noise like hell emigrating on cart wheels, and a big iron-gray horse with a cowboy a little bit bigger on top of him lit inside the stable door. Men don't grow that size any more. He was six-foot-six and as trim as an ash. His name was Yarborough. He didn't lose no words, and his voice shook the mangers back in the corral.

"By God," he said, "we're all ready to start up the trail in the morning. Herd counted, cook sober, a sackful of buffalo chips gathered, water keg full, whiskey jug nearly empty, everything in shape. We got to have a dance tonight and I'm hunting a fiddler. If fiddlers is thick in hell, damned if I know why they ain't populating Sherman, but I can't find even one. Tell me where in all outdoors I can find a fiddler. We just got to have a fiddler."

"Now hold your potatoes a minute," says I, "and I'll tell you something. There's a feller asleep back there in the hay that I'm pretty certain is a fiddler."

By this time Yarborough was off his horse and clanking back to the hay shed. I heard a scuffle and the man from Illinois came out rubbing his eyes. His name was Mathis, he said, and yes, his profession was fiddling.

"How'll I get out to the dance?" he asked.

"Right behind me," yelled Yarborough.

He was already on his big gray horse and had the horse headed towards the street. Mathis handed up the sack with the fiddle in it. It was evident he'd never mounted a horse in his life, and I kinder shoved him up. He'd barely locked his arms around the cowboy when that devil socked in the spurs and the gray gave a snort and a leap that landed them, I'll swear, more than halfway across the street. If you ever tried to look at greased lightning through a dust storm you'll know how the fiddler, the six-foot-six cowboy, and the iron-gray horse left town. The fiddler got back to town some time next day, and between him and some of the boys I learned about the dance.

As I've already said, he was dead tired to begin with — about as animated as a bag of meal. The ride out ten or twelve miles didn't rest him any, I guess. The crowd was already gathering. They gave him a good stiff drink, and he began sawing. He could make that fiddle talk. Every time he'd fag, they'd give him some whiskey. Between drinks of whiskey, they'd give him coffee, and they'd saucer it and blow it for him so he wouldn't lose no time swallering it. They shore wanted to keep on dancing. He played "Hell Among the Yearlings" so many times that some of the boys went to bawling like bull calves, and when he'd switch to "Rye Whiskey" they'd make out like they was swallering from bottles.

> Yuh could hear hands spankin' till they spanked each other raw,
> When he finished variations on "Turkey in the Straw."

> He could fiddle down a possum from a mile-high tree,
> He could fiddle up a whale from the bottom of the sea.

> Swing yore pardners — up and down the middle!
> Sashay now — oh, listen to that fiddle!
> Flapjacks flippin' on a red-hot griddle . . .

Along about midnight the fiddler got so damned fagged he said he'd have to rest. Two cowboys got some knitting needles and knocked time on them while the dance went on and the musician passed out. Say, I've danced many a time to the click of a pair of knitting needles. They harmonize like a bride and groom on such pieces as "Chicken in the Bread Tray Pickin' Up Dough."

The sun was coming up before Mathis played "I'm A-leaving Cheyenne," and everybody for the last time joined in on "My Horses Won't Stand." As the crowd broke up he wanted to know how he was going to get back to town.

"Well, me and that iron-gray has got to go to the herd and point it for the North Pole," says Yarborough, "and so we can't take you. But we'll get you to town all right. We'll get you there in a comfortable way, too, and won't punish you with riding double. Hey there, some of you fellers hitch up a pair of horses to that buggy."

The corral was full of horses, not one of which had ever looked through a collar and half of which would pitch at the sight of a saddle. The boys were all feeling juicy and they roped out a couple of browns as strong as buffalo bulls and as skittish as wild turkeys fresh trapped in a covered pen. Then they hitched this pair to the buggy.

"Git in!" Yarborough bellered to the fiddler. "Grab them lines, and we'll herd you off in the right direction. When you get to town, jest leave the rig at the livery stable, and somebody'll get it some time."

The fiddler got in and grabbed the lines. Two cowboys on each side of the team pointed them out of the lot and towards Sherman. There wasn't any road to speak of and the browns didn't seem to have any idea of going in any particular direction. In spite of all the herders could do, the team began making parabolas, circles, acute triangles and parallelograms and do-ce-do-ing over about five acres of prairie.

"Hold up, hold up!" Yarborough yelled, loping his horse up to the buggy. "Say, how much do we owe you for the fiddling?"

"If you'll put somebody in this buggy that can drive these horses you won't owe me anything," Mathis called back as the browns gave an extra wild tug.

Well, they gave the fiddler twenty dollars and put a man in the buggy who could, with the help of two herders, get the equipage to town. The boys were still gay when they whoaed down in front of my livery stable.

Mathis said they had treated him fine. "But I'll confess something to you," he added. "When that gray horse jumped into the middle of the street, my heart did something that will keep me from getting a life insurance policy as long as I live."

The fiddler slept a day or two after that. When he woke up, I asked him what he was going to do with his money. He didn't know.

"Well," says I, "your reputation as a fiddler is made. From this time on you'll have all the playing you want. Now the thing for you to do is to get a place of residence. Look over there across the street and you'll see an empty hotel. The proprietor went broke the other day. It's as empty of furniture as a last year's bird nest with the bottom punched out. You can rent it for a song, take in lodgers, and make money on the side from fiddling."

Mathis rented the hotel — just a big box cut up by partition walls. He got half a dozen cots and stuffed cotton-picker sacks with shucks from my stable for mattresses. He aimed for cowboy patronage. The cowboys didn't need any bedclothes. They could cover their backs with their bellies when it was hot and pull saddle blankets over their bellies when it was cold, and they could roll up their leggins for a pillow the year 'round.

Away late one night not long after he opened his hotel, Mathis came over to the stable, where I was still up. "Say," he says, "there's a cowboy over there on one of those cots yelling for somebody to come and pull the feathers out of his back. Says he's being ruined by such luxury. Hell, I'm not going to charge anybody for such accommodations."

But I guess he charged, for before long Mathis owned the best block of land in Sherman and had a first-rate hotel. He died a wealthy man. The last I knew of him he was still fiddling. He was a fiddler from who laid the chunk.

The Dream That Saved Wilbarger

O N E cold night soon after he came to Texas, Bigfoot Wallace was sitting in the warm cabin of a settler down the Colorado River when a man wearing a strange-looking fur cap entered, stood bent over the fire a few minutes, and then removed his headgear to warm his head better. At sight of the raw-looking, hairless scalp thus exposed, Bigfoot Wallace broke the social code against asking questions.

"My friend," he ventured, "excuse me, but what is the matter with your head?"

"I have been scalped by the Indians," the stranger replied.

Josiah Wilbarger wore a cap or hat, even at the dinner table, from the pre-dawn hour of rising until bedtime, when he put on a nightcap. The story of his scalping and of the dream that saved his life is still told by descendants of early settlers and may be read in reminiscences of those times.

In 1830, Josiah Wilbarger, lately from Missouri, located on a headright survey along the Colorado River about ten miles above the crossing of the *camino real* — the royal road, as the Spaniards called it — between San Antonio and Nacogdoches. His nearest neighbor was thirty miles or so down the river. Two years later his friend Reuben Hornsby built, with slave help, a double-log cabin up the river, nine miles below the present city of Austin, and moved into it with his wife Sarah and eight children. Although separated by several miles, the families were close neighbors. The names Wilbarger Creek and Hornsby's Bend fix permanently the locations of these two outposts of colonization.

Early in August, 1833, Wilbarger went up to Hornsby's to join a party of men scouting for headrights. The Hornsby home had already become a kind of land's-end headquarters. After spending the night, Wilbarger, in company with four men named Christian, Haynie, Standifer, and Strother, set out to explore to the northwest. On Walnut Creek they sighted a lone Indian, who ran and escaped into the cedar hills.

After the chase the party turned homeward. Near Pecan Spring, as the place was later named, they halted to noon. Wilbarger, Christian, and Strother unsaddled their horses and hobbled them to graze; the other two men staked theirs with the saddles on, merely removing the bridles. While all five were eating, Indians skulked up in the brush and fired on them, some with only bows and arrows. The white men got behind trees, which were small, and returned the fire, but soon Strother received a mortal wound and a ball broke Christian's thigh. With an arrow through the calf of a leg and a flesh wound in a hip, Wilbarger dragged Christian behind a tree. About this time an arrow went into his other leg. Haynie and Standifer now made for their saddled horses. As they mounted, Wilbarger started running toward them, calling upon them to wait. They saw him pitch headlong to the ground. Then they saw "fifty Indians" rushing for his scalp. They got away and reached Hornsby's house in safety.

There they told how they had seen the savages scalping their dead comrades and heard them yelling the blood yell. For the present, all the men agreed, the dead would have to care for the dead. The Indians were in such force and had met with such success that they might well be expected to attack the Hornsby outpost. A rider was sent below to carry the tidings to the Wilbarger home and to summon help.

At last the house was still and Sarah Hornsby fell asleep. About midnight she jumped awake from a vision as sharply defined as the peaks of clouds under sheet lightning. She shook her husband, speaking so loud that the men in the other room of the house heard.

"Wilbarger is not dead," she cried. "I saw him in a dream. He sits under a large post oak tree, naked, covered with blood from wounds, scalped. But he is not dead. I saw him plainly."

Reuben Hornsby tried to pacify his wife by going over the details she had plainly heard from the two survivors. He laid the dream to overwrought nerves. She quieted down and went back to sleep.

But about three o'clock she sprang from the bed, more excited and intense this time than before. "I saw him again," she cried. Her husband could not pacify her now. She threw a dress on, lit a candle, aroused all the men.

"As sure as there is a God," she repeated, "Josiah Wilbarger is alive. He is alive out there, all alone under a large post oak tree. His only covering is the blood from his own wounds. He is scalped, but he lives, suffering tortures, hoping and waiting for help."

"But" — started to explain once more one of the men who had left Wilbarger.

"But me no buts," Sarah Hornsby went on with rising voice. "I saw him as plainly as I now see you safe and sound in front of me. If you are not cowards, go at once or he will die."

"I'll say it again as I have already said it many times," the escaped man now got his word in. "I saw Wilbarger shot down. I saw at least fifty Indians around his body. They were even then lifting his scalp. They never leave a victim breathing."

"I don't care what you saw," Sarah Hornsby retorted. "Maybe you were too busy running to see anything straight. Anyhow, I have had the last look. I know that Wilbarger is alive. Go. Go at once."

There was no arguing, but Reuben Hornsby now pointed out that if he and the other men left before the expected recruits arrived from below, she and the children would be in grave danger.

"Never mind me," his wife flared. "I and my children can take to the elbow bushes and lie hid. Go, I tell you, to poor Wilbarger."

She was a little, black-haired, black-eyed woman of pure Scottish blood off a plantation of traditional refinement in Mississippi. She sang Highland ballads, read the Bible to her children, and taught them to read the box of books she had hauled in an ox wagon all the way to Texas. One time when all the men were gone from her home in Hornsby's Bend she dressed in man's clothes and showed herself armed with a rifle in order to scare off lurking Indians. Another time while her husband was away she sent two of her boys at milking time to bring in the cows from the wild rye that stretched out from the house like a field of wheat. From the window, gun in hand — for there was never a relaxed minute at this habitation in the wilderness — she watched them. Then, powerless to give aid, she saw Indians raise up with a yell behind the boys, but the boys got into the house unharmed. Another time she saw savages kill two young men hoeing in the field; then after dark she and her young sons buried them. In time she buried one of her own sons and another youth who were fishing in the river when Indians killed them.

Against such resoluteness Reuben Hornsby and the other men could not now stand. Still, they refused to leave until daylight, by which time the recruits from below were expected. Sarah Hornsby made coffee, cooked breakfast. Daylight comes early in August. With it came the expected reinforcements. Then the searching party prepared to ride.

"Take these three sheets," Sarah Hornsby called. "Two to bury Christian and Strother in. One to wrap around Wilbarger. You will have to bring him home on a litter. He cannot ride a horse."

The last sentence of her prophecy alone proved erroneous. The men went to the campsite where the Indians had attacked the day before. They shrouded the bodies of Christian and Strother, from whom all clothing had been stripped. After much search, late in the afternoon, they sighted a red-hued figure under a big post oak tree. An advance rider, mistaking him for an Indian, called out, "Here they are, boys!"

At this, the figure rose up, saying, "Don't shoot. It's Wilbarger."

His body was caked with blood. The only particle of clothing left to him by the Indians was a sock. This he had torn from his foot, swollen from the leg wound, and placed on his peeled skull.

With the sheet wrapped around him he was placed in Hornsby's saddle, the light-weighted Hornsby riding behind and holding the wounded man in his arms. Very slowly the horsemen filed towards the cabin in the river bend, six miles away.

There they found all in readiness for the rescued man: a bed, warm water to cleanse the wounds, poultices of wheat bread —

a bread too scarce to eat — and bear's oil to dress the scalpless head. "I knew you would bring him," Sarah Hornsby said.

Wilbarger's own story made Sarah Hornsby's dreams seem even more remarkable. The shot that knocked him to the ground had gone into his neck from the rear and come out at his chin. It only creased — temporarily paralyzed — him, he said. He did not feel pain; he could not move a muscle; yet he was conscious. He knew when a savage cut his scalp around with a knife and jerked it off. He did not flinch; there was no pain to flinch from. The only sensation he experienced was a sound as of distant thunder. He knew when the Indians were stripping off his clothes. They had cut the throats of the other two men; the sight of the bullet hole under his chin perhaps made them think that act unnecessary with him.

There was a lapse of time during which Wilbarger knew nothing. The sun was halfway down the western sky when he recovered consciousness and felt pain and knew that he was alone and could move. Dried blood was all over him, and he was still bleeding. He felt a thirst that was agony. He tried to stand up and walk but could not. The directions of the compass were perfectly clear to him. He knew where the camp waterhole was. He dragged himself to it. He drank and lay down in the water. He lay there until he was almost numb with cold. Then he crawled out on dry ground, to be warmed by the sloping rays of the August sun. At last he fell into a deep sleep.

When he awoke green blowflies were buzzing around his head. It does not take the eggs they lay long to hatch into flesh-eating worms. His wounds had ceased to bleed. He was again consumed with thirst. When he had drunk again, sharp hunger came upon him. His wonderful constitution was crying for nourishment to rebuild what his body had lost. He crawled to some bushes and ate a few snails that he found. He drank more water. He felt the maggots in the naked flesh of his head.

About nightfall he determined to crawl to the Hornsby house. But he had gone only about a quarter of a mile before, utterly exhausted, he halted under a large post oak tree. There in semiconsciousness he rested until roused by a cold wind on his naked head. The only sounds that came to his ears were the pulsing of the crickets, the hoot of an owl, and the long, long wail of a wolf. The dying moon came up.

Then, as he lay under the tree, he saw suddenly, distinctly, without warning, the figure of his sister Margaret Clifton. He saw her; yet she, he well knew, was living in Missouri, near St. Louis, more than seven hundred miles away. It was not until many weeks had passed that he learned she had died the day before he was wounded and even at the hour of his vision was spending her first night in the grave.

Standing near him, the sister said, her voice calm and restful, "Brother Josiah, you are too weak to go any farther by yourself. Remain here under this tree and friends will come to take care of you before the setting of another sun."

When she had spoken thus, she began to move away in the direction of Hornsby's house. Such was Wilbarger's state of mind, and so vivid was the visitant's form and so clear were her words that he did not question her reality. As the vision vanished, he raised himself and with an imploring gesture called after her, "Margaret, my sister Margaret, stay with me until they come! Margaret!"

But the air was empty of either answering sound or sisterly form.

Josiah Wilbarger recovered, though the skin never grew entirely over his skull bone. He lived for eleven years, leading an active life, until an accidental blow on the exposed skull hastened death. No one who knew him or Mrs. Hornsby ever doubted the veracity of either in their accounts of the dream — or spirit — visitations. Wilbarger told his story long before he heard of his sister Margaret's death. He was very definite in saying that the vision faded from sight while moving in the direc·· tion of the Hornsby home. As near as could be figured out, Mrs. Hornsby's first vision of the wounded man occurred shortly after Wilbarger heard his sister's voice and called out after her vanishing form.

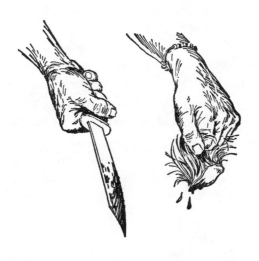

Bigfoot Wallace and the Hickory Nuts

BIGFOOT WALLACE had big feet, certainly — and thereby hangs more than one tale — but they were not out of proportion to his frame. He stood six feet two inches in his stocking feet and had the trunk of a Hercules. He could go for days, like an Indian, without food; then he had a vast space to fill. Once while he was driving the mail from San Antonio to El Paso, Apaches left him afoot and foodless three days' walk from the nearest Mexican *jacal*. When he came to it, he bolted twenty-seven eggs, and then walked on to a square meal. Captain Dan Smith used to tell how Bigfoot rode up on camps one evening just after they had killed a maverick yearling. Captain Dan Smith was cow-hunting with two other men. Bigfoot and a man with him had been scouting after Indians and hadn't eaten anything to speak of for two days. They hadn't shot because they did not want to make a noise.

They got down and built a fire. Bigfoot pulled out Old Butch, as he called his knife, came over to where the other men were skinning the yearling, hewed off a forequarter with a side of ribs, and then began roasting the meat on a mesquite fork. "The other fellows," Captain Dan Smith said, "didn't eat more than three or four pounds of beef apiece, but Bigfoot gnawed off and on until midnight, besides putting away a good part of a sack of biscuits we were carrying."

Anyhow, Bigfoot Wallace was an enormous man. You'll have to understand that in order to appreciate his military tactics. His brother had been killed by Mexicans in the Goliad Massacre in March, 1836. Not long after that he himself came to Texas to "get even with the Mexicans"; yet he was too easygoing and openhearted to be vindictive. He was descended from the great Scottish chief of his name, belonged to a Virginia family of education and stability, and used good English. He had been in the fantastic Mier Expedition and drawn a white bean — life — while every tenth man among his comrades drew a black bean of death. As ranger captain:

> He kept the Comanches from off the ranches
> And fought them far o'er the Texas frontiers.

He could trail like a bloodhound and read sign like an Apache. A bachelor, he lived alone for many years in his cabin west of the Medina River, but he loved genial company and was as convivial a soul as ever sat by the blazing ingle with Tam o'Shanter or sang:

> If the ocean was whiskey and I was a duck,
> I'd dive to the bottom and suck it all up.

He was as honest as daylight, which didn't keep him from stretching the blanket when it was blanket-stretching time.

Wherever he went, "Old Big" was a character. People were always after him to tell a story and asking for his "most remarkable experience with Indians." When he knew they were expecting something extra, he did his best to deliver. Captain Dan Smith said he had heard Bigfoot tell one story in particular many times, and I imagine it did not lose much in the captain's retelling.

Captain Dan Smith, when I came to know him and heard him tell this Bigfoot story, was an old man, trembly all over. His hand shook even when, sitting, he rested it on his cane, and his voice quavered; but his eyes were as bright as mesquite coals with the ashes blown off and his laugh was a tonic. A long, sharp-pointed beard seemed to sharpen his tall, spare frame. When a story possessed him, agility came back to him and he would flourish his cane with Hotspur fire. He drew the small pension granted to Confederate veterans, and added to it by selling a patent medicine. I never saw him offer it for sale, but he always had with him a little oblong tan satchel labeled BROWN'S HERB TABLETS. He would sit in the lobby of the cowman-dominated Gunter Hotel in San Antonio, the tan satchel on the floor beside his chair, while men stood around delighting in his reminiscences and yarns. He read books as well as newspapers and was conscious of the art of storytelling. A storyteller belonging to campfire life on the open range, he had brought his stories to a city of the machine age.

When the moon was full — the "Comanche moon," as people called it — Indians were expected, and then Bigfoot Wallace kept his horses shut up in a picket pen back of his cabin, except one in the cabin lean-to or else staked in a little natural clearing down in the brush about three hundred yards away. He had some mongrel dogs that could be depended upon to set up a racket when Indians came within smelling distance. What with horses penned, dogs watching, and himself sleeping lightly, plus the reputation he had among Indians, he never lost an animal — until one November night not long after the Civil War ended.

In the early, foggy morning he looked out and saw that his

horses were gone. The dogs had not whined or barked once during the night. Some people claimed that Indians could mesmerize dogs. Bigfoot figured the Comanches had mesmerized his. Going around to the back side of the corral, he saw where the thieves had cut the rawhide strips holding the upright pickets together and pulled several pickets out of the ground. Moccasin tracks were as thick here as pig tracks around a corncrib. It was against Bigfoot's religion to let Indians get away with his horses.

He walked down to the clearing in the brush where he had staked a gray mare named White Bean. She was still there. He led her up to the corncrib, threw his hull on her, crawled up into it, and took out on the trail. He was armed with Old Butch and Sweet Lips — as he called his long-barreled, muzzle-loading rifle — along with powder horn, some molded bullets and cloth patches to hold them snug in the gun barrel. He used to say, "Varmints don't seem to like the kind of kisses Sweet Lips gives." For him, not all varmints were four-legged.

The ground was moist, and as he followed the trail of the stolen horses, moccasin tracks seemed to get thicker, even though some of the Indians were undoubtedly riding. Bigfoot said he began to wonder just what he was going to do when he caught up with all those Comanches. Still, he kept on going, trailing as fast as White Bean could gallop.

After a while, as he topped a hill, he saw smoke rising from a flat maybe a mile and a half ahead. He knew then the Indians had stopped, close to a waterhole, and were cooking their favorite breakfast food, colt meat — one of his colts. The deed made him as hot as a bush red all over with ripe *chiltipiquins*. Yet, now that he was catching up with the Indians, he wondered more than ever what he was going to do when he struck them on that prairie. He kept on going.

Before long he came into a heavily wooded swag in which

grew many hickory trees. It was hickory-nut time. The nuts were thick on the ground and thick on the low-hanging branches. There wasn't much to them but the hard, thick shells, but they gave Bigfoot an idea. One time when he was going out to fight Indians he had hung two window shutters on himself as protection against arrows. That's what he told. He didn't have any window shutters along today. He didn't have one of those shields made out of buffalo bull hide that Indians parried against arrows and bullets. He didn't have a Spanish coat of mail. He decided to armor himself with hickory nuts.

He wore buckskin breeches and a buckskin shirt, and he always, in Carlyle's phrase, wore his clothes "cynically loose." Until the day he died, he liked roomy clothes as well as a roomy range. Gloves "choked" his hands; a collar choked his neck. Now he got down, pulled some buckskin strings out of a pocket, and began tying his clothes so they would hold the hickory nuts. He tied the cuffs of his shirt about his strong wrists, and he tied the bottoms of his breeches legs at the ankles above his big feet. Then he began gathering the hickory nuts and stuffing them in. He picked hickory nuts until he thought he'd go blind, he said. He stuffed them into his shirt and breeches until he was padded out bigger than Santa Claus. Finally there wasn't a cubic inch of space between his own skin and the buckskin not fortified with hickory nuts, and they were so evenly distributed that not a finger space of his body was unprotected. He took off his hat and filled it half full of hickory nuts so the top of his head would be protected.

Thus armored, he started to get on White Bean and ride for the attack. But he could hardly walk, much less pull up into the saddle. The mare went to snorting at him and cavorting around as if a bear were trying to mount. At last, though, Bigfoot led her up to a fallen log and gingerly stepped from it into the saddle. He got himself balanced, and with the hickory nuts working against his tough hide rode on towards the Indians.

Just before reaching the edge of the big prairie, he rolled off the horse — for he could not dismount in the usual way. He peeped- through the brush fringe and saw smoke still rising and Indians lolling around after their big bait of colt meat. In those times the waters were all clear and the grass was stirrup-high. Through this tall grass Bigfoot began crawling, Old Butch in his belt and Sweet Lips trailing even with his right leg.

He crawled until he was within maybe a hundred yards of the Indians. He took time to count them, and there were forty-two, including three staying with the horses. Then slowly, still keeping well hid in the grass, he squinted one eye and lined up the sights on Sweet Lips. She spoke, and a Comanche buck answered with his last yell. The shot was such a surprise that the Indians did not even locate the smoke made by the black powder, the only kind used in those days.

Bigfoot poured a charge of powder from his horn into the barrel, put in a bullet, rammed down the wadding, and again aimed. Sweet Lips sent a kiss as fatal as Cleopatra ever gave, and another Indian was converted.

This time the Indians were wildly alert. They saw the gun smoke, and now, all on foot, they took out for it lickety-brindle, hellety-split, a-yelling and a-drawing their bows. Bigfoot had prepared another charge of powder and lead. As quick as you could say "scat" he rammed it home. But this shot, if he had to use it, would, he knew, be his last. He was saving it for hard times.

Meantime, Sweet Lips in position, Bigfoot raised up in all his majesty and all his stature and all his hickory nuts. He said the whole bunch of Comanches halted "like they had been paralyzed by Davy Crockett's grin." (Davy Crockett could grin a knot on a log into splinters.) They didn't seem to know whether they were facing some sort of supernatural giant swelled out worse than a dead mule or "just Old Big." They knew whose horses they had stolen. They knew he was "pizen" unadulterated to Comanche depredators everywhere between the Nueces Canyon and the San Antonio River. Now, they seemed to debate with each other and within themselves for a minute or two. Then they must have decided that it wasn't a giant but the Patas Grandes (Big Feet) they had so often had on their trail.

This time they came not only a-yelling but a-shooting. It was a mighty lucky thing for him, Bigfoot said, that not a buck had a gun. But they were the most unerring marksmen with bow and arrow a man could imagine. Every time a bowstring twanged, an arrow hit — a hickory nut, split it, and then fell to the ground. Bigfoot said the arrows got stacked up so high in front of him that he stepped up on the pile and stood three inches taller. Then the Indians made a right flank movement and bombarded him from that side, then a left flank movement and poured in the arrows from that direction. The hickory nuts were getting shelled faster than a Missouri mule could bite the grains off an ear of corn. Every once in a while an arrow aimed high would hit his hat and split a hickory nut there.

Finally, all the Indians concentrated on a rear assault. By gravy, he said, those arrows kept jamming the hickory nuts in under his knee joints until he got so tickled he had to bust out laughing. Then he whirled around, and just as he did the last Indian shot the last arrow left in the last quiver of the whole band.

Well, sir, when they saw that their ammunition was all gone and that, though not an arrow had missed, the enormous target was still unharmed, they acted as if a bolt of lightning had struck the ground in front of them. For about a minute they stood with their eyes rolling and their tongues hanging out. Then all at once they stampeded like a herd of longhorn steers jumping up off the bed ground. They made a beeline for the Rio Grande, seventy miles away. They didn't even give the horses a look.

"I stood there in my tracks," Bigfoot said, "as still and solemn as a cigar-store Indian, until the devils were clean out of sight. Then I untied the strings around my wrists and ankles, and the hickory nuts just rolled out. If there was a peck of them there were two bushels, and you can kick me to death with grasshopper legs if a single, solitary hickory nut in the whole passel hadn't been split open.

"I thought what a pity it was to lose all those hickory nuts when they were so good at fattening hogs. I walked back to White Bean hid there in the brush and got on her and rode up to the battleground. Then I tied up the colt skin the Indians had peeled off and filled it with hickory nuts until it looked like a Mexican's goatskin full of pulque. I loaded it on White Bean and got home before dark with all my horses, except the et-up colt.

"I guess this was the most remarkable experience I ever had with Indians."

The Robinhooding of Sam Bass

I N July, 1978, it will be a hundred years since Sam Bass, at the age of twenty-seven, met his fate while he and his gang were preparing to rob the bank at Round Rock, Texas. He remains the best-known and the best-liked bad man of what used to be considered — before oil men took over — a bad man state. While he lay a-dying, he said to inquisitors of the law, "It's agin' my profession to blow on my pals. If a man knows anything he ought to die with it in him." So far as the records go, he never killed anybody until the end.

A deputy sheriff had walked up to Sam Bass in a store at Round Rock and asked for his pistol.

"I'll let you have both of them," Sam Bass said.

Before the deputy could draw he was dead. He left three little children. They and their descendants have never regarded Sam Bass as a knight of goodness and generosity. The people in stagecoaches and trains that he robbed did not knight him either. It has never been the victims who made sob ballads about outlaws. Stories about Sam Bass by people of adverse feelings seem not to persist. What people like to believe does.

As the ballad goes, "A kinder-hearted fellow you seldom ever see." What follows here is mostly anecdotes by people who liked Sam Bass. They, more than biographies, have kept Sam's name green; they and that ballad — swifter and vivider in detail than any ballad about any other frontier notable.

Sam Bass had been in Texas only six years when rangers killed him. He had been an outlaw on the dodge only ten months. He had spent most of the time around Denton, specializing in horse racing. He never was much of a cowboy.

> Sam used to coin the money, he spent it just as free;
> He always drank good whiskey wherever he might be.

In the spring of 1877 he rode down to San Antonio and threw in with Joel Collins. They bought a small herd of cattle on credit, drove them up the trail, and somewhere north of Dodge City sold out for cash. They soon spent all the money in riotous living and then got their names on the map by robbing, in Nebraska, a Union Pacific express train carrying California gold. Each of six robbers took $10,000 in freshly minted twenty-dollar gold pieces. They split up and

> Sam made it back to Texas, all right side up with care,
> Rode into the town of Denton with all his friends to share.

In the months following, his reputation for lighthearted generosity began to grow into legend. Now he had something to be generous with — something that did not belong to him. He and his followers made a few poor-paying train holdups in north Texas. He tipped the porters and brakemen — so people said. The rangers were after him; the people were for him. He had not been robbing people — unless they happened to be on board a train he stopped. He had been robbing corporations. Going into a town to buy supplies became increasingly risky. He was on the dodge, covering lots of country; he had to take, and when he took he put those twenty-dollar gold pieces into circulation.

Sometimes Sam was sorely pressed for grain for his horses and food for his men. One morning a farmer named Hoffman missed shelled corn out of his crib. It had been carried off in a sack with a little hole in it. Hoffman trailed the grains until he saw he was approaching a camp known to be occupied by the Bass gang. He turned back home. A few days later Bass saw him, and, handing him a twenty-dollar gold piece, explained, "I had to have some corn in a hurry the other night."

One morning a woman on a farm on Elm Creek was alone in the house when Bass and his men rode up.

"Do you have anything cooked?" Sam asked.

"No."

"Well, we are terribly hungry. We haven't eaten anything for some time. Would you cook us a snack?"

"Nobody ever left this place hungry yet," the woman said. She flew in and cooked a big bait of biscuits, eggs, bacon, and coffee, to which were added butter and molasses. After eating heartily, Sam Bass, hat off, asked, "How much we owe you?"

"Nothing."

"Many thanks. Let's ride, boys." But as Sam passed out, he placed two twenty-dollar gold pieces in the farm woman's hand.

In 1927, the proprietor of an ancient-looking plank hotel at Van Horn was an old-time Texan named Jackson from Denton County. He was a great admirer of Sam Bass, and one winter night while he and Asa Jones and I sat by the wood stove that warmed the hotel lobby he regaled us with stories of the daring good outlaw. Sam, he said, was sandy-haired, kept a sandy mustache well trained, and habitually wore a grin that showed sandy-hued teeth. He was good nature itself.

One day Jackson, then just a kid, and his small brother were carrying a bucket of water apiece from the well to their house when they were overtaken by Sam Bass and his crowd. "Give us a drink, kids," Sam said. The boys had a gourd, and they proudly ladled out water. Bass noticed that Jackson's brother was crippled with rheumatism, and as he started to ride away he pitched the cripple four silver dollars. He was headed toward a neck of woods.

He had hardly got out of sight when a posse of law-bringers led by Riley Wetsel came fogging up. "Clear out, kids!" Riley yelled. "There's going to be a battle." Of course the kids did not clear out. A battle was what they wanted above all else. They climbed up on a stake-and-rider fence to watch half the law-bringers go on one side of the neck of woods and half on the other, both parties shooting into the woods. One of the cross-fire bullets hit Riley in the leg. He thought Sam Bass had killed him, but by that time Sam was far away.

Sam Bass was a fool about good horses. One time rangers

raided a little pasture where the fine horses belonging to the outlaw gang were kept. For several days the rangers paraded those
horses around, keeping them in a livery stable at night. The
stable was across the road from where the Jacksons lived.

"I woke up one morning hearing voices," Jackson said. "I
thought I recognized Kid McCoy's. He was one of the Bass men
and rode the best-looking horse in the outfit. I ran to the window and peered out. The livery stable doors were wide open and
there were Sam Bass, Kid McCoy, and other men, pulling saddles off some little, sorry ponies and saddling up their own
horses. It did not take them long to change. Then they came
out of the stable yard hellety-split, yelling like Comanches and
emptying their six-shooters into the air. Shirttails were dodging
behind every door in town. My father was a very quiet religious
man — never even said *doggone*. 'My, those boys are making a
great disturbance,' he said."

If Sam Bass wasn't a killer, it wasn't because he could not
shoot. While galloping by a live oak tree near Belton, they say,
he six-shootered his initials into it. A vendor of mounted horns
from old-time Texas steers named Bertillion used to sell at fancy
prices pairs of longhorns purported to be from steers that Sam
Bass had shot down in night stampedes.

"One day," Shelton Story of Denton County used to remember, "a neighbor who had butchered a fat cow said he'd give
me a dollar to carry a hindquarter to a certain spot in the Denton Creek bottom, deliver it to men camped there, and ask
no questions. The meat was wrapped in an old slicker and I tied
it behind my saddle. That saddle was the first new saddle I
ever owned. The skirts were fancy stamped; it had long strings
of tanned elkhide, and its creaking sounded sweeter to me than
waltz music.

"Along in the middle of the afternoon I found the camp.

Four men were there, all wearing six-shooters. I said I'd come to bring some meat. One asked if Pete Lenoir had sent it. I said he had. 'Well, get down, kid, and stay a while,' this man said. I didn't want to stay but got down to untie the old slicker.

"After I had delivered the beef, the man said, 'That's sure a fine saddle you're riding.'

"I agreed with him and was prouder than ever. Then he said, 'Kid, how about trading your saddle for mine?'

"I looked over at the old hull he pointed to. I looked at the six-shooters he and the other men were loaded down with and the saddle guns laying around in easy reach. I didn't have any say coming, and I didn't say anything.

"After the saddles were changed, this man asked, 'Do you know who I am?'

" 'No.'

" 'Well, I'm Sam Bass.'

"I left with a heavy heart. I wasn't so much scared as I was just down at having lost my fine new saddle. If it had been left up to me, I'd not have put the old hull on my horse. I'd a left bareback. Sam Bass put his old saddle on my horse and girted it up himself. The leather on it was fair and it had good saddle pockets, but it was coming apart. I felt I had been taken advantage of by the meanest, low-downdest man in seven states.

"I rode on home. When I got down, I yanked that saddle off and threw it on the ground like I was trying to split the tree. When I did, I heard metal chink. I looked in a saddle pocket to see what it was. It was three twenty-dollar gold pieces; in the other pocket were three other pieces. Well, I bought a rig sure enough with all that money — new saddle, silver-plated bit, pair of Petmecky spurs, Navajo blanket, fancy-stitched boots, leggins, everything."

In the spring of 1878 a youth named Chunk Porter was

clerking in a dry-goods store owned by a Mr. Cates in the little town of Kaufman. Early one morning, as he told hundreds of times in later years and as his descendants and others still tell, he had just opened the store and was sweeping the plank sidewalk in front of it when three strangers rode up on good horses. Two got down and walked into the store; the other remained mounted, looking up and down the roads. Chunk was alone at the store that day, his employer being sick in bed at home.

One of the strangers, pleasant-featured and pleasant-voiced, said he wanted to buy a suit of clothes. Chunk was able to fit him with the best grade of wool in stock. The purchaser handed over two twenty-dollar gold pieces and said he would put the new suit on now. Chunk went to the safe, which he had not yet opened, for change. After he had worked the combination, opened the door and pulled out a tray full of money, he became aware of the man in the new suit standing at his side.

"Son," the man said, "that is a good deal of money."

Chunk explained that the town had no bank, that their cash had to be sent by stage or taken in person to Terrell for banking, and that the illness of his employer had prevented his attending to that matter. The stranger advised him not to let everybody who came along see how much money the safe held, and then rode away. After Sam Bass was killed in Round Rock the clothes he wore were identified as having come from the Cates dry-goods store in Kaufman.

Railroads, express companies, and the governor of Texas all offered rewards for the capture of Sam Bass, and these offers induced some citizens to join sheriff posses, out to get the money. They were all fiascoes. While the Sam Bass gang was dodging about the breaks on the Clear Fork of the Brazos in Stephens County, the sheriff set about organizing a posse. A settler named Hide, who was proving up a section of land, decided he'd join the posse and rode to the Caddo store to enlist another brave or two to go with him.

As he was dismounting with his artillery, a man carrying a sack of provisions from the store asked him where he was going.

"I'm going to hunt down Sam Bass," the settler replied.

"Then you don't need to go any farther. You've found him," the stranger said. "What are you going to do with him?"

"Nothing, I guess," Hide answered. There didn't seem to be anything else to say.

"How many children you got?" Sam Bass asked.

Hide told him. He had a big litter.

Sam went back into the store and brought out a dozen apples, a lot of candy, and a package of Arbuckle's coffee. "Take the candy and apples home to your children," he said. "When you get there make yourself a big pot of coffee and never tell a soul you have seen Sam Bass."

Hide waited thirty years to tell this story, so he said.

One night soon after a train robbery by the Bass gang in the vicinity of Dallas, a deputy sheriff named Boyd from Denton County and several citizens ambitious for reward money were in a saloon at Pilot Point. None of the posse knew Sam Bass by sight, but they were full of plans for capturing him. Presently a stranger in cowboy garb came through the door, glanced over the crowd, moved to the bar, and invited everybody up for a drink. Everybody accepted. After the stranger downed his whiskey he took a seat at a long table at the rear end of the room, his back to the wall and to one side of an open window. He asked for coffee and bread. Several of the men sat down at the table also, ordering coffee, Boyd opposite him.

The talk naturally drifted to the recent train robbery. Not in the least reticent, the stranger revealed a marked familiarity with circumstances attending it. Boyd was growing suspicious, but the stranger remained drawlingly calm. When the coffee came, he stirred his slowly and then asked Boyd to pass the plate of bread. Boyd was by now flustered. He seemed to feel that some action was expected of him as a peace officer. He paid no attention to the request. Rising, the stranger pulled his six-shooter, fired a bullet into the plate, scattering its contents over Boyd's lap. Then he stepped through the window. By the time the deputy and his posse got outside, Sam Bass had disappeared into the night. The country had another joke at the expense of Sam Bass hunters.

Most people who met Sam — and some who didn't — told of their encounters with pride. In one town that Sam had entered to buy ammunition he saw a sheriff and dodged into a dressmaker's shop. She had a mountain of ruffles on the floor; in those days party dresses were trimmed with yards and yards of ruffles. The dressmaker, recognizing Sam Bass, told him to get under the ruffles. He did. The sheriff came in and saw nothing that interested him. When she was a grandmother, the dressmaker used to end her story by saying, "Lots of folks loved Sam."

A peddler and auctioneer named Samuels didn't, but even he harbored no hard feelings. One time he and his teamsters, driving three wagonloads of merchandise to be auctioned off in Denton, had made camp when Sam Bass's company rode up. Bass introduced himself by name and asked if the merchant had any whiskey.

"We only have five gallons," Samuels told him.

"Well," Sam said, "we don't want to swim in it. Five gallons ought to quench our thirst."

The Bass men made camp, put out a guard, helped themselves to food as well as whiskey, played poker a while, slept, and next morning breakfasted with their hosts. At parting Sam

Bass was more than gracious in expressing appreciation for hospitality. "You'll probably see some rangers this morning," he said. "When you do, tell 'em which way I went."

A few weeks before Sam's betrayal and death, a well-armed rider dismounted in front of Dr. Isaac Mayfield's little office in the village of Deanville, away east of the Bass gang's usual range. Young Doctor Mayfield was fresh out of medical school and eager for practice. His horse, saddled and bearing saddlebags loaded with a county doctor's full equipment, stood at the hitching post. The stranger said the doctor would have to make a considerable ride to get to a sick man. What kind of sickness, the doctor wanted to know.

"You'll see when you get there."

The stranger led over what passed for a road for about ten miles west and south to Yegua Creek, and then along a dim trail into the Yegua Thicket, still noted for the dense growth of yaupon and other shrubs and trees. Then they came to a camp that had apparently been occupied for several days. Eight men were visible. Their leader did not give his name. He told the doctor that a man lying on a pallet of blanket-covered moss had a wounded leg.

The doctor uncovered him and saw that he had been shot through the fleshy part of the thigh and that gangrene was setting in. He called for a pot of boiling water. It was soon brought. He washed the bullet hole at entrance and exit and applied an antiseptic. Then he told the leader that he must probe in order to remove pus and needed some clean cloth. The leader went to his pack and brought three plain silk handkerchiefs, new and clean. The doctor had no narcotics to give the wounded man; anesthetics were then unknown.

"This is going to hurt," he said. "You all will have to hold him."

The men were standing around, back out of the way. The leader said, "Boys, those new silk handkerchiefs are going to be pulled through that bullet hole, hurt or no hurt. Now let a man get to each leg and arm and one to his head and hold him steady. No matter how much he hollers, hold him till the doctor says quit."

Five men stretched out the wounded man while the doctor ran the silk handkerchiefs through the bullet hole. The sun was low when he finished. He said that he would stay through the night if there were anything more he could do but there wasn't. He would return if called. Now he had better ride in order to get through the Yegua bottom before dark. The leader asked how much he owed.

"I guess ten dollars will cover the bill," the doctor said.

The leader handed him a twenty-dollar gold piece, adding, "Doctor, I would be obliged if you'll not mention this day's work, where you have been, or what you have seen."

The doctor replied, "My patients and practice are private, and I make it a point to keep my mouth shut on personal matters."

He rode away, and as there was no further word he presumed that the wounded man got well. He had concluded that the leader was Sam Bass; descriptions in the papers following the killing at Round Rock confirmed the opinion. He believed in law and order and was against robbers, but had a sympathy for the hunted man.

Almost immediately after news raced over the country that Sam Bass had been betrayed to the rangers by one of his own men named Jim Murphy, and killed, the ballad of Sam Bass came into existence. Nobody knows who composed it. In years that followed, millions of longhorns were soothed on their bed grounds and steadied on their long, slow trailing by the strains of the song. Two lines in particular express the sympathies of the singers:

> Oh, what a scorching Jim will get
> When Gabriel blows his horn! . . .

Relic pirates went to chipping away the headstone that a sister put up at Sam's grave in the Round Rock graveyard. Meanwhile, according to a minor legend, Sam Bass, like Billy the Kid, Jesse James, Bill Longley and many another outlaw,

SAM·BASS
JULY·21·1851
JULY·21·1878

was not in his proper grave at all. There is no boundary to human credulity. Shelton Story, who as a boy found six twenty-dollar gold pieces in the pockets of Sam Bass's discarded saddle, so developed his power of memory that he got to recollecting this end to his hero:

"Not many days after the Round Rock trouble, I took the

T. and P. train at Eagle Ford to go to Fort Worth. The minute I stepped inside the coach I noticed a man hunkered over in a seat by himself like he was sick. I took a close look and recognized Sam Bass. He was sick all right. In fact, he was dying from his wounds. I didn't say nothing. He didn't say nothing neither — not there on the train. When we got to Fort Worth I put him in a hack and drove him to a house out towards Grapevine — a house where we both knew he'd be safe. Blood poison had set in. He lived only two days. We buried him decently, and nobody will ever rob that grave. The man buried at Round Rock was just one of the gang. While he was dying he pretended to be Sam Bass so's to protect his leader."

An artist in storytelling does a great deal more than repeat verbatim what he has heard. Bill Kittrell is an artist. After having begged him at least fourteen times to write the story down, I have written it for him — in my way.

Sam Houston Hall was a very modest, very unferocious-looking and not at all loquacious man, but at a certain stage of fortification by liquid brave-maker, he had to tell a story — his story — his passport to glory, as he considered it. He wore a handlebar mustache that had once been jet black. At proper points throughout his narrative he would twirl first one side and then the other of that mustache like a het-up turkey gobbler swiping his bill right and left on the ground. Only Sam Houston Hall never got het up; he lived, drank and narrated as cool as a cloud sailing on an east wind. From here on is what he told — according to at least two constructive memories. Quotation marks would be an impertinence:

Well do I remember the day that I was born. But I'll have to go back a little before that. While Sam Houston was living with the Cherokees up in the Indian Territory, my pa gallivanted around with him some. Pa got to Texas in time to smell some of the gunpowder Sam Houston set off. Then in time he married and settled on Brushy Creek in Williamson County, up from Round Rock, where, as the ballad goes, "Sam Bass met his fate."

I was born about two o'clock in the morning, and about two o'clock that afternoon Sam Houston come riding through the country and turned off the main road to see his old friend. Pa was proud as everything and brung him right into the room where Ma was lying comfortable with me by her side. Sam Houston said, "Let me see that boy," and Ma uncovered me and sort of handed me over.

"What's his name?" Sam Houston wanted to know.

"He ain't got no name yet," Pa said.

"Well," Sam Houston said, "a lot of razorback-headed brats not likely to add to my honor have been named after me, but I wish you'd name this boy Sam Houston."

Ma was just as pleased as Pa over the idea, and Sam Houston Hall has been my name from that minute to this. I can't recollect exactly when the next valuable possession was added to my life. It was a rim-fire, copper-lined, .30-caliber English sporting rifle, and there was not another like it in Williamson County, or, for that matter, in any county joining Williamson.

I wouldn't say it myself, but they do say that by the time I was ten years old I was as sure a shot as ever drawed a bead between the Colorado River and the Brazos. There were lots of times in those days when food for folks was mostly meat, and wild meat at that. Meat for the Hall family got to depending on me and that rim-fire, copper-lined, .30-caliber English sporting rifle, and not another one like it south of Arkansas. Pa's earmark for cattle was underbit in each ear, and I got so I'd aim a bullet to nick out an underbit in the ear of some yearling deer

I didn't want to kill. A year or so later when it grew into a prime buck I'd take it for venison. That earmark sort of made it private property.

When I unsaddled my horse I never did unbuckle the buckskin scabbard that carried my rim-fire, copper-lined, .30-caliber English sporting rifle. Some horses never do get over flinching and spoiling the aim when a man draws a rifle to shoot from the saddle, but I had a horse that kept as steady when he heard the trigger cocked as that rifle itself. I wouldn't want you to get the notion he didn't have plenty fire power too. I always rode him when I went to town, and the more people he saw looking at him, the more fire he seemed to get in his blood. His name was Lightning.

One day I saddled up Lightning and took out for Round Rock. I was just twelve years, five months and three days old. I never can forget that date. Something like a magnet seemed to draw me to Round Rock that day. Of course I had my rim-fire, copper-lined, .30-caliber English sporting rifle in the scabbard.

As I rode around a motte of live oaks overlooking Round Rock I beheld an excitement that the town never had before and hasn't had since. Men on horseback were chasing this way and that, acting like they were after something they couldn't see. Some seemed to be shooting at the sky. But I saw one man empty his rifle after a man running on horseback through a cornfield with corn growing in it head high. Something told me that fleeing man was a dangerous criminal and that it was my duty to stop him.

I drew my rim-fire, copper-lined, .30-caliber English sporting rifle out of its buckskin scabbard and setting there on Lightning while he seemed to quit breathing drew a bead on the criminal right where his suspenders crossed. He fell over into the corn out of sight. I didn't have to see him to know his travels had ended.

I rode into Round Rock and asked what the excitement was all about. "Why, Sam Bass has robbed the bank and killed a man and got away scot-free," they said.

"I don't believe he's got away quite yet," I says.

About this time three rangers and a sheriff dashed up, yelling out to know which way Sam Bass was headed. I told 'em if they wanted to see where he'd stopped I'd show 'em. We rode down into the cornfield. They got down to examine what was left of Sam Bass and pointed out to each other how a .30-caliber bullet had drilled into him exactly where his suspenders crossed. I never did make any noise about it, but everybody that knowed anything on such matters knowed that Sam Houston Hall had the only rim-fire, copper-lined, .30-caliber English sporting rifle anywhere in fifty miles of Round Rock that day.

A millionaire can buy propaganda agents, a king can knight, a president can decorate, a pope can decree sainthood; but nobody but just folks can robinhood an outlaw. In order to get robinhooded, the outlaw must, like Jesse James in the song, be "a friend to the poor"; he must be daring and gay.

Yaller Bread and Pa'tridge Pie

T O get the point of this yarn, one has to remember that a long time ago on southern frontiers, where the climate is too hot for wheat, corn bread was the staff of life and flour biscuits were so rare that a certain boy upon seeing his first one put a coal of fire on it. He had taken it for a small terrapin and wanted to see if it would crawl.

Well, back in those times a family who had settled up Goose Creek was giving a wedding dinner — in the middle of the day, of course — for their daughter and her groom. They were putting the big pot in the little one and had thrown the skillet away. They were having not only flour biscuits but pound cake, golden with egg yolks and butter. It was already baked and sliced and on the table when a settler named Bullock who lived away up above the last fork of the creek — where the owls mated with chickens — came along in his ox wagon.

He and his family had not been invited to the "infare." They belonged to another community and he did not belong to this company anyhow. His hair looked as if he used it for a napkin and had not had the bear grease washed out of it for years. His buckskin clothes were "cured" not only with tallow rubbed in to turn water but with blood of butchered animals and all variety of dirt mixed with frying fat. Yet it would never do to let him go on without dinner.

"Now, Mr. Bullock," the hostess beamed, "I know how far you have to travel before dark and how bad the road is and all that, but you must eat something before going on. Dinner's about ready and you won't have to wait until all this crowd gets settled. Come on and sit down."

Mr. Bullock washed his hands and face in a washpan on the back gallery, dried on the common towel, lumbered into the big hall, and sat down in a broad rawhide-bottomed chair near a great plate of sliced pound cake. Soon plates of fried chicken, fried venison, beef roasted over coals, bowls of mustard greens and potatoes, jars of mustang grape preserves and jelly from wild dewberries, and other good things were within his reach. There was plenty of butter and gravy too, next to the golden-brown corn bread.

Mr. Bullock began peeling drumsticks at about a bite and a half each. He ate a piece of corn bread sopped in gravy and then he tried a slice of pound cake spread with butter. He sampled venison and approved of the beef, but a combination of fried chicken, pound cake and butter was evidently what his system called for. After he had consumed two or three pieces of pound cake, the hostess moved the corn bread nearer to him. The yellow corn from which it was made gave it a rich look, but Mr. Bullock was too deep in pound cake, butter and fried chicken to notice it.

Now the hostess was truly alarmed. Mr. Bullock had let his belt out a notch. It was a wide belt encased in rattlesnake skin. He appeared to be really settling down to business when he took it off and hung it over the back of his chair. While he was un-cinching himself the hostess ran out the back door and into the kitchen, a room separate from the main house, and returned with a platter of biscuits — flour biscuits.

"Oh, Mr. Bullock," her voice came with an anxiety that any-body else would have noticed, "do have some biscuits. We don't have them very often, you know, but I have just finished a big baking of them."

"No, thank you, ma'am," responded Mr. Bullock, who had resumed operations on the pound cake. "You jes' save them biscuits fer company. This here yaller bread is good enough for me."

Then he "blowed" some coffee in a saucer and swallowed it with another slice of "yaller bread."

My mother used to tell an anecdote of a similarly oblivious character of a similar architectural construction. He came by our ranch one day about dinner time and of course stayed to eat. Mama had baked a large quail pie, the quail having, I suppose, been trapped by us boys; men living in our part of the country in those days seldom shot for sport, but ranch boys often trapped for meat. Trapping game birds was probably not against the law. There were several extra guests at dinner that day, and the children had to wait for the second table.

Mr. Bud, as I'll call the rancher who stopped at dinner time, had hearty ways of talking, walking, bragging, and eating. He was, outwardly at least, enormously pleased with himself. He took to that quail pie with enormous gusto. With thoughts on her children waiting for the second table, my mother watched Mr. Bud's pile of quail bones mount. He had begun by piling them on one side of the plate, but the pile grew top-heavy and finally he cleared them all out onto the tablecloth.

I suppose he was eating beans, hot biscuits, potatoes and other food in proportion. He ended by picking the flesh from another quail or two, arranged the bones neatly on the pile, reared back and said, "Ella, that pa'tridge pie is good all right, but it would have been better if you had fried the pa'tridges before putting them in with the dough to bake."

My mother always ended the story by observing, "I felt like telling him I was glad I hadn't done anything to the dish to make him eat more of it."

Taller and Too Much Pepper

A F T E R fighting his way out of Texas, Isom Like continued to fight Indians in New Mexico a while, and then, with his horse stock, settled down near the Colorado line. He had six sons, and after he was seventy, he and they had a riding contest annually on his birthday. Old Isom always won, his wife habitually acting as judge. He lived strictly at home, but along in the 1890's buyers quit coming for his horses and he decided to drive a bunch east and peddle them out. Arriving in a town, he would go to the hotel to eat. This was back in the days when hotel meals were served "family style." When a waiter set boiled custard before him for dessert, he shoved it aside, saying, "Oh, that's children's food." When toast was offered him for breakfast, he calmly stated, "I ain't sick."

After he had celebrated his hundredth birthday, Jack Potter paid him a visit and asked his *remedio* for long life. He got it! "Live temperately in food and drinks. Try to get your beefsteaks three times a day, fried in taller. Taller is mighty healing, and there's nothing like it to keep your stummick greased up and in good working order."

Tallow was a substitute for both lard and butter. Melted and poured sizzling hot into a tin plate of black sorghum molasses, it helped end a meal with a dessert as good as a hungry man ever flopped his lip over. But melted tallow will quickly congeal in the mouth and stick to the roof of it. My grandfather, Rufus Byler, who was murdered in south Texas immediately after he came home from the Civil War, was bald-headed. "When I was a boy," he would explain, "I complained once about tallow that glued up in the top of my mouth. They put a hot skillet on top of my head so's to drive the heat down and melt the tallow, and that way burned all my hair out at the roots."

While Grover Cleveland was president of the United States, a terrible drouth struck many parts of the West. There was a move in Congress to appropriate money for the distressed, but Cleveland said it was the business of people to support their government and not the business of government to support people. In Boston, New York and other centers of population and wealth, money was raised to send food to drouth-struck areas. All the drouth-sufferers could do was pray for rain — and a good many of them were like the old preacher who said, "It won't do any good to pray for rain as long as these dry winds keep blowing from the west."

In Jack County during this drouth small ranchers and other citizens decided to hold a camp meeting. It was election year, and, of course, all the politicians in the county came with pious faces. Among them was the district judge, a candidate for re-election and also a pillar in three churches. One service was to be devoted to intense prayer for rain. The ramrod of this serv-ice was a blunt cowman named Brummett, a strong partisan of the judge's. He invited the judge to lead in prayer, kneeling at his side.

In the beginning the judge prayed for "copious showers to

moisten this thirsty earth and cause it to produce crops for the farmer and grass for the rancher," but he soon took to plainer talk.

"Now, God," he issued instructions, "we don't want no mizzle-drizzle dripping. We want a gully-washer and fence-lifter. Let it rain pitchforks and bobtailed heifer yearlings. Send enough water to make the frogs holler once more. But now, God, if you can't see your way clear to send us rain, soften the hearts and open the purses of people in the East. Give them to understand how hard up a lot of us are. Cause them to send us sufferers barrels of meal, barrels of flour, barrels of rice, barrels of bacon, barrels of lard, barrels of molasses, barrels of beans, barrels of coffee, barrels of sugar, barrels of salt, barrels of pepper, bar—" Here the old cowman became excited, nudged the judge in the ribs and whispered not at all low, "Oh, hell, Judge, that's just too damned much pepper."

It was a broiling summer day when a settler, one of the unnamed heroes who helped "redeem Texas from the wilderness," halted his wagon by the public water trough on the square of a little town west of woods and water. A box of panting chickens was lashed to the footboard on one side of the wagon; on the other side was a water keg. Dangling from the rear end was a washpot. From under the raised wagon-sheet peered a half dozen freckle-faced urchins. A brindle dog with a grotesquely long, red tongue, with which he had been lapping water, lay in the shade cast by the wagon and panted. A woman in a sunbonnet, with a baby at her breast and a twig of hackberry with snuff on the end of it in her mouth, sat on the wagon seat. The man was taking out his team.

This team was what gave the outfit distinction. It consisted of a rawboned old gray mare and a dun ox. The pair of beasts was certainly an oddity, and a native of the village was not long in crossing the ground from a shed in front of a grocery store and showing his curiosity.

"Well, you see it was this way," the mover explained with mighty little emphasis in his voice. "I had another horse but the critter died, jest starved because the drouth dried up even the mesquite leaves out there. I told the old woman there wa'nt no two ways about it, that we were going to move back where it rains. Then I traded for the ox."

"How are oxen selling out in that western country?" the native pumped.

"Well, I dunno as they are selling. I had two sections of land and I traded one of them for this ox."

"That looks purty steep to me," the native commented.

"Well, I'm satisfied," the mover gloated. "You see the damned fool I traded with couldn't read and when it come to making out the deed I just slipped both sections off on him."

Esau the Hunter

F O R generations stretching back to the horizon of chronicled time, the hairy one called Esau has been held up as a sermon against improvidence, thriftlessness, surrender to appetite, foolish evaluation of the offerings that life makes.

Esau was a cunning hunter, a man of the woods and field. He could read sign; he knew all the shepherd lore about weeds, snails and stars. Walls cramped him; cushions smothered him; the smallness of small people wilted him. Only out in the open could he expand. "Canst thou bind the sweet influences of Pleiades, or loose the bands of Orion?"

His twin brother Jacob was cunning too — cunning in getting and holding. He never went hunting, but dwelt about the tents, where he kept tally on every lamb added to the estate and on every ephah of wheat advanced to a servant. His old father Isaac loved Esau, saw in him the vanished strength and freedom of his own youth, delighted in the wild taste of the venison he brought home. The mother of the boys loved Jacob and took pride in the way he saved, hoarded pieces of string, and spied on the hirelings. Jacob would some day sit in the seats of the mighty, and God would listen for his advice — given in the form of humble prayer, of course — on how to run the country.

One winter morning, long before daylight, Esau went out to hunt. He was making for a hollow on the other side of the last line of hills. He did not need sun or stars or wind to course by; something inside him was as true as a compass. He did not see the sun that morning. A bitter wind driving rain blew up against him at dawn. He knew it would send the deer into coverts, but he kept on going. He crawled through mud, slid on rocks, crept through brush. Water dripped from his eyebrows. By the time he turned homewards his feet were leaded and his soaked clothes weighed like a heavy drag.

When he plowed into the big tent after dark, empty-handed, he was trembling with cold and hunger. Nothing makes a man so hollow as walking all day, sodden and chilled to the marrow, in biting wind and rain. Now, in the warmth and light, he smelled the stew that Jacob had been comfortably and calculatingly seething. He was so faint that he reeled. Every fiber in his being called out for the steaming nourishment, as cracked soil yearns for moisture. He was a part of the good earth.

And Esau said to Jacob, "Feed me, I pray thee, with that same red pottage . . . I am faint."

And Jacob said, "Convey to me thy birthright, and I will give you to eat."

And Esau said, "Behold I am at the point to die. What profit shall my birthright do to me unless I eat?"

And Jacob said, "Swear to me this day."

And Esau sware away his birthright for something to eat.

Then Jacob gave Esau bread and pottage of lentils; and he did eat and drink, and rose up, and went his way.

The years passed and Jacob, going his way, gained property and power. He cheated his father-in-law, schemed to circumvent nature, and became the model for all graspers after unearned increments that the world has since rewarded. He became the upholder of all respectabilities and was the main pillar of society. He advanced the orthodoxy of all royalists of all times: *Keep on top by keeping others down.* When he gave a gift it was to win a favor. When in the stillness of evening he heard the chirp of crickets, he wondered if the shepherds of his far-spread flocks were listening against wolves. When he gave a farthing to a blind singer of ballads, he silently accused him of shiftlessness. The ballad bore no meaning for him.

And the way that Esau went was still the way of the hunter, over the hills and far away, the sun and the rain in his face, free from the bondages of property, free from the gnawing lust to possess everything he saw and to outsmart all his fellow men. He did not consider himself wise enough to give God much advice. Yet he was no shiftless rabbit-hunter of Rip Van Winkle irresponsibility, with an outcast cur for his only respecter. Despite Jacob's craftiness and his own appetite, Esau had tents, family and flocks. He owned things, but things did not own him. On warm spring days he could lie on the grass and listen to it grow and receive a joy beyond that of watching his own sheep fatten on it or of wanting, like Nebuchadnezzar, to eat it himself. When the wind blew fresh, he could sniff it and gladden within himself at how the old does were sniffing it too and working their ears and nostrils. He could stretch out for hours on the ground, his back to a log, watching over a valley, the light clouds drifting one way, the cawing ravens flying another, and, thus lingering, feel something sweet and clarifying to his soul, a kind of liberation, seep into him. He gazed into spring dawnings to hear the lark's faltering notes come dropping down. In his heart he thanked every ballad singer that he heard. Jacob said he was childish; Rachel said he was childlike; his nephew Joseph and other boys thought him a hero. He presaged another treader of the open lands who long afterwards liked to lie down in green pastures and wait by still waters and who sang a song: "I will lift up mine eyes unto the hills."

In time Esau grew too wobbly in the knees to follow a trail, too weak in muscle to draw a bow, too watery in the eyes to pick out the flick of a stag's antler in the bush. Like his father Isaac before him, though, he still craved strong venison and remembered free days with the wild things. Poet Whitney Montgomery has pictured "Esau Grown Old." *

> Make room for him
>   By the fireplace;
> He is done with the hunt,
>   He is done with the chase.
>
> He is done with the hills
>   And the torrent's thunder
> And the deep, dark woods
>   That he loved to wander.
>
> Let him sit in
>   His chair and nap,
> With his hairy hands
>   Crossed in his lap.
>
> And when he would
>   Recount old glories,
> Be kind and listen
>   To his stories.
>
> Despite the hate
>   Of God and his mother,
> He has had more
>   Than his crafty brother.

* Quoted by permission of author and publisher from *Hounds in the Hills*, by Whitney Montgomery, The Kaleidograph Press, Dallas, Texas, 1934.

Animals of the Wild

The Voice of the Coyote

At twilight time, when the lamps are lit,
Father Coyote comes to sit
At the chaparral's edge, on the mountain side —
Comes to listen and to deride
The rancher's hound and the rancher's son,
The passer-by and everyone.
And we pause at milking-time to hear
His reckless caroling, shrill and clear —
His terse and swift and valorous troll,
Ribald, rollicking, scornful, droll.
— GEORGE STERLING, "Father Coyote"

A S the "father of song-making," the coyote, though a slight creature, has gone deep into the imaginations of Western people. "We'll have singing tonight," my father used to say at the supper table following the butchering of a beef. Not long after dark the Mexican vaqueros down the hill from the ranch house would, from good spirits helped by the fill of fresh meat, lilt some ballad or love song toward the highest star, and then the coyotes would, from gladness at smell of the blood and offal and in response to the vaquero singing, wail out their song in still higher notes. English-speakers living with the coyote usually call his noises "yelping," "howling," "barking," "chattering," "yapping," maybe "mourning," maybe "laughing," but to the vaquero people they are *cantando* (singing).

"Next to God, the coyote is the smartest person on earth," an old Mexican saying goes. Then may come a tale making a fool of this "sagacious" personage. Well, it's no fun to make a fool of a fool. To Indians of coyote land, he is the supreme trickster. To everybody who knows him, even a sheep owner, he is a character.

Old Crip

THE coyote will not eat while we are looking," Luke Stillwell, government trapper, said, as at dusk he put a grown jack
rabbit just shot into a cage under some live oak trees, far
enough removed from the house that its stench did not permeate
the domestic air. "In the morning there won't be anything left
of this rabbit. Coyotes have to have hair with their meat. One
would starve on clean beefsteak."

After suppering on Mrs. Stillwell's hot biscuits, venison,
honey, gravy, and apple pie — though never shall I admit any
dessert to surpass honey of mesquite blossom, hot biscuits and
fried venison, especially if some glasses of cold raw milk be
added — I maneuvered to get the trapper down to bedrock on
Mister Coyote. "In the tradition of American wildlife," I said,
"the Custer Wolf, Snow Drift, and other big wolves became
symbols of cunning. Have there been any individual coyotes to
equal them in foxiness?"

Luke Stillwell was silent for longer than a minute. He
shifted in the rawhide-bottomed chair. A wrinkle stood on his
forehead.

"I called her Old Crip," he began. "I set my first trap on this ranch the twelfth day of September, 1943. There had been trappers ahead of me, and they had taught some coyotes a lot. I began right away catching crippled coyotes — escaped from their traps. I caught fourteen cripples and then there were two coyotes left. They were really educated. Finally I caught one of them, and the trap held. It took me fifteen months and five days to get Old Crip.

"She had two toes off her left front foot. While I was still clearing the other sheep-killers out, she put her right front foot into one of my traps. She pulled, gnawed, twisted and broke that foot off just above the steel jaws. What she left there was all I ever saw of her until the end. The average coyote when caught in a trap becomes frantic. It bites bushes, the trap cover, steel, sometimes its own tail. The part of its foot below the steel jaws becomes numb, and often the animal will chew that part, not with the purpose of cutting itself loose but in blind desperation. Another trapper told me of a coyote that chewed both front feet out of a trap and then just sat there without a struggle while he came up to kill her. I am absolutely sure that Old Crip knew what she was about when she set to work to free herself.

"Within thirty days the stub had healed and she was killing sheep again. She killed sixty lambs within a month's time. She went from one pasture to another and killed three thousand dollars' worth of sheep during the fifteen months and five days I kept after her. I didn't let up for a day. Her track was unmistakable and her habits were individual.

"She killed often for sport. Any killing leaves plain signs. But Old Crip never seemed boastful and reckless in her killing like some coyotes. One night four bold ones came into a clean pasture, killed sixteen lambs, gorged, went on, met a skunk, killed him, tore him up and rolled on him without taking a bite of his flesh, went on, met a big fat possum, killed him, and left him untouched beside the trail. These coyotes were out to shoot up the town. Old Crip would slaughter sheep right and left; then she was gone. When a coyote with any sense kills a sheep, he knows he is in danger. He eats in a hurry. He takes one gulp and then looks up. As soon as he is full, he makes tracks — no lying around the carcass for him. This was the way of Old Crip. She killed without reason at times, but always on the alert. After the killing was over, she seemed never to be playful or loggy. She stayed unceasingly careful.

"She never traveled stock trail or road. Coyotes that travel in that way — and it is natural for a coyote to trot down a road — are easily caught. All the time I was after Old Crip, fresh coyotes were coming into the ranch from the big cattle pastures joining us. They had regular entrances, and they regularly got into traps. A coyote seldom learns anything by seeing or smelling the carcasses of his mates. A dead coyote seems to mean nothing to a live one — excepting always the highly intelligent — and Old Crip was the most intelligent of them all. During five and a half years of trapping on one big ranch before I came here, I caught fifty-four coyotes in a single trap at one location, just resetting it and hanging the carcasses of the victims, one after the other, near by. This was at a wire-netting fence corner. I had some other traps close by, and altogether caught between one hundred ten and one hundred fifteen coyotes at this location. The easiest kind of coyote to trap is a young male. The females even when young are more distrustful.

"Old Crip had already depredated on the ranch for several years when I took up her trail. She would never go under a fence unless another coyote preceded her, showing that the way was clear. She had probably been caught at a hole under a fence. She avoided all lures, scent or bait. I caught her that first time in a blind trap — just a naked trap hidden in the ground —

placed where I thought she might go to water. That was on the night of October 31, 1943. She had miles of Los Moros Creek to water in and she was not fixed by habit to any one watering place. After she stepped down the bank to water and had drunk, she backed out, putting her feet in almost the exact tracks they had made coming in.

"In the spring I found her den with the pups in it. Her mate had no doubt been caught. I set a blind trap at the den. A sheep got into it and fell into the hole, rather large at the mouth. That night the mother coyote beat a trail around the sheep and the den. I took the sheep out the next morning. Old Crip never returned to her pups. The mother instinct in coyotes is strong; in Old Crip it was not blind. She plainly suspected — and she was right — that a hidden enemy would not let her pass if she stepped into her den to move her young ones. She left them to perish.

"In any coyote country you frequently see coyotes moving about by day, though it is their nature to be nocturnal. I never once saw Old Crip. It is my belief that she never roamed during daylight hours but kept herself absolutely hidden. So far as I know, she never howled. Except at mating time, she ranged alone. She killed alone. She went in the night and she went in silence.

"It is a habit with some coyotes, not with all by any means, to gorge a bait of sheep meat, six pounds say, go off maybe forty or sixty yards, in open country farther, to where there is brush and shade, and there dig out a hole. Then the animal throws up the meat, still fresh and undigested, into the hole and covers it with earth, just as a dog buries a bone. The coyote that does this will almost invariably come back the next night, dig its meat out of earth that has kept it fresh, and eat. By that time flies and buzzards would have ruined the carcass, provided other coyotes had not made away with it. A coyote will rob another coyote's cache if he finds it. The caches make good trapping places; sometimes I bury a piece of meat or bone, mound up earth over it in a natural way, and set traps. After a coyote fills up on meat for the purpose of burying it and has buried it, he goes straight back to the carcass and eats again, either to digest the food or to carry it to the young.

"Now, if Old Crip ever buried a piece of meat, I did not know it. If she ever ate carrion, I did not know it. She had lost the scavenger habits of her species. She was always choosy about her meat. She liked it warm and fresh, and she was particular about the cuts.

"It was on the night of December 17, 1944, that I caught her the second time, in a blind trap, on a bluff overlooking water. She must have realized that she could not free herself this time. I found her drowned. She had dived off the bluff and gone under some wire netting in the water. The hook on the trap chain caught in this wire. She aimed to kill herself, so it seems to me. She had just cut the throat of a choice lamb, had eaten, and was on her way to water. I examined her stomach. It contained five or six pounds of select meat — kidneys, small intestines, leaf fat, loin, and tender ribs. I never heard of a lobo smarter than Old Crip. I came to admire her while she was baffling me. She seemed to belong to the hills that I belong to. I think of her lots of times in the night. I'll never forget her."

―――――――――――――――――――――――――――――――――

Playing Possum

―――――――――――――――――――――――――――――――――

WHEN a possum plays dead he does not know what he is doing any more than a sensitive plant knows what it is doing when upon being touched its leaves close together. The possum and the sensitive plant merely exercise reflex action; but when Brother Coyote plays dead, he is just cunning — so they say.

One time there was a coon who lived up in a hollow tree overlooking a kind of open-air distillery where mezcal was made. This coon was curious and often sat back in the hollow of his tree and watched without being seen. He watched men bring in goatskins of honey-water from the maguey plant. Then, after it was distilled, he watched them pour it into bottles. Often when he was sleeping down in the hollow tree he would hear sounds of laughter and gaiety. If he came up and looked out, he would see the laughers drinking out of bottles, some acting like lunatics. He wondered about the stuff in the bottles.

One day all the people left the distillery to go to a fiesta. Then the coon came down to investigate. He was a solemn kind of person, but in his heart he loved laughter and wished he could laugh too. He took up a bottle of mezcal, stood on his hind legs just as he had seen men stand, and pulled out the stopper with his teeth. Then he took a drink. *Hombre!* Fire blazed through his insides! Zigzags went up and down his backbone! He coughed, water flooded his eyes, and then he felt better. He felt springy.

He took another swig, not quite so much, and let it trickle down. Then he laughed, his spirits seemed so light. He took one more drink and shouted with glee. He wanted to find somebody to share his joy with, and so, carrying the bottle, he went walking down the road. Once in a while he would sip, just sip, the mezcal and laugh. His shoulders were thrown back, and he was looking at rainbows.

Now it happened that a hungry coyote passing across the country heard Señor Coon laughing. He stopped behind a prickly pear bush and looked. What fine eating the fat fellow would make, he thought; but he knew from experience that if he started after him, he would run up a tree out of reach. After he watched the coon dawdle along a little while, he said to himself, "This fellow is drunk. He won't ever get up another tree."

The coyote struck a long trot, keeping down low, and made a circle so as to come into the road ahead of the coon, but out of his sight. There he lay down on his side, kicked the dust as animals do when they are helpless, made other signs, and then became as lifeless as a chunk of mud. His face was turned in the coon's direction.

Coming up, the coon saw the dead-looking coyote. Before he got too close, he stopped, laughed out loud and said, even louder, "H'm, I've always heard that the way to see if a person is really dead and is not just acting, is to kick him in the stomach. Then, if he is dead, dead, dead, he will open his mouth and stick out his tongue."

Señor Coon took three steps forward, put down his bottle,

reached into his pocket, pulled out his specs, put them on and leaned away over. "Absolutely dead," he said to himself out loud, "but it will be wise to make the test." Then, very cautiously, he approached nearer, but not too near, and poked a paw into the coyote's belly. When he did, the coyote opened his mouth and stuck out his tongue.

At that the coon ran up a tree and there he laughed more than he had laughed in all the rest of his life put together. And the Señor Actor passed out of sight without saying one word.

A ranchero of Chihuahua had back of his house a corral of high and thick adobe walls. It was drained by a very narrow rock-lined ditch running under the wall. Through this ditch the ranchero's chickens entered the pen every evening and went out every morning. One night a coyote squeezed through and caught a chicken. Then the master ordered a servant boy to stop the ditch up with a rock every evening.

One summer morning this master went out early to enjoy the sight of his fighting cocks in the corral. All he could see was scattered feathers, heads without chickens, and chickens without heads. The boy had forgotten to stop up the ditch, and over in a corner lay the gorged marauder. With maledictions, the ranchero kicked it. It showed no sign of life. He thought that perhaps it had died of colic from so much fresh meat. Perhaps it had filled itself so full that it could not squeeze out through the narrow ditch it had entered. In a harsh voice he called the servant boy to come now and take away the stinking carcass of the destroyer of his finest gamecock.

After the boy had dragged the carcass through thorns and over sharp rocks about a hundred yards, he gave it a kick and was turning to come back when the master yelled for him to take it yet farther away, out of stinking range. The boy obeyed and dashed the carcass against a boulder. As he started back to the house this time, the ranchero, who was still watching and expressing himself, beheld the coyote leap to its feet and run away.

Magician with Chickens

I N the timbered Sierra Madre of northern Mexico I heard how the gunless Pima Indians catch wild turkeys. A roost having been located, a number of Pimas go to it after dark with a supply of pitch pine and gourd rattles. One Indian lights a torch and, holding it up in one hand and waving it, while rattling a gourd containing rocks in the other hand, circles around under the turkeys, all the while yelling and chanting. The turkeys begin to *put, put, put,* looking down this way and looking down that way, too distraught by what is under them to fly away, growing more and more uneasy. Before the pine torch is burned out, a second Indian relays the first, running, jumping, waving his light, rattling his gourd, splitting the air with his yells. Maybe two or three Indians run at the same time. They keep up their business until some of the turkeys lose their balance and fall out of the tree, *como borrachos* — like drunken ones.

I was discussing this subject with a kind and honest old Mexican in a village of Sonora. "You need not doubt the fact," said he. "Coyotes catch turkeys in the same way. They run around under a turkey roost at night, barking and shooting fire out of their eyes up towards the watching birds. After a while the turkeys get dizzy — sick, and just fall out."

The means employed by Don Coyote in drawing chickens out of trees vary according to the tellers. Supreme authority on techniques was Don Marcelo, gardener for the San Luis Mining Company's grounds at Tayoltita, in the state of Durango. Wonderfully pleasant grounds they were. Attending to Don Marcelo's words, I would forget their meaning while becoming enthralled by the sounds of his soft voice and the vividness of his gestures. Munden's "bundle of faces" could not have been more various than Don Marcelo's. Not content with acting out all his own characters, if I tried to tell something about a horse or a burro, he would throw his fiery sympathy into mimicry of every sound and motion made by the animal. He would crane his neck like a turkey. He would put up two fingers alongside his head to represent the sharp ears of the armadillo and then rustle a hand through leaves on the ground to imitate the armadillo's motion. He would contort his face into the jaguar's snarl before leaping on a dog.

With his own eyes Don Marcelo had seen one coyote magnetize chickens as a clown. Every morning at a certain place where he stayed, a chicken was missed from the tree roosts. There were dogs at this house, but the dogs never said anything against this thief of the darkness. Then one night Don Marcelo and another man sat up to watch. The moon was shining. They could plainly see the forms of the chickens in the branches.

Perhaps an hour before midnight, they heard the chickens make soft noises. Neither of the watchers had seen the coyote come, but there he was. He had just appeared out of nowhere. He knew how to awaken the chickens without making any noise himself. There he was under them, looking up, and there they were, all awake, looking down.

Presently the coyote caught his own tail in his mouth and be gan a mad whirl around and around under the chickens. They became so intent on watching him, trying to keep up with his dashing circles, that within a short time one of them lost its perch and fell to the ground. Some of the other chickens began squawking and cackling, but the coyote was already trotting out of sight with his chicken. As intent on the spectacle as the chickens were, the watching men had not tried to interfere with the performance.

I once considered all such tales as pure folklore. Now I neither believe nor disbelieve. W. J. Slaughter, a rancher of the last century on the Frio River, in lower Texas, used to tell his children of the following experience.

He was spending a night at some ranch down the Frio River. The moon was full. Out in the yard a number of chickens roosted in a mesquite tree. Slaughter's bed was a pallet on the floor of the unscreened porch looking out on the mesquite. He was a light sleeper, and had not been asleep long before he was awakened by coyotes under the mesquite tree. They were not making any noise but were running around. Every so often a coyote would while rising on its hind legs spring upwards, much to chicken excitement. Slaughter was too much interested in the procedure to draw the six-shooter from under his pillow and shoot. He was seeing something that he had often heard his vaqueros tell about and had set down in his own mind as mere fancy. Before long he saw a chicken flop downward. One of the coyotes caught it before it struck the ground and made off; the other two went with him. They got out of sight and no doubt divided the chicken. In about three shakes of a dead sheep's tail, here they were back under the mesquite. By now, however, the owner of the chickens was up, and a shot from his gun put a stop not only to the coyote magic but to any further natural history observations on the part of Mr. Slaughter.

Brother Coyote and Brother Cricket

ONE summer evening about sundown a coyote trotting across the plain put his foot down on a tuft of grass wherein a cricket was singing *"Sereno en aquellos campos"* — "Serene in those fields."

The cricket jumped out and cried, "But, Brother Coyote, why are you destroying my palace?"

"I really did not know you lived here until you exposed yourself," the coyote said.

"You are crude and you insult me," the cricket said. He was ready to spring away.

"Insult you!" the coyote jeered. "Why, you dwarf, I am merely seeking my living, and now that I have you, I am going to eat you up. I had rather have a red watermelon or a fat kid, but I eat a cricket or a grasshopper when it's handy. Maybe you will fill the hollow in one of my molars."

"But, Brother Coyote," the cricket said, now in his soothing way, "it is not fair."

The coyote sat down on the carpet of grass. "Brother Cricket," he said, "you know that when nature offers itself, it is fair for nature to accept."

"But, Brother Coyote, you haven't given me a chance."

"Chance?" exclaimed the coyote. "Why, what sort of chance do you expect?"

"I want to fight a duel."

"You fight a duel with me?" And the coyote laughed.

"Yes, fight a duel with you," the cricket said. "If I win, then my song will go on. If you win, then I'll fill the hollow in one of your respectable teeth."

The coyote looked away off across the plain, and saw a crow flying down in play at the waving tail of a striped skunk. "Well," he said, "perhaps the people need a comedy. All right, we'll have your duel, Brother Cricket."

"Oh, thank you very much, Brother Coyote."

"Now I sit here trembling at the sight of your armor and weapons," the coyote said. "But go on and name your terms."

"It is agreed," said the cricket. "You go and get your army together, and I will go and get my army together. Tomorrow when the sun is straight overhead, you have your army on the prairie just above the water called the Tank of the Seven Coons, and I will have my army in the thicket in the draw just below the dam to this tank. On the hour we shall engage in mortal combat."

"That is clear, General Cricket," said the coyote. "Until tomorrow at high noon, *adiós*."

"*Adiós,* General Coyote."

That night General Coyote went east and west, north and south, summoning in high voice his forces to gather on the prairie above the Tank of the Seven Coons. He summoned the lobo, the badger, the tiger of the deep canyon, the panther of the rimrock, the wildcat of the chaparral, the coon, the possum, the sharp fox, and all the other people with claws and teeth.

And in a singsong General Cricket summoned his forces —

the horseflies, the mosquitoes, the honey bees, the bumblebees, the yellow jackets, the black hornets, and even a colony of red ants — all the people that have stingers and can stick. He told them to gather in the thicket in the draw below the Tank of the Seven Coons.

Long before high noon, the people of fang and claw were assembling on the prairie above the water tank. General Coyote was trotting about, looking this way and that way, smelling and listening. The sun stood straight up, and still he could not see one sign of General Cricket's army.

Finally he called the fox and ordered him to scout out the position of the enemy. With his long nose pointed ahead, his ears alert and his eyes peeled, the fox went trotting down the draw. General Coyote was watching him. When he came to the edge of the thicket, the fox flattened to the ground and began twisting into the brush. Just as he was poking his keen snout into a clump of whitebrush to see and smell more closely, General Cricket ordered a battalion of black hornets to assault him.

They did, all at once. They stuck their stingers into his ears, into the corners of his eyes, into his nostrils, into his flanks, into every spot of his body where hair is short and skin is tender. He snapped and pitched, but only for a minute. He turned seventeen somersaults on the ground, and the black hornets came thicker. Then he streaked for the tank of water. He dived to escape his assaulters, and went to the bottom.

But in a minute he had to come back up for air. Then, sticking his long, long mouth out of the water, he cried at the top of his voice, "General Coyote, retreat! The enemy are upon us!"

General Cricket had already ordered the yellow jackets to attack the army of giants on the prairie, and the war cries of the bumblebees were in the air.

"Retreat!" the fox shrieked again.

General Coyote tucked his tail between his legs and retreated and every soldier in the army tucked his tail and retreated also — all except the bobcat. He retreated without tucking his tail. That is how General Cricket won the duel with General Coyote.

Thus a person should avoid being vainglorious and considering himself shrewder than he is. He may be outwitted by his own vanity.

The Panther's Scream

W H E N I was a boy, I heard stories of ghosts and phantom riders, but no tale of the spirit world ever shivered my timbers like accounts of the panther's scream and its readiness to leap upon a man carrying meat, upon a woman entering a shed room into which the big cat had stolen to devour a fresh deer ham, or upon a child in the dark to eat it up. Nobody then called the panther a "mountain lion"; backwoods people often called it "painter."

The favorite story was of a neighboring ranchman who located a wild turkey roost in the Nueces River bottom and rode out one evening for meat. It happened that he had only two loads for his double-barreled shotgun. He tied his horse at a barbed-wire fence, through which there was no convenient gap, and walked on about half a mile and hid himself near the roost. At dusk he saw and heard the wild turkeys fly up into a clump of live oak trees. They took their time and it was dark before they were all settled. He waited for the moon to come up so that he could skylight the big birds blended into the foliage. He maneuvered around until he had several lined up and then fired both barrels. Six turkeys fell to the ground.

He was carrying them back to his horse, making slow progress on account of the weight, when the scream of a panther right behind him in the brush curdled his blood — a scream always described as more terrifying than the scream of a woman in fright or pain. The man knew what the panther was after; he dropped a turkey. He had gone but a short distance farther before he heard the awful scream again. He dropped another turkey. The next time the squall came from brush to one side of him. Finally he had only one turkey left to drop. If the panther leaped out of the shadows, the man's gun, even as a club, would be of little avail. And now the scream came nearer, more terrifying. He dropped his last turkey. Just as he got to his horse, which was plunging against the rope, the man heard the panther again. But now, thank goodness, he was mounted, "tearing a hole through the brush."

After hearing this story — and it seemed never to be told except at night — I used to lie awake in bed for hours wondering what would have happened to the man had he killed only four turkeys, or maybe only five, to dole out to the panther instead of six, or if he had had a whole mile to walk instead of just about half a mile. But above any concern for human destiny the panther's scream dominated my imagination. Years later when I read,

> Tiger, tiger, burning bright
> In the forests of the night, . . .
> In what distant deeps or skies
> Burnt the fire of thine eyes?

— I wished that some poet of the panther would intensify the panther's scream as Blake in "England's green and pleasant land" had intensified the tiger's eyes. To this day I never look at a panther mounted in a museum without thinking what a lack it is that the scream — the very essence of the creature — cannot be mounted also.

Perhaps it would be, if the processes of petrifaction could be extended. Telling of the Petrified Forest of Arizona, Jim Bridger used to say, "Yes, them putrified trees stand up natural like any other trees. They are simply monstrous. You can ride all day and not get acrost the forest. And all up in the limbs there's putrified birds, some of 'em blue and some of 'em red and all other kinds of colors. And them putrified birds is act'ally singing putrified songs."

If a panther's scream could chill the blood, the deathly silent approach of one in the dark until it got close enough to touch would freeze the marrow. Jeff Ake's people were with Old Hickory in Tennessee but moved to Arkansas before he was born. He drove cattle up the Chisholm Trail and all the other trails and then went out into the Apache country. He could charm the heart out of a whippoorwill with his fiddle, and his grandchildren thought he was the greatest storyteller on earth. This was their favorite:

"I was up on the Flower de Lucy that time, staying at a ranch shanty alone. The Indians was pretty bad, and nobody knowed when they might jump us. One evening late, when I come in from riding all day, I saw that Charley Merritt and Bob Burch had left me the backstrap out of a deer and some bear steaks. They kept bach, down the country a ways. The meat was hung up high. You had to hang up everything eatable; coyotes would steal the spurs out from under your head to chew on the leathers.

"Well, when I unsaddled that evening I throwed my saddle down on the floor next to the door. There wasn't no yard fence to this place. Then I et about three pounds of fried venison and hit the hay. Like always, I had my six-shooter under the piller. In no time I was snoring hee-haw, like that.

"I don't know how long afterwards it was, but I woke up in pitch dark, feeling like something was wrong. It wasn't near time to get up, but I was wide awake. Then something touched me down the leg, like a hand just feeling, soft — that way. 'Indians,' I thinks, and lays as still as a log. D'reckly there was the same soft touch higher up my leg. I was inching my hands up to my chest so that if the Indian grabbed for my throat I could grab his. It seemed he didn't know my geography any better than I knew his. Next the touch was on my stomach, and it sorter pressed down like he was a-leaning over to get a look into my face.

" 'Well, by gravy,' I thinks to myself, 'I ain't going to the Happy Hunting Grounds without some company.' Then I makes one big grab for his throat and collars him. I whips him over on the bed alongside me, twisting out of the covers and trying to get them wropped around him. He's half under me and I throws my legs so's to hold his down. About then I discover the Indian has turned into a panther.

"He's clawing like a mowing machine, but them bed quilts is a shield of mercy. What I'm afeard of is his teeth. I manage to clamp his muzzle shut with one hand and got a good holt on a foreleg with the other. I am shoving him up and back and purty soon have him over by the saddle. I kinder wrap my legs around his hips so he ain't got no room to claw in and tie his muzzle up with the horn string. Then I get a buckskin thong out of a saddle pocket and half-hitch his forelegs together. He is still scratching me with his hind paws, but it's easy now to tie them up with saddle strings. I light the lantern and drag saddle, panther and all into a shed room and chain him up, and then go back to sleep.

"The next morning the owner of the Flower de Lucy came
along and when I told him about the panther he wanted to see
it. I told him he'd better go easy, but he was the kind who have
to have their way, and shore enough he got a little too close and
that panther took a mouthful out of his thigh. He started to kill
him, but I told him this was my panther and he had to let him
be. 'I'll give you fifty dollars to let me drill daylight into his
insides,' he says. 'All right,' I says, and he handed over the fifty.
He pulled his six-shooter and shot the panther dead. I don't
know what I would have done with him if he hadn't. He wasn't
no pet size."

Baby-Hungry

W H A T really made a panther hungry was the smell of a baby. Among the stories of early days that Queenie used to shiver her grandchildren with were these personal experiences:

"When our first baby was five months old, Sam said we had to go to Fort Worth, about ninety miles away, for supplies. He had made sideboards for our ox wagon, and we planned to bring back some furniture as well as cloth and food. Nothing much happened on the way, and it was the best time I'd ever had, seeing the people and stores and all. I never dreamed Sam had so much money. He bought me everything I admired — a trunk, a spinning wheel, a sewing machine and many a yard of pretty cloth. Then we started home.

"We were on the last lap of the journey and it was beginning to get dark. Sam happened to look back and saw what he took to be a man with a white shirt on a-galloping towards us. The baby had the colic and started to cry. As the galloping thing got closer, Sam said, 'That's no man. It's the biggest panther I ever saw.' The panther had heard the baby and smelled us, and musta been awful hungry, for he loped right close up to the wagon. Sam stood up and cracked his whip and let out a holler that would curdle your blood, and the panther stopped and trotted off a ways and sat on his haunches. Then he got out of sight a little off to one side and let out a scream that froze my blood. D'reckly he was back in the road.

"Well, this went on till we could hardly stand the strain, and the baby kept crying, and it got darker and darker. Finally, Sam said, 'Queenie, you'd better put the baby in the trunk.' I knowed then that he expected the panther to leap up on the wagon, and I reckon he thought we'd better smother the baby to death than see it torn apart by the panther. I did like he said, and stuffed my Sunday hat under a corner of the trunk lid so as to let in a little air, and sat there near dead from fright. Sam kept up his whip-cracking and yelling till our cabin came in sight. Never before or after did it look so good to me.

"A cousin of mine and his bride Sary took up a section of land close to ours, and I could cut across the woods and not have to walk over three miles to their house. Sam often told me I mustn't do this, but I loved to take baby on pretty, sunshiny days and walk over to Sary's. One day Sary was preserving, and I stayed late helping her, and before I got well started home the sun was down nearly to the treetops. I was hurrying along when something made me look back, and why I didn't just drop dead, I don't know. A big yellow panther was walking right after me. I started to run, and the panther ran too. When I slowed down, he would slow down, but still gain on me. It was getting darker and darker, and I was getting scareder and scareder. I seemed numb all over, but somehow I kept on running. The panther gained on me and I knew any minute he'd grab baby away.

"I snatched off baby's cap and dropped it, and the panther stopped to smell it. I gained a little. Then one by one I snatched off more clothes, mine and baby's both, whatever was handiest, and dropped them as I ran. Well, I made the cabin door and fell inside and managed to push the door shut. Thank Heavens, Sam wasn't there, and I come to enough to dress ourselves and start supper before he got in. He didn't need to ever warn me again to take my saddle pony and go around by the open pasture when I wanted to visit Sary."

Befriended by a Panther

T H E R E are stories of friendly panthers, too, but they belong mainly to the Spanish countries southward. No one has told them so well as W. H. Hudson in *The Naturalist in La Plata*. Here is one I heard one night in a camp of *sotoleros* in a desert of northern Mexico. Leaves of the yucca-like sotol plant afford an inferior fiber for cords and ropes; the distilled juice makes a fiery liquor; the head when roasted and split open by machete or ax provides nourishment for stock. With absolutely nothing growing on the parched earth for our horses to graze on, my *mozo* Inocencio and I were glad to camp with the sotol-cutters and feed our horses on sotol they had already roasted.

Another growth in that harsh country is the low-growing lechuguilla, every leaf of it a dagger. It is as bitter as green persimmon. "Did anybody ever try it for thirst?" I asked of the chief sotol-cutter, named Juan de Dios.

"I did. One time."

I waited.

"God saved me, not the lechuguilla."

Juan de Dios now with fervid energy began sticking bits of twigs into the ground. Near them he put the backs of his hands against the earth, holding up his gnarled fingers to indicate stubble.

"The land up there to the northwest where you are riding," he went on, "is like that — just tables and slopes of lechuguilla daggers. But in the land also grows the guayule. In 1907 I was gathering guayule to be sold to the factory of rubber. We had our camp at a big tank. There was no other water for a long, long distance. Each day we had to go farther and farther out from the tank to find the guayule. I was gathering it by myself. I went out in the morning with my tortillas for dinner, a bottle of water, and an old knife. It was in the time of the *canicula* — the dog days of July and August — and it was so hot that the rattlesnake crawled only at night.

"One day I went afoot because my burro was too lame. I would gather the guayule into piles and later carry it in. I went far out. *Bueno,* by noon I had drunk all the water. The sun in the sky danced up and down like a crackling frying in grease. The thirst came, but I had to keep on gathering guayule in order to buy frijoles and corn for my family. There was no *remedio* for this. I pulled until nearly dark, and then I started back to the tank. The thirst of the body was like that of the ground under a dead broomweed.

"And then — I do not know how, perhaps it was the thirst — I found myself lost. There was no moon. There was no trail. And lechuguilla everywhere. I cut out the heart of one to chew. The bitter juice gave thirst more thirst. I kept on, but I did not know where I was going. Sometimes I would stop to listen, to consider; then I would go on.

"Know you, *señor,*" and here the voice of Juan de Dios lowered into that tone of confidence I had already noted in him, "a man who lives all the time out sees some strange things come to pass. *Bueno,* according to the stars it was two hours past midnight when I sat down on top of a hill to rest. I did not know what to do. I am a man of the camps; yet I was northed.

"While I was sitting there, the moon, weak and thin, came up over my shoulder. And then right out in front of me, perhaps twenty feet away, I saw a *león* (panther). He was just sitting on his haunches, still, his face towards me. I could see the white of his breast.

"I did not wish to fight with this animal. I arose and started away from him. At once he made some jumps and galloped around in front of me. There he sat again, silent, not moving, just gazing."

Juan de Dios slunk his shoulders and held the palms of his hands outward in front of his body to simulate the posture of the panther.

"And now fear made thirst die. I gave a shout and leaped away from the *león*. Quickly he gave some jumps and again was in front of me, just sitting there silent as if he were going to say a prayer. *Por Dios,* I could not comprehend this. Then God seemed to give me valor and I stood up straight and I said to myself, 'This animal is not offering to attack me. He is not waving his tail and stretching out his body in preparation to leap. It seems that he is not my enemy. Therefore, he may be my friend.'

"I took one step towards the animal. He arose, but in a gentle manner like a dog. I took another step. He turned and started off. Another step and he was retreating slowly but with his head turned back as if to advise me to follow. I went on, following the adviser. He went this way and that way, twisting through the lechuguilla and the chaparral. Then in about half an hour we entered a trail. I did not know where the trail went to or where it came from. It was well beaten, but I knew not which direction of it to take. I followed the *león*. He went on and on.

"In summer the light comes very early. Not long after the time for the first rooster crow my guide stopped, looked at me, and then stepped out into the chaparral. Now I saw just ahead in an open place a cabin. I advanced. In front of the cabin was a little wagon with two barrels of water in it. They had been hauled from a hole three leagues away. Thus the lion, as a friend of man, saved my life."

Pablo Romero Roped a Bear

A L O N G time ago a certain bear that had been offended by a vaquero caught him and while chewing on him found his blood so good tasting that he ate the vaquero up. After that he lay in wait for men. Frequently he was shot at, but no bullet ever seemed to harm him.

Because of a white spot on his black-haired front, this bear was called Star Breast. He haunted glades and woods around a fine spring of water where two mountain trails crossed. The place was called La Quiparita. All travel over this part of the country was by horses and mules and all travelers favored the fine camping grounds at La Quiparita — wood, water, grass, and shelter by the big trees near at hand. In time the place came to be avoided because of the number of people Star Breast had destroyed there.

Now, a vaquero who worked on a ranch a long way off and had often heard of Star Breast was very brave and very ambitious. One day while he and another vaquero were hunting strayed horses in the Quiparita country, they saw the tracks of Star Breast — tracks so enormous that no man of the camps could mistake them for the tracks of any other bear.

"Listen," said Pablo Romero, "I am going to kill Star Breast. I know that it is useless to try to shoot him and we have no guns anyhow. But I shall rope him and choke him to death the way we rope Indians and choke them. I am riding as good a roping horse as a reata was ever thrown from. He has the strength of ten bulls in him. This rawhide reata is new. It would hold an elephant."

Pablo Romero's companion pleaded with him not to think of such a foolhardy undertaking. "Why, don't you know," he said, "that if Star Breast is proof against bullets he will be proof against rawhide. Right now he hides in those bushes listening to us and preparing to come after us. Instead of riding farther toward him, let us go the other way."

"No," replied Pablo Romero, "in this country lead is not superior to rawhide. A good roper, a good roping horse, and a good rope can conquer anything that breathes."

Pablo Romero would not be turned. His companion finally consented to stay and watch the roping from a distance. They rode on toward the bushes and, sure enough, as they approached, Star Breast emerged. He stood on his hind legs, waving his great hairy arms, rumbled a great roar, and then came on. The horses ridden by the vaqueros tried to stampede, but Pablo Romero, by untying his reata from the horn of the saddle and playing out a loop, persuaded his horse to keep going. A good roping horse can hardly be stopped when he realizes that the rope is being prepared for action. The other vaquero had halted.

He saw Pablo Romero fasten one end of the reata to his saddle. He saw him with swinging loop dash toward Star Breast, who had halted and was again reared on his hind legs. Then he saw the loop fall over Star Breast's head, while man and rider dashed on. When the end of the rope was reached, the horse was jerked back and the bear was jerked down. The loop had caught him under one arm and around the neck. Almost instantly the horse whirled so that he could get a better pull, and at the same time the bear recovered his upright position.

And now came a desperate maneuver between a gigantic, fierce, powerful and cunning bear at one end of the rope and an expert horse ridden by an expert rider at the other end. Several times the bear was jerked down. Had the loop not been under his arm, the pull about his neck would no doubt have choked him. The bear soon learned that by grasping the rope with his hands he could break the force of the jerks. Once he caught the tough rawhide in his teeth just at the instant it was tightening. A tooth was jerked out and he howled with rage. He did not catch the reata with his teeth again. He began to go forward up the rope toward the horse. As the length of the rope between the animals grew shorter, the horse had a shorter distance in which to run and therefore could not jerk so hard. He could not jerk the rope out of the bear's hand. He was panting hard.

Pablo Romero was a brave vaquero. He would not quit his horse. He had no gun of any kind to shoot. The rope was knotted so tightly about his saddle horn that he could not loosen it. Worse, on this day he had no knife with which to cut it. Had his companion been very brave, perhaps he might have roped the bear also and have pulled him away from his friend. He was not that brave. Besides, as he said, this roping contest was not his.

At last, panting and frothing, Star Breast got up to horse and man. Now the vaquero who was watching saw a strange thing. He saw Star Breast reach up and drag Pablo Romero from the saddle. He saw him take the rope off his neck, coil it up, and tie it to the saddle horn. Then he saw him mount the horse and, with the limp form of Pablo Romero across the saddle in front of him, ride off into the brush! That was the last ever seen of Pablo Romero or of Pablo Romero's horse.

The Bear Who Fattened His Own Pork

O V E R in piney woods edging the Mississippi lowlands an ancient colored camp cook named Kinley McCullock made himself famous for his bear steaks and bear stories.

"It war a long time ago," old Kinley used to tell. "Mister Cockrum he was my boss man. Hav war still a-sucking, I 'member. We named him William McKinley Havana, but everybody called him Hav, lak they still does. Bud was old ernough ter tote in wood fer the fireplace. One mawning early I was out a-milking when I heared some old mockingbirds jist a-cussing and a-stewing. I knowed right away an uppity squirrel was aggervating 'em. I thinks a little fried squirrel would package up mighty neat inside me fer breakfast. So I calls to Bud to bring the gun. He brung it and trots along with me.

"But Mister Squirrel musta got word I was making tracks his way. Anyhow, he warn't thar and the mockingbirds quit saying whar he wuz. I goes on, down the aige of Mister Cockrum's cawnfiel', looking up inter trees along the fence. I got squirrel meat on my min'. The roas'en years is shore fine that summer, and we been a-playing 'Green Cawn' for dinner every day without any banjo.

"Well, here me and Bud wuz way down the fence peering up inter all the branches on our side the fence and a-listening fer Mister Squirrel ter scratch the bark, when I heared somebody over in the tall cawn. I knowed 'twarn't Mister Cockrum out in the wet dew, and I knowed he wouldn't be sending enybody over ter this fiel' anyhow. I kin hear whoever 'tis breaking the roas'en years off, and sounds ter me lak he's mighty careless tromping over the stalks. I says low ter Bud, 'Cawn thief shore brung erlong plenty o' brass.'

"We steps back inter some bloodweeds growing aginst the fence and waits, jist ez quiet ez a hoptoad waitin' fer a fly. The cawn is still a-popping. Then d'reckly I catches sight uv the thief. He's wearing black, but I don't have no idees 'bout our preacher. He's got a cawn patch uv his own. Now this gentleman is coming right down 'tween two rows, kinder spraddling in his walk. His arms is full uv roas'en years, and then the first good light uv mawning hits him and I sees it's a b'ar. Jist as I seed this, he stops and stacks all the cawn in one arm, lak it wuz stovewood. Then he reaches down with the other hand and picks up a big yaller punkin frum a vine. He takes hit under his arm. Now he's all loaded up and ready to go home. I thought at first he wuz going to walk right over us, but he sorter takes out to one side, and Bud and me jist stands. I'se telling my eyes not to click too loud. That thief he steps over the picket fence lak it was the golden stairs. Befo' the Good Lawd, I never seen no plain woods b'ar toting off cawn and punkin lak dat.

"After he shuffles inter the thicket, I says ter Bud, 'We'll kinder track him.' So we snuck along behind, he being so keerless he never looks back oncet. Purty soon he come to a big holler stump 'bout six foot eround and high ez my shoulder. I seen he wuz a-going ter stop and so got behin' a big gum tree with huckleberry bushes growing all eroun' it. Sho' nuf, he stands still by the stump, listening and looking about in every direction, 'specially down the way he's come frum. He seems ter suspicion somebody's spying on his doings. He's ez smart ez any cawncrib thief that ever tuk off his shoes. D'reckly he 'pears to be satisfied.

"Then he pitches that load er roas'en years over the aige of the holler stump inside. Then he th'ows the punkin down so it's boun' ter bust. He looks over inside the holler a good while, lak he's watching sumpin'. Fin'ly he leaves, going inter thick timber.

"When he's good an' gone, Bud and me snuck up ter the holler stump and scramble roun' ter get a good look inside. What yer reckon we see? Jis an old narrow-face with a crop in one year and a swallerfork in the other! That's Mister Cockrum's mark. There's mighty little meat on the hawg, but he's going to grow plenty if Mister B'ar keeps perviding and he keeps on wrapping hisse'f roun' cawn and punkin lak he's doing now. His jaws is champing ez happy ez a banjo talking to 'Little Brown Jug.'

"B'ars don't fancy lean pork, you know. No, sah, they's choosy. This one's going ter have pork that'll make cracklin's.

I guess he stole that shoat frum Mister Cockrum's pen in the dark and maybe couldn't pick very choosy. We go over and tell Mister Cockrum, and he jist laugh lak he thinks I'm trying to 'splain away some shoat in my pen. No, sah, he don't wanter come and see what kind uv a hawgpen a b'ar uses. But after a while he consent, and when he see that hawg in his own mark and the cawncobs and punkin stems and b'ar sign and all, he scratch his haid. Then he taken the hawg out and turn him loose to rustle fer hisse'f till the fall mast will fix him up fer bacon. But I made a mistake when I didn't go back next mawning to see how Mister B'ar look when he come with another load uv cawn and find his hawg ain't nowhar."

In a Hollow Tree with a She Bear

J IM I N G R A M was raised on bear-lard biscuits and bear bacon, and was twelve years old, they say, before he tasted his first hog-ham gravy. When he started balding, he began greasing his scalp with bear oil to bring back the hair. He never would admit that rattlesnake oil is as good for rheumatism as bear oil. He hunted mostly in a great tangle of brush, vines, fallen trees and soaring timber known as Hurricane Rake. He always hunted alone and he had no use for a dog, because a dog couldn't get through the kind of places he crawled into. He would ride to the edge of Hurricane Rake, tie his horse, take his gun, a strong rope to string the bear carcass up with, and a gunny sack to put the fat off the insides into, and strike out looking for sign.

When Jim Ingram discovered the enormous cypress stump, fully twelve feet high, that came to be called "Ingram's Snag," he was in a tangle of sweet gum and other growth almost against it. A scratching he heard told him the stump was hollow. He looked up and saw a big bear emerging from it. Two cubs, apparently intent on following her, stuck their heads up, but the old bear turned and gave each a slap that sent them back down. Then while Jim Ingram was trying to find an opening for his gun and a shot, the old she made off upwind, disappearing in the jungle.

Ingram felt sure she was out for food. His best chance for bear grease, he decided, was to wait for her return. While he waited and waited, he got to thinking how much fun his five small children, not to mention the older ones, would have with those two cubs as pets. He knew as well as anybody that the timidest kind of bear would fight like a circular saw for her cubs, but as he waited some more, he decided that the mother of these cubs had gone off on a long hunt and that he could capture them and get away before she returned. His plan was to rope one of the snags along the rim of the hollow stump, pull up to it, let himself down inside by the same rope, put the cubs in his gunny sack, climb out and get gone.

He leaned his gun against the cypress, roped a snag, and a few minutes later was down inside a hollow ample enough to camp in. Leaving the rope dangling, he located the cubs by their whining and snarling away back in the darkness of a hollow root. While he paused to figure how he might get hold of them without making a trip up for a stick to twist them out with, he heard an echoing scratching noise against the hollow wood. He looked up.

There old Susie was, all four feet bunched on the rim, balanced like a hen on a limb, peering earnestly down into the shadowed hollow. She did not appear to find fault with the musky smell of bear and damp decayed wood that emanated from her home.

"No," Jim Ingram later reported, "there wa'n't nary a twitch to her nose. I was jest hunkered there, my mouth opened about as wide as the gunny sack I had ready for the cubs. I guess my eyes were bugged out like a pair of purple grapes on a mustang vine. I don't remember ever staring so hard in my life at any-thing else as at that bear. I didn't have no right to be supprised, but I was. The bear was supprised too, but she was still madder. She was the maddest bear I ever see, and I've saw many a mad bear. There she squatted and there I squatted, and I couldn't have moved a finger. Then she started down."

Bears don't climb down trees headfirst, like squirrels. Old Susie had to reverse ends to start down. The posture placed her head outside the hollow so that she could not possibly see what was going on beneath her descending rump. Not at all slowly, the rump began wabbling downward, claws feeling for holds.

And now the spell that held Jim fixed was broken. "God-a'mighty!" he yelled. "Git out o' here!"

The yell rumbled and echoed in the deep hollow. The bear was more than startled. She obeyed directions with great alac-rity, hauling her body out. Then, turning around and balancing all four feet on the rim, she again peered down.

Jim was on his feet now, one hand grasping the rope. He gave it a flap against the bear's nose. She put out a hand, swept the loop from the splinter that Jim had roped, and let it fall at his feet.

Again she reversed ends and began her rearward descent. Again Jim gave his war whoop. He'd been saving his energy most of his life, and now he threw it all into his voice. The bear scrambled out again, and then started down again. Jim be-came more than prodigal with his vocal productions. Six times in all, the bear retreated before the sounds that Jim sent up. The seventh time she started down she kept coming. Jim hadn't be-gun to lose his voice; the bear was merely getting used to it. Jim had his knife out, but there was a mighty poor prospect of digging it into a vital spot.

"There wa'n't but one thing fer me to do," Jim afterwards

told, "and I done it. When she backed in good reach, I grabbed her by the tail with one hand and give her a good knife-spurring with the other. At the same time, I yelled like nobody ain't never yelled before nor since.

"She started back up again, and this time I was with her. Yes, sir, she set out like Sam Bass's race mare. I had to drop my knife so's to hold on with both hands. She took me up by that tail like a coon pulls crawfish out o' the mud with his'n. When I got to the rim, I made a dive that landed me on my feet. At the same time, that she bear made a dive into the hollow that must of landed her on her head. No, sir, she wa'n't going to make no more rear movements into that holler tree.

"But it didn't hurt her none. While I was a-getting my gun, I heard her talking mama-talk to them cubs. I didn't stop to cipher out exactly what she was saying. I jest pulled my freight fer Jericho. I'd done decided I could go a spell longer without bear grease in the corn bread."

Bear Nights in Mexico

COMING down the corkscrew trail, Inocencio and I and our pack mules saw the ranch named Golondrina a full hour before we drew rein in front of a house of three rooms thatched with bear grass. Four men were lounging under a wide and deep *ramada,* or shed, attached to the house. They had, no doubt, seen us when we rode over the pass. As soon as the ranchero and I had stepped within, while Inocencio with help tended to our beasts, he halted in front of me, standing up very straight and looking me straight in the eye, and said: "You are now in your house. I am Santiago Blanco, at your orders. This is my wife."

Don Santiago and I had introduced ourselves to each other by name when I dismounted, but he wanted me to be doubly assured of hospitality. Doña María placed herself also at my orders. Before we finished supper I had learned that Don Santiago was a teller of extraordinary experiences, that a hanger-on kinsman named Pantaleón was a loutish puncturer of Don Santiago's claims, and that this was a bear country in every sense of the word.

"With bears all around so plentiful," I said, offering cigarettes, first to Doña María, "in the morning I go hunting."

"Yes," responded Don Santiago, "they are so plentiful that they are a barbarity. One in particular I wish you would kill. He has damaged me much."

There was a pause of silence. Then Don Santiago shifted himself to look towards the northwest in the direction I was facing.

"You see that bright star," he asked, "with its spurs in the top of a bluff?" I saw it. "In winter time," he went on, "that mountain breaks the cold northers trying to blow away this ranch. The wind up there growls and grumbles and rumbles so that the mountain is called Cerro del Gruñidor."

"But why," I asked, "is it named the Growler?"

"Because," interposed Inocencio, who had heretofore been among the silent ones, but who considered it his prerogative to answer any general question I asked — *"porque es el nombre que le pusieron* (because it is the name they gave it)."

"No," Pantaleón put in, "it is called Gruñidor because the wind up there makes a growling and a grumbling and a rumbling that would terrify *el demonio* himself. The pass over it is called the Pass of the Bad Overcoat, for not even a sheepskin coat is sufficient when one comes through it against the wind. The wind up there is fiercer than fierceness itself. One time when I was coming through this Pass of the Bad Overcoat with a burro loaded with grass, the wind caught him and blew him over the bluff."

"*Bueno,*" Don Santiago went on, a patient tone in his voice, "here under this very *ramada* where we sit a kinsman of mine named Tranquilino Molino used to play the accordion every evening and night and often also during the mornings. [Anyone named Tranquil Mill should be a musician!] The accordion belonged to me, and if Tranquilino were playing it after I went to bed, he would leave it on this table, where no dew could fall on it.

"Well, one morning he came over to play the accordion, and it was gone. We searched everywhere, but we could not find it. The people here are all honest, and nobody could think what had come to pass."

"How *triste* it was without any music!" Pantaleón commented.

"Then about three nights later," Don Santiago continued, "I heard and all the other people of La Golondrina heard the music of an accordion coming down from the Cerro del Gruñidor. I could not think who might be playing it. In the morning we went up the mountain but we could find no tracks of any Christian being, only of bears, deer, and other animals. And other nights the accordion sounded. It was a thing very curious. Then the serenades stopped.

"About that time I went to Múzquiz. I had to sell some goat hides and buy provisions. A *mozo* carried the goat hides on a mule. First I must tell you that I have a goat camp two leagues away behind the Cerro del Gruñidor. Sometimes I do not visit it for a week or ten days. It is called Majada Escondida because it is so well hidden. It is a good camp — a cabin for the *pastor* to live in, pens made out of rock, and a well to supply water for the little animals."

"And what beautiful little animals!" Pantaleón exclaimed not without diplomacy. "There are more pintos, red-and-white and black-and-white, and more black goats, and more yellow goats, and more brindle goats, and blue goats and brown goats and tan goats and more billy goats with long, long beards than in anybody else's herd. How they can climb! What billies they are!

And fight! *Por Dios,* Cousin Santiago, tell how those black billy goats fought!"

"Oh," Don Santiago hesitated, "that is just a joke, a thing put together."

"Tell it, tell it anyhow," Pantaleón urged. "What a barbarity!"

Plainly not unpleased, Don Santiago told "the thing put together."

"One time," he began, "I went over to the camp and on a knoll this side saw two black billy goats fighting. When I found the *pastor,* I told him to get the two goats and put them in his herd, where they belonged. Five days later I was there again and saw the billies still at it. But all that was left of them was their two tails just brushing through the air and going at each other. I rode up closer. The tails were plainly the tails of my billy goats. Not another thing was left of the animals. Their heads, their horns, their legs, their bodies — everything was worn away, vanished. When I asked the *pastor* why he had not separated the black billy goats and brought them to the herd, he declared he could not make them quit fighting. What fighters!"

"*Bravos* to the tail-end!" Pantaleón exclaimed.

"But I come back to history," Don Santiago announced. "*Bueno,* that day I went to Múzquiz with the goat hides to sell, the first man I saw was my *pastor* — my own shepherd — the shepherd I supposed to be tending my fine flock of goats at the Escondida.

" 'What,' I said to this *pastor,* 'are you doing here?'

" 'I,' he answered, 'came to get from the old herbwoman some bark of the wild cherry to cure a pneumonia that I felt approaching me.'

" 'But how long have you been here?'

" '*Patrón,*' he answered, 'I came eight and one-half days ago.'

" 'Por Dios,' I said, 'what did you do with the goats?'

" 'I left them,' he said, 'shut up in the pen so they could not stray off. I intended to return to them immediately, but God did not will for me to go back so soon.'

"There I was. There that idiotic *pastor* was. And — my goats? They must all be dead of thirst and hunger, I thought. I did not even take time to sell the goat hides or buy provisions. I told Don Mariano of The Fifteen Letters, the store, to send coffee back by the *mozo*. I almost killed my horse getting back to La Golondrina. There I caught a fresh one. Spurring him to the goat camp, I melted his tallow.

"When I ascended the last hill, I looked to see if buzzards or ravens were flying around over the pen. I saw none. I had a little hope. As I drew near enough to catch a vista over the top of the walls, I thought I saw a goat standing on the trough. Perhaps, I thought, God has remembered me and I can draw water from the well and pour it in the trough and the goats will drink and then they will eat and grow fat again. The trail went down into a low place and I could no longer see over the wall. I rode now at a walk, for, as you know, it is well to let a horse cool slowly at the end of a hard ride. Riding slowly that way, I could hear. My ears were open for the bleat of a goat. I heard no bleat, but I heard the creak made by a rope pulling up water. *Por Dios,* I thought, who can have come to this tail-end of the world to water my goats? There is but one trail into this Escondida place. I had seen no tracks on it.

"Then I came nearer, so near that I could see plainly inside the corral. The goats were alive and some of them were drinking water out of the trough. And, *por Dios* and all things most pure, the one who was drawing water was a bear!

"I sat frozen on my horse and watched him. The goats seemed well contented. They are such stupid animals! The bear kept on drawing water with his hands. He could manage the rope and bucket as well as you or I. Then, all at once, he smelled me. *Wuh!* he said, dropped the rope, and ran through the gate and tore out into the sierras.

"I made examination. By tracks and other signs all was clear. The bear had been herding the goats out of the pen every morning, bringing them in to water in the late afternoon, and then killing one for his supper. What other animal would know to fatten his meat? I went to the little cabin, where the *pastor* always sleeps. There I found my accordion. I understood now who had played it up on the mountain. What a wretched bear! *Qué barbaridad!*"

"What a barbarity!" echoed the others.

I hunted until late the next day without seeing a single bear sign, old or new. Back at the rancho I found the company increased, and also Don Santiago seemed to have increased. First there was his son Hilario, a colonel in the Mexican army. As a respectful son he spoke little before his father; he did not even smoke in his presence. Don Santiago was exuberant with pride, which several swallows of cognac from a bag of bottles brought by Hilario as a present had not diminished. Next there was a cow-buyer.

Supper was very late coming, and the longer it was put off the more generous Don Santiago grew in paternal pride.

"Now just look at my son Hilario," he finally burst out. "A colonel, and so young! He is going to make a general. He has always been *extraordinario*. While his mother was big and we did not know what day he might be thrown into the world, a rider appeared yelling, 'There the revolutionists come down the cañon.' We had to get out — at once. No time to hunt horses. We mounted what was at hand. The only beast for my wife to ride was a blue mare heavy with foal. I had a man follow at her heels so that he could help my wife beat her.

"On, on we went down the cañon, and I at every bend in the trail calling upon my family to spur, to quirt, to hurry. At the Puerto de Santa Ana the mare stopped, and right there she dropped her colt. But still my wife had to ride her. 'Come on!' I said. 'I can hear the horses of the revolutionists hoofing the rocks behind us. There is no time to wait for additions.' And so we left the colt and rode on.

"When we got to the crossing on the Río Sabinas below Las Rucias, my wife said she had to stop and have her baby. There was no remedy. We stopped. 'The Comanche that groans will not get to camp,' I warned. She brought forth quick. I cut the cord with a machete that one of the men happened to have, but because I was always keeping my eyes in the direction from which we were flying I cut it off six fingers from the navel. There was no time to be a certified surgeon. There was no time to do anything with the new boy but leave him. Just as he was giving his first squall, I saw dust raised by the *revolucionario* horses. 'Come, come!' I yelled. 'The recruits have picked the wrong time to join us.' My wife got back up on the blue mare and again we were following our direction.

"Thus I brought my family to safety, but it was after dark when we rode into Múzquiz. I was grateful to God that the barracks there had plenty of legitimate soldiers to defend us. We went to a house.

"About daylight I heard the blue mare nickering. I looked out and there she was nosing her colt. In the natural way, it had smelled her trail and followed, but its legs were wobbly and it could not follow fast. On this colt's back was the boy we were compelled to leave at the Río Sabinas. He had seen the colt coming by on its way to its dam and, in the natural way, crawled on so as to get to his dam also. It was beautiful to see with what gusto they both sucked.

"And that boy was Hilario, my own true son. *El coronel!* Look at him! If you wish proof of what I have told, examine his navel. It is the most ample in all the army of the Republic of Mexico."

This detail, however, I had no opportunity to verify. As naturally as Hilario mounted the colt, there followed allusions to my bear hunt, along with questions concerning experiences — or lack of experiences — with that animal.

"Yes," commented Don Santiago, "the bear is a very curious animal, very smart."

Now that a fresh audience was provided, I prepared myself to listen again to the story of the bear and the accordion.

"My father," continued Don Santiago, "was a famous hunter of bears. He lived in the Sierra Madre and one time set out alone after a certain bear. When night came he made a little camp down in a valley and turned his mule loose. This mule could be turned loose anywhere and she would never go far away. She was little but very strong. Her name was Tabaco, because one time she pitched a sack of Lobo Negro tobacco out of the pocket of her rider. Ah, what a mule she was! Well, my father turned her loose, ate some little thick tortillas that he warmed on a little fire, and went to sleep. He had yet a long way to ride, and so, very early, before the Morning Star was up, arose.

"He took his reata in hand and stood listening in order to locate the mule. He heard a little sound in the grass and brush and went towards it. When he was near, he bent over the ground to skylight the animal. He saw a dark shape and whirled the reata to lasso it. Then he started to lead the beast towards his saddle, but it would not follow. He wondered what was the matter, for this mule had been trained to lead. He walked towards her to place the rope over her ear; the creature snorted and tried to pull away. One can never tell what a mule will do. Finally he got up to the animal's head. Then he found that he had roped a bear. Because he had left both his machete and his gun at the camp and because the bear was becoming very restless, he had to let it go."

The cow-buyer wanted to say something here, but Don Santiago was in the saddle — his own saddle.

"Even a good hunter, like our friend here," continued Don Santiago with a complimentary gesture towards me, "may not always get a bear. Another time my father was chasing a bear and shot it while it was running. He saw it stop, seize some grass, and stuff it into the hole made by the bullet. He was taking careful aim to shoot it again when all of a sudden the bear picked up a rock and hurled it. It missed my father, but it hit the horn of his saddle with such force that the rawhide covering was torn off. The bear picked up another rock and my father wisely retreated."

"Don Santiago," I said, "your story brings to mind an account I once heard of a vaquero who roped a very violent bear. This bear seized the rope, quickly drew horse and rider up to him, pulled the man off, mounted, and then rode away with the man dangling over his saddle like a meat goat."

"Do you recall the name of the vaquero?" gravely asked Don Santiago.

"Why," I replied, "he was named Pablo Romero."

"I knew him well," Don Santiago declared. "The encounter was at a pass called Salsipuedes in the Burro Mountains. This vaquero was noted for a very wide and long red sash that he always wore. One night he foolishly lay down to sleep near some coals on which he had boiled coffee. A wild bull, attracted by the smell of the smoke, rushed upon him, hooked him between the sash and his body, and went off with him. Thus the bull carried him on his horns eight days. Whenever the bull drank, Pablo Romero lapped water with his hand; when the bull grazed up near a prickly pear, Pablo Romero reached out and gathered the tuna fruit to eat, for this happening was in the fruit season. Pablo Romero, however, knew nothing at all about bears."

Diamond Bill, Confederate Ally

T H E Y tell me that Jeb Rider's log cabin still stands, about a quarter of a mile up the slope from the spring on Elm Creek. Nobody has struck oil in this part of east Texas yet, and so things out of the past live on there. People still talk about the Civil War, and call up the names of Jeb Rider and certain other Confederates reduced long ago to earth in the little graveyard where wild trumpet vines cover the fence with red flowers all through the summer months and into fall. Old Bill — called also Diamond Bill — disappeared long before the last Rebel disappeared, but Jeb Rider's story of Old Bill keeps on blooming with the trumpet vines. This is the way he told it:

When me and my wife married, it was her idear having the house so fur up the slope from where we got water outa the spring on Ellum Creek. She was skeered of floods and strong on a hill breeze. Also, she didn't like bottom land mosquitoes. I was nacherly agin having to tote water so fur, but 'fore long I sometimes wished it was further. Don't ask me why she didn't tote it like other wimmen. I could walk down the trail and set on the cypress log there at the spring and kinder get peaceful.

She was always badgering me to clear more land and plant more sweet pertaters and hoe the corn cleaner and keep stovewood chopped up, and put my God-given time in on a lot of other nothings. I'd always been used to squirreling 'round with the dogs or jest being quiet and letting whatever was going on kinder soak into me. Stewing about always has went against my grain.

The best dog I ever had was Old Bill. He was out of a bitch Pa brung from Tinnissee; that is, figgering in several ginerations between. I never can remember whether it was July 13 or July 14 he died, the year before the War started. Anyhow, one cloudy day about a month after he died I was going down the trail to the spring uncommon low in the mouth and was about halfway when, kinder unconscious-like, I heared sump'n behind me. Maybe it was a rustle in the leaves. I didn't pay no 'tention till I heard a low rattle. Then I looked, and I'll be dogged if it wasn't the biggest diamon'back rattlesnake I ever see, right in the trail, not more'n six steps back.

When I stopped and looked, he stopped too and raised his head up in a curious way and looked at me without shaking his tail a-tall. It's that tail-shaking that makes a rattlesnake so fearsome, puts the j'ints in a human's backbone to shaking too. Well, I didn't have a thing along to hit with, not even a water bucket, and when I glanced 'round fer a stick there wa'n't none in reach. I started on down the trail agin to a dead dogwood I could break off. Then I looked back and that diamon'back was coming on too, keeping a respec'ful distance, and all at once he sorter seemed to me like a dog that wants to foller you and be friends but's afraid to come too clost. Well, I stood there a-holding the stick, and he had his head up a little watching me, and his eyes jest seemed to say he understood. They looked a lot charitabler than some human eyes I've peered into.

Then I done clear contrary to nature. I throwed the stick away and started agin on down to the spring. Ever once in a while I'd turn my head and look back. The rattlesnake was still follering, humble and respec'ful. When I set down on the cypress log, he coiled up and kept looking right straight at me. D'reckly I begun to kinder talk to him. I was still youngish and a blamed fool about feeling sorry for myself. And that old snake would nod his head around and look like he felt sorry too.

No telling how long we mighta kept up the conversation if about half a dozen mockingbirds hadn't got to diving at the snake and jabbering and disturbing his peace and mine too. Still, I felt a lot better. When I started up to the cabin, he started too, jest follering like a dog. About halfway up he dropped out, and I didn't see nothing more of him till the next day. I was going down to the spring agin to fetch water fer Abbie to wash with. Right about the halfway place, he fell in behind me like he'd done the first time, and now his follering seemed jest as nacherl as a dog scratching fleas.

"See here," I says to him after we got settled at the spring, "I'm going to call you Bill. Bill, he was the best coon and possum dog I ever had, and he always understood me. When I wanted to squirrel around, he never had no idears about weeding the corn or putting poles in the fence to keep the hawgs outer the field or anything like that. Yes, sir, you're Bill to me from now on."

And Bill jest nodded his head and looked grateful out of his eyes and shore woulda talked if he could of. It was real soothing to be with him, and when Abbie went to squalling fer me to hurry up and bring on the water he acterly winked.

Well, after that we was together lots at the spring. Whenever I went to the store I'd hear talk about the Aberlitionists up North working to take the niggers away from us Southern folks and make 'em our equals, and more talk about the Black Republicans. When I got back I'd tell Bill about 'em — sometimes afore I told Abbie — and, by hokey, he'd coil up and look fierce enough to bite a crowbar.

Then the War did come. I volunteered fer Captain Abercrombie's company and traded off some corn and a mule fer a good, gentle horse and bought Abbie a new ax and got all ready to go. The evening afore I was to set out, I went down to the spring to kinder ca'm myself and tell Bill good-by.

It looked like he understood all about the Yankees. I told him to look after things around the spring as best he could and I'd be back some day. The next morning after Abbie got my things all packed and I'd told her good-by and started fer the county seat, I rode to the spring to water my horse.

Well, jest as I was coming out under that leaning ellum over the trail between the house and the spring, I felt sump'n drop acrost my shoulders. It woulda scared me if it hadn't been so nacherl.

"So you want to go to war too, do you, Bill?" I says. He nods.

"I don't know how the fellers in camp would take to you," I says. "They're all Texians, you know," I says, "and got about as much use fer a rattlesnake as a wildcat has fer a lost puppy." You see, I hadn't told a soul about Old Bill — not even Abbie. I jest didn't think anybody would understand. But if Bill was so set on going with me, I decided right then I'd try to convert the heathen.

"If you'll promise," I says to him, "not to bother nobody and stay put where I puts you, I'll take you. I'll explain to the fellers and maybe they'll git the idear."

He nods and we rode on.

Some of the fellers seemed to think at first that I was a plain idiot, but they left Bill alone and he left them alone. I shore didn't have no trouble with anybody trying to steal my blankets, and the way Jim Bowie — that's what I named my horse — and Old Bill got to be frenly with each other was a caution. Sometimes Jim Bowie would kinder nose Bill along the back, and many a time when Jim Bowie was a-grazing I've seen Bill crawl out in front of him and scare off devil's horses so Jim Bowie wouldn't accerdently chew one up. You know how a devil's horse, once it's inside the stomick of an animal, can kill it. I fixed up a bag for Old Bill to ride comfortable in, and when we moved, hung it on the horn of the saddle.

Fer months we jest practiced marching and squads-righting and squads-lefting and so on. I'd leave Old Bill on the edge of the parade grounds, and I got to noticing how interested he seemed in our movements. When we paraded, he'd get exciteder than the colonel's horse. The band music was what set him up. "Dixie" was his favorite tune, and he got so he could sorter rattle it. It shore was comical to see him histing his tail fer the high notes.

Finally our training was over. We crossed the Mississippi and joined Gin'ral Albert Sidney Johnston's forces. Then when Shiloh opened up, on that Sunday morning in April, we was in it. We fought and we fit all day long, sometimes going forwards and sometimes backwards, sometimes in the bresh and sometimes acrost clearings. We didn't know till next day that our gin'ral had been killed. If he'da lived and if we'da had a few more like Old Bill, things would have turned out mighty different.

My regiment was camped on Owl Creek, due north of Shiloh Chapel, and jest before we went into battle that morning I took Old Bill over to a commissary waggin and told him to stay there and told the driver to kinder keep him. Late evening found us coming back into a long neck of woods that our colonel told us we'd have to clear of Yankees. They'd worked in between us and Owl Creek. We found 'em all right, but they was the deadest Yankees I ever see. At first we was bellying along on the ground, keeping behind trees and expecting fire. Then when we kept finding more and more dead uns, we figgered some other outfit had beat us to 'em. We got to breathing easy, and then somebody noticed that none of the dead Yanks showed bullet marks. It was all-fired strange, and the trees wasn't none of 'em creased neither.

I decided to examine a little closter, and I pulled up the britches leg of one Yank. Jest above his shoetop on the outside, where the ankle vein runs, I noticed a pair of little holes about the size of pinpoints. I found the same marks on the leg of the next Yank; on another, on another; and then, all of a suddent, I knowed Old Bill'd been there. I told the boys. They went to looking at the dead Yankee legs and couldn't he'p being convinced.

We kep' going through the neck of woods and counting dead Yankees till we got to Owl Creek, a little below camps. My ricollection is that the count run to four hundred and seventeen, but it may have been a few more or less. Course, too, some few might've been counted twicet. I guess the official report would show, if it didn't git burned up at Richmond.

It wa'n't more'n a rifle shot from the near side of the woods to camps. We got in a little before sundown, and there Old Bill was stretched out under the commissary waggin. He looked plumb tuckered out and as ga'nt as a gutted snowbird. Well, the night before, one of the boys happened to set a trap fer possum right in camps almost. He went to it as soon as we got in and found a big wood rat. He brung it in alive and put it in front of Old Bill. As a rule, Old Bill never et nothing hardly, but the way he nailed that rat and then swallered him whole was an education in appertite. We all shore was proud of him. After that the boys quit figgering on frying him up fer beefsteak. They took to calling him Diamond Bill and looked on him as a mascot. Some of 'em said he was the most valuable soldier in the Confederate Army. Why, the Colonel used to git me to send him out on scout duty. No telling how many Yankees he cleaned out of thickets it was dangerous fer a man to enter. He knowed the difference between Confederate gray and Union blue jest as well as Ab Blocker's cow dog knowed the difference between a branded critter and a mav'rick.

Well, 'tain't no use fer me to tell about all the battles we fought in. At Appermattox I was still alive and so was Diamond Bill. Jim Bowie wa'n't, though, and we rode home on a borrered mule. One day 'way long in the summer I put Bill down at the spring on Ellum Creek and afore my saddle blanket was dry I was breaking land, putting up the old fences, hoeing weeds out of the patch Abbie had planted, and doing all sorts of work. The dogs was all dead and there wa'n't no time fer nothing else. Lots of days I didn't even think about Diamond Bill.

Then one day in the spring of '66, while I was going in a hurry down to the spring, I heard something that made my mind whirl back. I wheeled around and saw a big diamon'back running towards me. Afore I could grab fer a stick, I seen who it was. "Why, Bill," I called out. "Bill!" He nodded his head the way I'd seen him do a thousand times. But he made a new kind of motion that says he wants me to foller him. He turns off the trail and I follers.

About a hundred yards off he sidled up to another rattler, and looked back at me. "Mrs. Bill?" I says. He nodded, and the two went on. D'reckly we come to a clearing 'bout the size of our courthouse maybe. Diamond Bill stopped, raised up like a nacherl-born commander, and give the durnedest rattle a man ever heared. Then he moved on ahead about ten paces and rared up agin. By that time, squads and troops and companies and battalions of young rattlesnakes was coming out of the bresh on all sides. I'm afeared to say how many there was — hundreds, maybe thousands. They come out in regular formations, squads-righting and squads-lefting and fronting-into-line like old soldiers. Bill lined 'em up fer dress parade about the middle of the field. Then he sounded one rattle fer a signal and, keeping a perfect front, they begun advancing towards me, all rattles a-going and every dadgummed one of 'em a-playing "Dixie."

Diamond Bill knowed what he'd done in the War. A thousand pities he was the only rattlesnake in it. He didn't seem to realize the war was over. Here he'd come home and raised this army, and now he was offering it to me. I ricollect how the Confederate boys uster always be quoting Gin'ral Bedford Forrest. He said, you know, that the gin'ral wins who gits there fustest with the mostest. Well, it was jest too late to have the mostest, or to be firstest either. I tried to explain to Diamond Bill. And that was the last in a military way I ever seen of him.

In Realms of Gold

The Broken Metate

LONGWORTH and I were in a Mexican restaurant beside a window looking down on the San Antonio River. It was away past noon, and our waiter seemed to have disappeared for a siesta. Dishes shoved to one side of him, Longworth was indenting lines in the red-and-white oilcloth with the point of his knife, occasionally dipping it into the cheese-yellow sauce left on his plate for a drop to indicate where a hill stood or where a copper peg had been dug up. He was a tall, spare man, perhaps nearer sixty than fifty, not a white streak in his mop of coarse black hair.

"But where did you get this map?" I asked. "It must have a history."

"Yes," he replied, "it has a history, and God knows in trying to follow it I have had a history too."

The story was told with many backings and windings, and I did not get the whole of it until nearly a year later, when I found Longworth one day in a little room out in the yard behind the boardinghouse kept by his wife. He was working on his "radio sleuth," an electrical device for locating minerals. After explaining its mechanism, he brought out a thick pile of documents. From them and from his own testimony I have put Longworth's story together. Like all good stories, it begins far away and long ago.

The story had been going on even before that day in February, 1756, on which Lieutenant-General Miranda of the province of Texas set out northwards from San Antonio with a small company to investigate "mineral riches long rumored" in the hills draining into the San Saba and Llano rivers. The magnified rumors of magnificent veins of silver that Miranda brought back, the mission that the Spaniards soon set up on the San Saba River and that the Comanches promptly destroyed, the Spanish presidio (fort) built three miles distant from the mission that was abandoned forever in 1769 — these are facts in documented history. By the time Jim Bowie of Bowie knife fame

reached San Antonio, legend was asserting that the Spaniards had worked very rich veins on the San Saba and been forced to hide away tons of bullion in underground caverns or tunnels. A daring plunger, Bowie made expeditions in search of both the mines and the cords of silver bars. After he died in the Alamo (1836) rumor decided that he had found what he was looking for.

But now to get back to Longworth's story told there in the Mexican restaurant in San Antonio:

About the time of Bowie's battle with Indians not far from ruins of the San Saba mission, a man by the name of Dixon settled on the San Marcos River near the present town of San Marcos. He didn't belong to any colony. He was one of those frontiersmen who couldn't endure being crowded. A poor man, he was not too poor to keep an Indian in his hire. This Indian, it seems, had rejected or been rejected by his tribe. One day an aged Mexican appeared at Dixon's cabin inquiring for rocks marked in a certain way. Dixon knew of some rocks on his claim — a claim without a deed — that bore the signs described. He, his Indian, and the old Mexican went to them, and in a short time the Mexican dug up a small olla of silver coins, which he divided with Dixon.

The next day, as soon as the Mexican was gone, the Indian asked Dixon if it was his desire to possess a great deal of silver. Dixon admitted that it was.

"Then," replied the Indian, "I will lead you to it. Yonder to the northwest in Summer Valley is a cave full of it. The mouth of the cave is stopped up with rocks, but I have been inside. I can go inside again."

It turned out that "Summer Valley" meant the valley of the San Saba River. When Dixon and his guide got to the first pecan trees on the San Saba, they saw Indian sign everywhere; the Comanches and the Apaches were at war. Dixon's Indian was afraid of both war parties, but from a concealed position he pointed out the vicinity of the cave. Dixon took a good look at the features of the country, for he expected to return at a safer time. Then the two men went back to the San Marcos. The next year the Indian died. This was not long after the close of the Mexican War, maybe 1850.

The country was settling up, and Dixon now took into his confidence three neighboring settlers: Sam Fleming, G. B. Ezell, and Wiley Stroud. The four partners felt that they needed something more definite and reliable than the Indian's tale to guide them. (On other occasions he had not distinguished himself for veracity.) They decided to send Dixon at common expense to Monclova, Mexico, once the capital of the united provinces of Texas and Coahuila, to find out what he could from the archives there — though not a one of them could have told the difference between an archive and an angina pectoris had he seen the two side by side.

Upon arrival in Monclova, Dixon found that the archives were in the custody of the Catholic Church and that outside examination of them was prohibited. He was on the verge of returning home when he met a Spaniard whom he had known in Texas. He frankly told him his difficulty.

Now it happened that the Spaniard had a daughter, named Carlota, who was engaged in some minor capacity by the priests in charge of the archives. Her father thought she might help in getting the desired information. She readily assented to the plan. She declared that some of the reports in the archives bore on the San Saba mines, though she had no idea of their contents. They were kept secret. She could copy them, she added, only at risk to her soul. She would probably have to wait a long time for a chance to get full information. With the understanding that he would hear when it was obtained, Dixon came home.

Months went by without a word, then years — so many years

that Dixon and his partners had almost given up hope of ever learning anything from the Monclova documents. Then one day in 1858, the north-bound stage through San Marcos brought a letter from Carlota. She was in San Antonio and she had, she said, information too valuable to trust to the mail. She asked Dixon to come to her immediately. He went.

In the interview that followed, Carlota was at once open and secretive, definite and indefinite. She was willing to tell only part of what she knew, though that part she disclosed without reservation. She had dug out, she said, documentary evidence concerning fourteen mines located around the old San Saba fort, some of them more than six leagues distant from it, the richest being Las Iguanas. In the bottom of the shaft leading to the Iguanas mine reposed two thousand bars of silver weighing fifty pounds to the bar. To this vast storage she agreed to furnish a detailed *derrotero* (chart), with the understanding that a fifth of the silver should go to her. Once the silver was secured, it could be utilized in reopening and working the great mines from which it had been extracted before hostile Indians ran the Spanish miners out of the country.

"Dig up this silver," she said, "and then you shall have all the other charts."

Dixon could not read Spanish, but he brought home the *derrotero* to the two thousand bars of silver, and Wiley Stroud, the only "Spanish scholar" in the company, read it. It stated that the shaft was filled up with rocks. The partners agreed that it and the old Indian's "cave" were one. They were on fire with enthusiasm and confidence.

But it always takes lost mine hunters a good while to organize for work. The greater the wealth at stake and the poorer the searchers, the longer the time required. The San Saba wealth was immense; Dixon and his company were as poor as Job's turkey. It took them over two years to get ready to go to the San Saba. Just as they were at last about to set forth, the Civil War began. All four entered the Confederate Army; when the war was over, all four were still alive. Meanwhile Carlota had gone back across the Rio Grande. The Texans lost all trace of her.

In 1868, exactly ten years after Carlota's appearance in San Antonio, and nearly twenty after the Indian's guidance towards a cave in "Summer Valley," the San Marcos adventurers, with several grown sons accompanying them, reached the San Saba. They carried along a few spades, axes, picks, grubbing hoes, a crowbar or two, rifles for meat and Indians — and a keg of home-made corn whiskey.

Carlota's *derrotero,* as Wiley Stroud spelled it out, directed that they go three leagues towards the west up the San Saba River from the old fort and then turn north and follow up Silver Creek one league. The searchers had no trouble in finding the ruins near Menard. Approximately three leagues (about eight miles) to the west they came to the mouth of a creek called Silver and proceeded another league up it.

The *derrotero* now called for a mound of stones on a hillside. They found a mound of stones. Under the stones, buried shallow, should be the half of a Mexican *metate* (a stone used to grind corn on). They found half of a *metate.* Now they were to measure off thirty varas due south and dig; there they should find a copper peg. They found it. Another thirty varas to the south should be another copper peg. It was there. Still another thirty varas to the south they should go and then turn west. At intervals of thirty varas each they should on this east-to-west line find three more copper pegs. They found them all. Next, going on west for an unnoted distance, they should come to two mesquite trees growing close together; in the ground between these twin trees they should dig up the other half of a *metate*.

As the men ran their lines and dug up copper peg after copper peg, their excitement, as may be imagined, was intense. They worked in a trot. Finding the two mesquites with the piece of *metate* at their roots proved a tedious business. Finally, however, the stump of one tree was located, and, surely enough, excavation around it brought to light the half of a *metate*. This half fitted exactly with the other. Across the lava-gray surface of the rejoined halves the letters of one word showed plainly. The word was EXCAVAD — Dig. Dig where?

The chart directed that a tree with three prongs would be found to the south of the second half of the *metate*, and that fixed between these three prongs should be a flint rock "about the size of a turkey egg." It was only after three or four trees had been chopped down and forks made by branches cut into that the flint was found deeply embedded.

The next step was to sight from the flint in a northeast direction to the initial mound of rocks. The intersection of this line with the east-and-west line was the place to dig into the old shaft. The point of intersection proved to be almost in the bed of Silver Creek, which is generally dry. According to directions, the shaft must be opened for sixty feet straight down; then a complicated tunnel that twisted in various directions on several levels must be cleaned out before the "storeroom" of two thousand silver bars could be broken into. Dixon and his men began tearing into the earth. As they worked, it became evident to them that they were clearing out a big hole that had been dug through solid rock and then later filled. It did not take them long to realize that they could never remove all the rocks without hoisting machinery and the expenditure of an immense amount of labor. Some of the men became discouraged and skeptical. "If it is necessary to tunnel this whole damned hill out to get the silver," said one, "I don't want none of it." Another swore that "the whole business was a cheat"; another that "no Spaniard would go to so much work to hide his stuff."

During the discussion several of the malcontents had frequent recourse to the whiskey keg. Finally G. B. Ezell's son grabbed the *derrotero* out of the hands of Wiley Stroud, who was for the fortieth time interpreting some item, and threw it into the fire. It was immediately consumed. But Stroud had spelled out the chart aloud so many times that its contents were indelibly impressed upon his own mind and the minds of his partners.

Discouraged and quarreling, the San Marcos men gave up the search, never to renew it. The first rise in Silver Creek after their departure filled up with rocks and gravel the shallow excavation they had made to mark the site of the original Iguanas shaft. The six copper pegs were scattered, and now, as far as is known, not one remains. The pieces of *metate* were carried home by Sam Fleming, who cemented them together. Later he moved to Benton, in Atascosa County, where he ran a blacksmith shop, and it is remembered that his wife used the repaired *metate* as a clabber trough for her chickens. After her death he went to San Antonio, where for fifteen years he lived with his niece and her husband, a man by the name of W. J. Parker.

Now Parker, likewise a Confederate veteran, was for years keeper of the West End Pavilion. Here in 1902, W. M. Longworth met him and was taught the history of the San Saba Mine as it has thus far been recorded.

"Night after night," Parker assured Longworth, "I have heard old man Fleming tell how Dixon was guided by the Indian, how he represented his partners in Monclova, how the Spanish lady, Carlota, brought the *derrotero* to San Antonio, and then how the hunt for the two thousand bars of silver came to a dead end. Fleming never varied in a single detail. His story had to be true."

It took Longworth a long time to act. Before he ventured greatly he wanted to make sure of the alleged chain of fourteen mines from which the great storage of silver bars had been extracted. He wanted to see those documents that Carlota claimed to have found in the archives of Monclova but would not show to Dixon.

So, about ten years after becoming interested, he raised five hundred dollars and turned it over to a trusted Mexican, instructing him to go to Monclova and "use the money right." The Mexican must have "used the money right." He came back with a copy of a very long document purporting to have been written by one Pablo Bernal. This document recites how two thousand miners under the direction of a certain José de la Amelgamese worked "fourteen rich mines" on the San Saba in the eighteenth century.

"The San Saba hills are bald hills of limestone," so the document quotes José de la Amelgamese. "They are without surface indications of minerals. But we prospected in caves and found a lead to much silver."

True, the directions to the "fourteen mines" seem vague. Yet Longworth felt recompensed for the five hundred dollars he had spent to get them. He went up Silver Creek to a place that he verified as being where Dixon and company had made their location. There he set to work. When he had cleaned out the shaft for sixty feet straight down, he struck a wall that appeared to have been cemented. He broke through it into "a kind of natural cave" — the Spanish tunnel. But the tunnel was also filled with rocks and dirt, *"mostly surface material."* For months he and his helpers carted rocks in wheelbarrows and hoisted them up the shaft. Then he struck a powerful vein of water.

His funds were exhausted, but he managed to buy a good pump. It proved to be inadequate. About this time the United States entered World War I. Longworth made good money working on the cantonments around San Antonio. He bought another pump. It would not do the work. Thus alternating between cantonment jobs and pumps, he spent two years.

Meanwhile he became acquainted with a major in the United States Army who owned an island off the coast of Florida on which pirate loot is buried. As soon as the war was over, this major sent from his home in Kansas City a new kind of "radio machine" guaranteed to indicate any mineral in its vicinity. When the machine got near the San Saba diggings, it "squalled," "bellered," "roared," simply "cut up" beyond all precedent. Longworth felt more certain than ever that he was over a room full of silver bars.

But there was the water. He could find no pump to control it. He was at his row's end, it seemed. Then he heard that a San Antonio lawyer owned some powerful pumps that had proved very successful in a Mexico mine. He went to see the lawyer.

"When I told him what I wanted with pumps and where I

was working," Longworth said, "he jumped straight up out of his chair. 'Man,' he exclaimed, 'I've been looking for that location myself. Undoubtedly you are at the right place.'"

In short, for a half interest in the project, the lawyer agreed to finance the search. He secured long leases on the land around the workings. He installed adequate pumps. He put a crew of Mexicans to tunneling. For weeks they carried out from twelve to twenty tons of rock a day.

To describe the labyrinth of holes that Longworth and his moneyed partner made would be tedious. The farther they dug, the more ambiguous became some of the directions inherited from the San Marcos adventurers. One night, however, Longworth had a dream that set them straight again. Then a series of floods in Silver Creek refilled the tunnel with silt. It had to be reopened.

At last report, the lawyer was still spending money. "It may be tomorrow," he'd say, "it may be a week from now — it may be a year. But some day we are going to break into what is perhaps the biggest treasure chamber known to history. It will create a sensation equaled only by the tomb of King Tut."

This is the dream that never dies.

Where the Gleam Led Captain Cooney

A L O S T mine — of notability — is a Proteus, appearing in so many shapes that it may not be recognized when seen. It is a chameleon varying its hues according to background and light. It is a cloud in the sky changing its form according to winds and temperatures and also according to the fancies of the beholder, now a camel, now the devil with a pitchfork, now Rodin's "Thinker." It is the Lorelei luring by her grace and form; it is the Pied Piper of Hamelin. It is the *ignis fatuus*, the will-o'-the-wisp, signaling in brightness to somewhere and floating away to nowhere. But "it is better to travel hopeful than to arrive," and who wants to put out the lights, deaden the singing, lump into formlessness the beckoning shapes of enchantment, mock into humdrum the promises that keep the hopers hoping?

No lost mine of the Western Hemisphere has had the lure of more plausibility, more gold and more fine hunting than the Lost Adams Diggings, somewhere in northwestern New Mexico, northeastern Arizona — or elsewhere. No golden hoper lured by it has been more luring to me than Captain Cooney.

Years before the Apaches could be cleared out of their New Mexican stronghold, Jim Cooney entered it and made a gold strike in the canyon named for him. Then in 1880 a band of

Victorio's Apaches got him. His brother Michael Cooney came out from Louisiana to take over the properties.

The first thing he did was to blast out a tomb in a great boulder forty feet high, place the body of his slain brother therein, and then seal it with a marble slab. Next, Captain Cooney drafted a dispatch to the young and gay Silver City *Enterprise* announcing that Mogollon, over the mountains from Cooney Canyon, held "the wealth of the world." He had an interest in the strike there. Then, with Morris Coates as a partner, he began looking for something even richer than the "wealth of the world" — the lost Adams Diggings. He was a kind of spiritualist, and he used to wake Coates up of a morning to tell him where a vision in the night had revealed the gold.

Before long he was hunting by himself. Then he quit the search to go to Santa Fe as a legislator. There a story he heard put him back on the trail that was to lead him deeper and deeper into solitude and finally through the door that never opens outward.

The story he heard goes back to the early '80s, when the western boundary of Socorro County, bigger yet than some states, was being surveyed. Along with the surveyors was a boy whom two of the axmen took to deviling unmercifully. He was sensitive, and one day after these tormentors had goaded him to desperation, he left them swearing he would never go back to camp. Unarmed, with nothing but the clothes on his back and a pocketknife, he took out across the mountains in the direction of Silver City, towards the southwest.

On the very first day of his foolhardy flight he came to a canyon of running water. He was very thirsty, and it happened that the spot where he got down to the water was immediately below a waterfall. While he was kneeling to drink, he could see the base of the bluff over which the water plunged, the cascade making a kind of curtain that hung out a foot or more in front of it. Back in this sheltered recess a ledge of "color" caught his eye. He broke some pieces off and put them in his pocket. By good luck he got through to Silver City. There he showed his samples to a mining man named Burbank, keeping quiet to everybody else. Burbank had the samples assayed. They ran one hundred and fifty thousand dollars to the ton. Nuggets as big as frijoles were imbedded in the rocks.

The boy wanted to go back at once, but Burbank would not risk the Apaches. He did risk them in another direction, however, by going with Langford Johnston on another lead. After the Indians had killed Burbank, Johnston buried him and came back to look for the "Lost Boy Mine." Burbank had not told, or had not been able to tell, him much about the location.

Meantime the boy had gone to his home in St. Louis. There he stayed two years before returning to develop his find. He found Burbank dead. The memory of men who had abused him and cut his soul to the quick came back. He would not have another "pardner." He was used to being alone anyhow. He had a little money. He outfitted and set forth alone. It is known that he made camp between Sycamore and Turkey creeks in the Mogollons. He came back to Silver City once, posted a letter, got supplies, and slipped out again.

The letter was to an uncle in Kansas City, a printer. In part it read: "I have found the richest mine in the world. The country is so rough I cannot get my pack outfit nearer than three miles to it, but I have blazed a trail from my camp to the ledge. The Apaches are getting thinned out, but I write you in case . . ."

Maybe the Apaches were getting thinned out, but the thinner they became the more desperate and relentless they grew. The boy never came back.

It was the printer uncle, with the boy's letter, whom Captain

Cooney met in Santa Fe in 1892 while he was attending the legislature. Captain Cooney certainly must have known that the boy's ledge of gold was not the placer gold, picked out of gravel, that Adams had found. Nevertheless he somehow identified the one with the other. He felt sure that Boy's Canyon — as the unknown came to be called — and Adams's Zigzag Canyon were identical. Henceforth there was to be no surcease for him in the quest.

The boy had not been seen for ten years when Captain Cooney located three blazed trees on the divide between Turkey and Sycamore creeks and found indications of a camp. That was all. He could find no trail blazed anywhere, and there was not a waterfall within many miles — in so far as he could find.

If no canyon waterfall could be found, then the gold — always associated with the Lost Adams Diggings gold — simply had to be somewhere else.

Captain Cooney had no "pardner" now to awaken in the morning with news of a directing vision. As the years went on, he became more and more a man of utter solitude. Perhaps his closest confidant was a chunky little pack burro named Black Pete, with whom he habitually shared his beans and sourdough bread. Many a morning he would say, "Which way, Black Pete?" And whichever way the little burro pointed his ears would determine the direction of the day's search.

There were quiet nooks like Dutchman's Spring, away up close to the Continental Divide, where Black Pete seemed to like the wild rye particularly well, and many a time Mike Cooney would spend a day traveling to such a place just to humor his burro. Then on a summer morning while he was waiting for the sun to come over the peak and warm his joints and dry the dew off his bedding, he would sit around and watch hummingbirds suck wild horsemint or fight a pygmy battle. What sense was there in hurrying anyhow? Besides, the whole country was good to prospect in, for everybody agreed that the Adams gold was not in a mineralized area. While Black Pete got slicker and fatter, the aging Cooney must have spent uncountable hours dawdling around camp doing nothing but watch a striped chipmunk peel seed out of a pine cone. He would whistle at a squirrel to make it bark, and then the two would keep at each other until the squirrel quit. Crossing some valley, he liked to stop and watch the wild turkeys grazing on the beans of the tall pink-flowered turkey weeds, which hard-pressed squatters later cut and hauled into their chicken yards.

At night he had for solace the flickering patterns made by the light of his campfire on the great tree trunks and the boulders and drifts of straw on the ground. Again he would look out in the moonlight upon the mountains beyond — always mountains and always beyond — standing gray and mystical.

Some years were dry, with the thunder of August a mockery and only the flirt of a canyon wren to reveal a tin cup of seep-spring water — too dry for the wild dewberries and raspberries. Then prospecting was a cramped business, but generally it rained on the mountain crags when it didn't rain anywhere else. Out of rain clouds there was a great wind, and at night there was a great moon. The whole world was buoyant, and the lode of gold had to be great.

The longer Captain Cooney lived in solitude with his own quest and his own visions for company — and always Little Black Pete — the richer and more real to him became the Adams Diggings. He would never hunt in the lava beds, but he circled all around them. He hunted in the red bluffs of the Zuñi country, where the boys who herd goats stand like sentinels hour after hour on the cliffy points and, looking out over the forbidding waste lands, seem to guard some secret — a secret more mystical than material — that only their eyes have seen. He stood on Inscription Rock, where the name of Oñate carved with a dagger point still attests that he passed here in 1606, and looked towards Mount Taylor to the east and the Zuñi Buttes to the west and wondered which way Adams passed. He climbed the astounding butte called Acoma, where the Indians have their "city in the sky," perhaps the loneliest and eeriest point of habitation north of the Andes. Somewhere, in all the immense world of mountains and canyons spread out beyond, the Adams gold lay waiting. Captain Cooney could wait too.

One summer he decided to prospect into the Taylor Mountains, away to the north of his usual haunts. He always liked to get up high so that he could see out. From his camp he watched the golden mist of sunset fade slow, slow on the Sandia Mountains fronting the Rio Grande a hundred miles east. The mystery, the vastness, something forever undefinable in such vistas, lured him back to the Mogollons and the Tularosas. There he could gaze upon familiar crags out in the pure blue — blue above them, blue around them, blue under them.

William Henry Wright, the great observer of grizzly bears and recorder of their ways, came to the conclusion that in the Selkirks they bed and loiter on the heights partly at least to enjoy the grand views, which they spend so much time seemingly contemplating. It must not have been altogether fear of enemies that caused Indians of the Southwest to build their homes on the most inaccessible mountaintops, far from wood, water and tillable soil, but also a desire to look out. Captain Cooney, of Irish blood and of Louisiana swamp experience, came to belong to the mountains as truly as grizzly bear or Zuñi Indian belonged; and many and many a time he worked up to the summits for a look beyond anything that a miner could ever touch with his pick.

And so, for Captain Cooney, it was on and on. Prospecting

down some prong of the Gila River, he would get down to mistletoe, and then begin working back up again — into alligator junipers, some as old as the sequoias of California; from junipers into oaks and pines; out of oaks into great Douglas firs mixed with gigantic pines, the air about them ever as fresh as the mountain ferns growing in the shadows; and above the level where piñon jays warn the deer of a man's approach. Then around patches of quaking aspen, dazzling in the sunlight, into a waste of black, volcano-smelted rocks, acres and acres wide, not one sprig of vegetation visible amid their sterility.

On some eastern slope of these summits Captain Cooney would stand or sit and gaze for hours at the vast spread-out Plains of San Augustine, the flecks of blue shadows, the intensifying sunshine making the grass look as white as a freshly laundered sheet. The Plains of San Augustine seem destined to preserve the character of Magdalena as a cow town, but nobody ever dug gold out of them. Still, as Captain Cooney used to tell, when he saw them glistening and luring far away, he could never keep from thinking that his friend Beauchamp might be right.

Beauchamp was a kind of "jack-jeweler," in Clifton, Arizona. He claimed to be a seven-months child, and, therefore, to have powers of divination. He had maps and more maps. He would buy any waybill a Mexican tried to sell him. Every summer he would go to Mogollon, outfit, and maps wrapped in oilcloth, strike for the canyons running down out of the mountains into the San Augustine Plains. To him every crag and canyon draining into the Plains of San Augustine was a possibility for the Adams gold.

Captain Cooney had far rather watch an eagle soar, and mark where its shadow skimmed the ground — ground hiding gold — than be where men might watch him. Sometimes when he was going down for provisions, he would turn aside from the trail and "lay low" until a rider he had sighted was past. However, there were not many riders to meet. He did not like the inquisitiveness and curiosity of most people. No man likes to have the deepest thing in his nature, the purpose of his life, made light of. More than that, the years of solitary living were making him shy, like a Tarahumare Indian who will slide behind a tree to keep from being detected, or like a deer that instead of running in fright will merely cover himself with a bush and watch. He would go out of his way, though, to meet one of those lone hunters named Ben Lilly, Nat Straw, Ed English, so as to ask if he had noticed the leaning pine with Adams's initial cut on it.

When the ice binds the high-up world and snow covers it depth over depth, the elk, deer, birds and other creatures have already come down — all except the bear, and he is sleeping the winter through. Man must come down too. As a rule, Captain Cooney wintered on his old stamping grounds along the San Francisco River. Adams had time and again come here, looking for his own trail — and that made the valley a better place for Captain Cooney to linger in.

When he could look out and see on the mountainside a brown patch that had been white, he began to overhaul his equipment and watch for the sure sign of spring's opening. That sign, good for both season and luck, was a wild turkey-hen setting. Whenever he could spy or hear of a nest, he was ready to head out. This was as a rule along towards the first of April. Meanwhile, waiting for the long winter months to pass, he usually heard something to increase his fervor. Maybe it was nothing but another talk with Charlie McCarty, up at Milligan's Plaza, who had kept one Adams party from getting lost, helped them run out of whiskey, and in the end traded for the very horse that Adams rode. Captain Cooney was on the San Francisco when Bear Moore's body was found.

The facts that came out about Bear Moore gave him immense encouragement. During Bear Moore's lifetime everybody who knew him was certain of just one thing — that he wasn't knowable. He always wore long whiskers, which, like his hair, were matted with bear grease and dirt. He might have his hair roached once a year, but never his whiskers. He kept them to hide two sets of scars on his face — one set from a knife, and the other from the claws of a grizzly that gave him his name. He lived out in the mountains nobody knew where, occasionally showing up at Pinos Altos or Silver City with gold, which sometimes he sold but usually shipped to the mint at Denver. One time in Pinos Altos he got twelve hundred dollars for a buckskin of flour gold — gold fine in grain like flour. He did not come into the settlements of a winter; people said he holed up like a bear, living on meat he had killed and put away. He was never known to possess a horse, mule or burro.

Then Nat Straw and another prospector found Bear Moore's body not far from his camp. Under his chest, clutched tight in his hands, was a baking powder can half full of black sand mixed with flour gold and also containing a big nugget. The camp proved to be a cave, the ash heap at it six feet deep. People figured he had lived there for twelve years. It was two miles from any water, as remote and unapproachable as the walled-up cavern of some prehistoric cliff-dweller. It was estimated — by other hunters for the Lost Adams Diggings — that Bear Moore must have buried at least one hundred thousand dollars of minted gold. Whatever he buried is still where he put it.

His cave held a kind of clue to the source of his gold — a set of rawhide horseshoes. He himself never had any use for any kind of horseshoe. He had long been accused of being a friend and ammunition-supplier to the Apache Kid. Therefore, those rawhide horseshoes must have belonged to the Apache Kid, who often used such. The Apache Kid must have brought gold to Bear Moore.

I have known four men, out in New Mexico, each claiming to have been in on the killing of the Apache Kid at four widely separated places. I wonder how many men in Arizona shot him. His best biographer says he was not shot at all but died a natural death. He ranged all the way from the White Mountain Apache Reservation in Arizona down into the Sierra Madre of the Sonora Yaquis, and east to the Rio Grande. He was more of a killer of Apaches than of whites, though for years whenever a lone prospector or rancher in Arizona or New Mexico was found murdered, the Apache Kid got the blame. At times other renegade bucks were with him, but generally he was alone except for some young squaw he had kidnaped.

When he was not in a region too rough for any horse to travel, he rode the best horses the country afforded. When a horse could no longer carry him, he killed it and cut out the loin-straps to eat. Before he became this pariah of two nations, this Ishmael of mankind, the Apache Kid had been foremost among the native scouts at San Carlos in Arizona, had learned the white man's language, his way of preparing food, and his expert marksmanship. At the same time no warrior of Geronimo's band, no lone wolf among the remnant of Chiricahuas yet hiding like wild dogs in the mountains of western Chihuahua, ever attained to more cunning in tracking an enemy or covering up his own tracks.

Not even a gold hunter who waylaid ghosts would dream of trying to take the trail of the Apache Kid. Nevertheless, to Captain Cooney the gold that the Apache Kid presumably brought in to Bear Moore and the gold that Bear Moore most certainly possessed went further to prove that gold lay somewhere — somewhere where Adams wandered — waiting to be found. Captain Cooney had additional evidence.

One of Butch Cassidy's "Wild Bunch," who had drifted down from Jackson's Hole in Wyoming to work on the W S range along the San Francisco, told Captain Cooney of an old Indian trail leading around Bullard's Peak. The description made Cooney think it might lead to Adams's Zigzag Canyon.

The trail had been traced out, though in many places the tracing was only a shadow, generations back by Apaches who wanted to travel unseen. It dived into impassable cracks; it went over a hundred feet of steep-sloping, solid, slick rock where more than one horse had started sliding and shot to his death far below; it hugged cliffs and twisted through fringes of timber. Finally it went down into a tunnel-like canyon, a thousand feet deep from rim to bottom, so narrow for an hour's travel that a rider threading it could in many places reach out his hands and touch the walls on both sides and at the same time look up and see driftwood lodged far, far above — a sight to set any man speculating on the result of a cloudburst at the head of the canyon. But this trail took the old quester only to a rincon where a horse thief in no way related to the Apache Kid had some horses shod with rawhide.

In the summer of 1914 Captain Cooney decided that if he went to Socorro and worked back westward, instead of as usual starting in on the San Francisco to prospect eastward, his luck might change. It did. In October somebody ran across him away up in the blue. Next May, three searchers located his skeleton. In his vest pocket was a brief diary, the last entry in it: "Nov. 15 — Let in a little sun." Also there were four or five little nuggets evaluated later at twenty-six dollars. They could hardly have come from the Lost Adams Diggings.

Pedro Loco

PEDRO LOCO, some say, was one of old Victoriano's Apaches before a Mexican woman trapped him. Others say he was as Mexican as anybody, a descendant of the peon that the Conde de Majalca left to guard his property when the War of Mexican Independence ran all the Spaniards out of the country.

Whatever his antecedents, no particular interest or property had been attached to his person until one day in 1890 when he appeared at the Banco Nacional de Mexico in Chihuahua City with a few flat-cut emeralds, some jewelry that might have adorned a churchman or a holy image, a small chunk of crude gold, and one of the old-time bars of silver weighing two thousand ounces — twice as much as the regulation bar has weighed since Spain lost Mexico. The banker struck a bargain and was curious; Pedro took the money and was silent. Within a few months he was back again with another parcel of treasure stuff. The banker paid for it, was more curious, and set spies to watch Pedro.

Pedro did not come to him again, but there were other buyers and Pedro sold to them. Traffic in bullion and stuff out of old hoards is still not foreign to Chihuahua City. The banker's spies learned nothing. Before long, people began calling Pedro "Don." He set up an establishment. It was not so magnificent as it was ample, its adobe walls and patios squandering over a whole square of ground. It had to be ample to accommodate all the uncles, aunts, cousins unto the remotest degree and even the kin of godfathers and godmothers that settled down on Don Pedro and his wife. It took money to keep such a household in corn and frijoles, and during the dark of the moon at irregular intervals Don Pedro continued to bring in modest amounts of silver to barter.

His movements were more and more watched. It was daylight knowledge that when he left Chihuahua City, he went northwest to Sacramento. Thence his movements blurred and faded out, as if he had turned into a "fool" (Mearns) quail that squats unseen against a rock in open view. All interested parties, however, were sure that Don Pedro went on from Sacramento into the mountain region not far distant called the Victorino, a name that memorializes one of the strongholds of Victoriano of the Apaches. In the Victorino, the Conde de Majalca had his mine, enormously rich in silver output, before the War of Independence ended him. It is told that, carrying four hundred bars of silver, he used to make a trip to Mexico City once a year, his guard, servants and muleteers numbering four hundred persons. The little village of Majalca, in the Victorino, bears his name. Before he was killed on the long road to a ship that would sail him over the sea, he had hidden not only his own fine possessions but the riches of the Chihuahua Cathedral in a cave near his mine, or in the chamber of the mine itself.

Now, among those who dogged Don Pedro, trying to find the store from which he got his silver, was one Carlos Avalos, a "tiger" of political notoriety. By many ways he brought pressure to bear against Don Pedro. He persecuted him through other politicians. He cajoled him, set traps for him, played the bloodhound himself. One time he waylaid Don Pedro in the Sacramento Canyon and there attempted by brute force to make him talk. Don Pedro remained calm and silent. Avalos tied him and tortured him, but the Indian in him was adamant.

"Then, damn you," concluded Avalos, "I fix you so you can't talk even if you want to."

Pedro was pinioned, arms and legs, helpless. His torturer drove two sixteen-penny nails into the jaws of the silent man, one on either side of his face, nailing the upper to the lower jaw. He rode off leaving Pedro tied and nailed. A wood carrier who happened along with his burro rescued Pedro. He recovered, but to the end of his days he carried deep scars in his face and was *"un poco loco"* — a little crazy. Henceforth he was Pedro Loco. But he was not too *loco* still to go in secret and come back in secret with gold and silver and jewelry and the flat-cut emeralds. And he was not too *loco* to keep his jaws closed.

Once, once only, he relented. He had a very dear friend who was in desperate need and who was very deferential. This friend was Felipe Jiménez.

"The first day," Felipe used to tell, "we rode our mules up the canyon maybe one hour, maybe two hours, past Sacramento and camped. When we ate our supper, the wild turkeys were gobbling around us in every direction. About dark Pedro Loco turned his mule loose, saying that it would go home by itself and that from now on he would go afoot and guide my mule. The next morning we went on for three hours maybe, and I knew we were getting into the mountains of the Rancho Guerachic. — (Another name for Majalca.)

"At a certain place Pedro Loco blindfolded me fast and hard.

On foot he followed behind my mule, driving it. Of course the canyon twists and the wind in it shifts and changes too. But I was keeping alert and noted every change of direction. I am sure that we left the Sacramento Canyon and turned up a canyon that cuts in from the north. We did not ride more than an hour before we stopped on rocks. Then Pedro Loco told me to get down. He led me over some boulders. For a short distance we crawled. When he took the blindfold off me, we were in a cave and two sotol stalks were burning to light it. It was not the light that almost blinded me; it was the heap of precious stones, of gold, most of all, of silver bullion, and also of jewelry. There were beautiful crosses and fine plate, candlesticks and holy vessels.

" 'Help yourself,' Pedro Loco said. I did. Then when my pockets were full, he put the blind on me, tighter than before. I crawled again. I heard the sound of loose rocks — very, very dim the sound was. My mule went forward. I knew we were not returning over the same route. My brain was not blind like my eyes. I began fraying the blanket I wore and dropping the shreds — marking the trail to come back over. I felt on my face the cold breeze of dawn. We kept traveling, Pedro Loco close at my mule's heels and I dropping here and there a shred of the blanket.

"At length we halted. I heard a dog bark. It must have been a dog at the Rancho Guerachic, for there is no other ranch in that part of the Victorino.

" 'Get down,' Pedro Loco said. These were the first words he had spoken since leaving the cave. I did not like their tone. I obeyed. I could smell the dawn. When the blind came off, I saw that we were on a mountain. Pedro Loco was standing there with his hands full of woolen shreds.

" 'Here is your blanket,' he said. 'Your wife can weave it back together.' Then he gave me a kick. I felt too cheap to kick back. 'You cannot betray me,' he said. 'Go home!'

"I left him standing there and rode back to Chihuahua City. I sent to San Antonio, in Texas, for my brothers to come and help me get the wealth. For five years we sought. All I know is that Pedro Loco showed me the treasure. He told me he had located it while he was a warrior with Victoriano."

In the fall of 1908 Victor Lieb and Bill Adams, two American mining men who had been in Chihuahua for years and were familiar with the facts and traditions connected with Pedro Loco and his secret treasure, determined to exert superior Anglo-American intelligence and find the wealth. They disguised their purpose by getting permits to prospect for minerals in the Victorino. Lieb sent for a bloodhound out of the stock employed by the state penitentiary in Texas. He engaged as a helper a Pima Indian noted for his trailing ability. The dog proved to be marvelously keen of scent and was soon taught to trail silently on the leash.

November passed and December was passing. Without doubt Pedro Loco would make a trip out before Christmas. Lieb and Adams had their camp above Sacramento in the mouth of the canyon gorge. On the evening of December 20, Pedro Loco rode up on his mule, saluted the two Americans in a friendly manner, drank some coffee, and rode on. At dark they followed, the bloodhound silently straining on the leash. The trail turned out of the main canyon and up a box canyon cutting in from the north — the route that the blindfolded Felipe was so sure of.

It was pitch-dark. About half a mile up this side canyon the bloodhound suddenly ceased to trail, whined in fear, bolted back the way he had come, and jerked with such violence on the thong, which Lieb for safety's sake had tied around his waist, that he broke it. Among the rocks and trees hidden in the pitchy darkness the winds were howling. Lieb and Adams turned back also. They found the dog in camp. Impatiently they awaited daylight. When light dawned, they took the bloodhound and the expert Pima trailer and set out. At the mouth of the box canyon, the bloodhound refused to go farther. The Pima proceeded, but soon it was apparent that instead of trailing he was merely going ahead. He could "trail a hummingbird almost," but he could not follow Pedro Loco's tracks. In places the steep slopes of the canyon wall are covered with talus. It seemed likely that Pedro Loco's cave had an entrance hidden by the talus, but not one sign of it could be found.

On Christmas Eve, Lieb and Adams were back in Chihuahua City. The cold norther and the bright sun were keeping most of the daylight population of the great plaza lined up against warmth-absorbing walls. Only the blanketed and the coated could be at ease on the benches. And there in the windy sunshine the two Americanos saw Pedro Loco. He was wrapped in the blue coat he always wore and sat humped up like an old buzzard. He looked at the pair of prospectors and grinned. They could not resist pausing for a few words.

"I thought you'd have that fine dog with you," Pedro Loco said.

One thing leads to another. Living in Chihuahua City at this time was a fairly rich and unfairly grasping American, whose name may be indicated by the letter C. C stands for coyote, but I never have understood why human beings want to libel coyotes and burros. C was, of course, in the mining business. At various times he had employed Victor Lieb and Bill Adams to examine properties for him and do other work. He now came to them saying that he wanted two or three locations out in the Victorino country examined.

They told him they had just been prospecting in that region, had geologized it thoroughly, and failed to find the least indication of minerals — no matter what the Conde de Majalca had found. But C had some money to spend on these prospects, he said, and was going to spend it. The partners engaged to make the examinations he wanted.

After they had spent about two weeks in the Victorino, C came out and agreed that further exploration was useless. The next morning the prospectors told their *mozo* to pack up, and the outfit started back toward Chihuahua City. But just as they were leaving camp, an oldish Indian whom Victor Lieb had once bought a panther-killing stallion from, and whom he had more than once hired as a helper, rode up. He was a Mexicanized Indian who lived away back in the mountains, where he had a few head of stock and a corn patch.

"Listen, Don Victoriano," the Indian said, "I have been wanting to see you for a long time. I know something that will interest you."

He got off his horse, pulled an old brass-bellied .44 Winchester rifle from the deerhide scabbard on his saddle, laid it between some rocks, and carefully sighted it.

"Look," he said.

Victor Lieb knelt and looked out beyond the line of sights.

"What do you see?" asked the Indian.

"I see the mountains."

"Yes, and you see the gap where the Arroyo de los Fresnos comes out from them. That is thirty miles from here. On a little mesa on the right-hand side of that gap is an old smelter. I have

seen it. Cutting into the gap, a little beyond, is the Cañon En-
cantado. Vaqueros tell me that between the smelter and the
mouth of this cañon there are ruins of a mining camp. Go
there and perhaps you will find something."

Lieb and his partner had supplies enough to last three or
four weeks. They had nothing to do. They decided to investigate. C wanted to be in on the chance also. He even offered
to finance the expedition, and on these terms he was taken in,
the three to share equally whatever might be found.

The gap of the Arroyo de los Fresnos proved to be an ideal
camp — water, wood, deer all around, turkeys so gentle they
would come into camp, grass belly-deep, and bear. The ruined
smelter had an oak tree growing out of it that appeared to be
hundreds of years old. Scattered about here and there were signs
of ancient workings, but the slag about the smelter — rich slag
— showed that it had not come from these workings. The prob-
lem was to find the origin of the slag.

Lieb decided to move camp from the smelter over to the ruins
of the old mining camp, not a great distance off. The outfit
moved, and Lieb took his horse to stake him out on a little
bench. While the stake-rope was being tied, a fly or something
caused the animal to stamp. The ground under the horse's
hoofs sounded hollow. At this moment Lieb's eye caught sight of
an outcropping vein. He yelled for the *mozo* to bring a pick.
The whole camp came running.

Digging down at the exact spot where the horse had stamped,
the men very shortly struck a layer of logs. They were of the enduring juniper and were as sound as they had been the day they
were buried. The rocks and soil above them having been removed, the logs were lifted out. They covered the mouth of a
shaft. Leading down into the shaft were the old-time chicken

ladders, notched logs, still slick from the wear of moccasins and bare feet of Indian miners. The ladders appeared to be as sound as the juniper logs. Getting lights, ropes, and other equipment, the discoverers began to descend.

For three hundred feet they climbed down in dry air. At the bottom against a highly mineralized ledge were the remains of a fire, which had no doubt been built to heat the rock, against which water would then be dashed to make it split. There were several *zurrones* — the bags of rawhide in which the native miners carried their burdens of ore upward, suspending them from the forehead. Truly this was a lost mine worth finding. This was the ore that had been worked at the smelter and that had left such rich slag.

Lieb drew up all the papers for staking their claim — "denouncing" the mine, as the Mexicans term it. He placed the papers in his instrument box, which was never locked. They would have to be filed with the government. That night C left, saying he had to get back to Chihuahua City and would meet his partners there. He rode to a railway station for a train, while Lieb and Adams traveled horseback with a mule-load of selected ore samples. When they reached Chihuahua City a week later and Lieb went to get his papers to file them, they were gone. They had been filed by C under his own name alone.

In a Drouth Crack

O N L Y two or three times in a century does a drouth scorch the life out of the central part of Texas as did that of 1886. Now it was late August. There had been no spring. The cedar elms along Onion Creek were already dropping their leaves. Some oaks were dead. Even the narrow, non-evaporating leaves on mesquites, beginning to take the prairies, were seared. The only winds were whirlwinds — the sign of more dry weather. The grass roots had died; the bull nettles in the fields were runty and withered. Drouth cracks seamed the black land everywhere.

Fanning his face with his hat, Tobe Pickett sat on the front gallery of his low house, which sprawled out on both sides of an open hall, among live oak trees on Onion Creek, near the Spanish Trail crossing, about eight miles from Austin. He had a way of grumbling to himself, interspersing his phrases with "my-my's" and long sighs, often with a kind of rhyme. He usually ended his soliloquies with a whistling sound that prolonged itself the length of time it took to expire all the air from his thick chest. Now he was going on to himself about the weather.

"My, my, ain't it hot!" he'd say. "Oh, ho, dead doe, how,

hmmmm! I wonder if it ain't ever going to rain. Rain, rain, gone to Spain. Hu, hu, hu" — and then that long, dying whistle.

The only person present to notice his ejaculations and groans and mutterings was his wife, Aunt Mat. She was so used to them that she had ceased to pay attention to them. Wiping the sweat from her face with her apron, she stepped from an ironing board in the hall to the wooden bucket hanging from a rafter of the gallery and dipped out a gourd of water. As she drank, her eyes swept the horizon.

"Seems like them dust devils get thicker every day," she remarked.

"It's too dry for the dry weather locusts to sizzle," Tobe went on. "My, my, my, looks like it jes' can't rain. Drier'n it ever was before, worser'n it was in 'sixty-four."

"You don't know how bad it was in 'sixty-four," Aunt Mat rejoined mildly. "You was stealing peaches in Georgia — between battles with Sherman's Yankees. That Meskin oughta be showing up."

"Well," Tobe retorted, "haven't you and everybody else left here during the War told me over and over how the cattle died too poor fer the buzzards to eat? And how the prickly pear took the dry rot and shriveled to nothing? And how half the dogies that didn't starve to death fell down into the drouth cracks? Don't tell me. Dry, dry, dry, and not a cloud to try . . ." — and Tobe was off again on one of his monologues.

The sun was still maybe two hours high. The Mexican hired man came up to the gallery, his feet, in rawhide sandals, touching the ground at each step in a manner of infinite repose.

"Maybe so I go haul the water now?" he queried. "She is more cool."

"Cool!" Tobe exploded.

The Mexican said, "Sí, señor," and took a restful stand in the shade.

"Ho, hi, hum, whirlwinds till kingdom come," Tobe went on, looking out over the baked land, apparently oblivious of everything else.

"Well, don't jes' set and go on forever," Aunt Mat exclaimed. "Tell Pablo to get moving and haul the water. When our well went dry, I predicted the last waterhole in Onion Creek would dry up too. If you and Pablo don't fence in that rock waterhole, we won't have any water fit to drink."

"My, my, call it dry! Yes, go on, Pablo, and hitch up that Gotch mule to the sled and haul the water."

As the Mexican made a motion to get going, Tobe added, "And mind out for them drouth cracks. Giles's horse stepped in one yesterday and nearly broke his leg, and his wife said the off wheels of their buggy got into one and they had to drag away down it before it got shallow enough to pull out of. You watch now. Drier than a lime-burner's hat and hotter'n a hotbox in hell. Pablo, maybe a cup of coffee would sorter cool me off."

"Sí, señor." Pablo went to the kitchen, where he could be heard lifting the stovelid off and raking up coals. After a while he brought out a cup of hot, black coffee. After watching and listening to Tobe sup the first sup, he left to haul the barrel of water.

He did watch out for the cracks. That night he told his wife María he had seen a jackrabbit try to jump a crack and fall into it. He sometimes exaggerated when he talked to María, particularly if other people were around to hear what he said. But very seriously he now added: "When you go to the back side of the field, María, to cut prickly pear for the pigs, watch out that you don't fall into a crack like the jackrabbit. Those cracks — they are a barbarity!"

Late the next day while going across the field to cut prickly pear for the hogs, María saw a crack that really was, she believed, too wide for a jackrabbit to jump. Bending over, she slowly moved along it trying to locate an imprisoned rabbit or something else in its depths. A few feet down, darkness obscured the opening, but presently she saw something that rushed into her memory an old tale known to everybody in the country.

Her eyes made out an iron chest, wedged between the walls of the crack. She could even trace a kind of cable that passed over the lid and through the handle on one uptilted end. That is what she always claimed. Could it be the chest of gold that the Spaniards left so long ago when they were held up on Onion Creek? Many strangers had come to the country looking for that chest. According to some, it was on one side of the creek and according to others, on the other side. As the story went, the Spaniards, when attacked, had thrown it into "a hole." But they hadn't had time to dig a hole. There was no known cave in the vicinity. Some old settlers argued that the hole was a drouth crack, which, of course, had closed with the first good rain, leaving no sign. There were supposed to be signs on rocks and trees in the vicinity.

Thinking of all she had heard, María stood beside the great crack and looked around to make sure that no one had seen her. It was time for Pablo to be coming from Onion Creek with his sled of water. She hurried to the gap, beyond a line of brush, to meet him. A neighbor was with him, however, and her news was for Pablo alone. She went on and cut the prickly pear.

It was after dark before she got an opportunity to talk.

"I tell you, Pablo," she imparted, "that chest has more than gold. Gold, yes, but what riches besides! It is too big. It holds, most certainly, a little saint and a silver cup for the holy wine, and a cross with red jewels in it. Look, it's big like that," and she measured with outstretched arms.

But it was Pablo's opinion that the chest contained nothing but gold. Had not a cousin to his *compadre's* uncle got the story from a priest, who had heard it in a monastery at a town far down in Mexico where another priest had confessed one of the dying bandits who had helped rob the pack train? The Spaniards were on their way to St. Louis with the gold and were right at the Arroyo de las Garrapatas (Ticks) — the old name for Onion Creek — when the robbers attacked them. This *historia,* coming down so directly, told of gold only, in a chest of iron "placed in a hole."

After their children were asleep, Pablo looked out and saw that the big house was dark. "The *patrón* and Doña Mattie are asleep," he said.

Then he lit the kerosene lantern and he and María set out across the field to feast their eyes on the chest in the great drouth crack. They had not gone fifty steps, however, before they heard the strong voice of Aunt Mat asking what was up.

"One *animal,* he catchee the chick," Pablo responded.

"The *animal* has gone and if you don't look out one rattlesnake will bite one Meskin," Aunt Mat's voice came back. "It's too hot for the rattlesnakes in the day, and they are crawling everywhere these nights," Aunt Mat warned. "Get back, I tell you."

The Mexicans put out the lantern. After a while, Pablo wanted to venture forth again without the lantern, but no,

María was too afraid of snakes — and only she could lead the way to the chest. "I will show it to you tomorrow," she said.

Pablo speculated how not only poles and ropes, but a team and a derrick might be necessary to get the chest up. He was afraid to let anybody else in on the secret. Yet how was he to haul the great chest out in daylight in an open field without being discovered? Well, he would see the chest in the morning and then settle on a plan.

But the next morning early Aunt Mat put him and her husband to building the fence around the one clear waterhole left in their stretch of Onion Creek. The cattle and horses would have to go on down the creek to the next waterhole. After dinner, instead of taking the siesta that even the lizards in this awful drouth took, Pablo got María to go with him across the field, as if to show her something about the prickly pear thicket. The heat was enough to sizzle the brains of a roadrunner.

The chest, María said, was at a place not visible from the house. But now she could not find it.

"Yesterday when you thought you saw it you were but sun-struck," Pablo accused.

"No, my head was as clear as the water out of Manchaca Spring," María returned. "My eyes were clear. The light down in the hole was clear. I saw the iron chest as clear as the Three Marys come up every evening." And she pointed to where Orion, with his belt of three stars, comes up every summer night.

"You are a fool," Pablo said.

Perhaps the heat was in his head. Quarreling, they went back to their cabin, built in the shade of a great live oak tree. There María bound around her head some fresh willow leaves she had brought up from Onion Creek. Pablo, perversely, placed only mesquite leaves in his hat to cool his head.

After he had had his siesta, María said, "This evening I mark the place, I alone."

When Pablo came in at dark, he asked, "You mark it?"

"Most certainly. I found it exactly, going to bring prickly pear for the pigs. Again I saw the lid and the strong cable going under the handle in one end. On the way back I saw it again and I placed three prickly pear leaves so that one hangs over the hole, just above the box."

"Perhaps the prickly pear will fall in," Pablo said.

"Perhaps the saint in the chest will lift it up on top of the ground," María retorted.

She was hard to argue with. They went on talking for a long time. Was the crack deep on down under where the chest was lodged? It was so deep that the bottom was in darkness. Then if the crack widened another inch, the heavy box might loosen and fall even to *infierno*. This heat and scorching of the world was all coming from that *infierno*.

"Tomorrow in the morning we go without fail," Pablo said. "The fence around the waterhole is finished and I will have time."

"*Mañana* for a surety," María said.

As they talked, they suddenly sensed a breath of freshness in the air. It had the smell that comes only out of clouds. Listen! The "carts of the giants," racing out of the east, were rumbling over their heads. Look! Lightning! Its tongues showed clouds of inky blackness covering the sky. From the big house came a great cry of joy. In fifteen minutes the sky was pouring down barrels, hogsheads, tanks of water; then the downpour turned into an all-night soaker. The next day Aunt Mat told neighbors how Tobe had rushed out into the yard, bareheaded and in his underclothes, and let the rain pour over him, how he had held his mouth open for the water to pound into until he choked, and how he had stretched out his hands and yelled: "The drouth's broke, the frogs croak, green grass, garden sass, slick cows and not a louse!"

Onion Creek boomed down like a regular river and carried away the fence Tobe and Pablo had put up around the rock waterhole. The next day and the next more rain fell. Not a crack was left in the land, the black dirt swelling and sealing up the contractions, leaving only hog wallows. They were little lakes. The sky was still full of water, and all creatures beneath it seemed to know that tomorrow green would be showing everywhere. The old mules were kicking up their heels and the cows were trying to play with their calves. Everybody in the country from the Carolina wren under the bluff on Onion Creek to the Governor of Texas on Capitol Hill was lighthearted.

Everybody but Pablo and María. At daylight after the big night rain, they had floundered together across the field. Deep mud gave the ground uniformity except in the hog wallows, where it was deeper. They couldn't find even one prickly pear leaf to mark the spot where the crack had opened over the chest of gold. María knew where the place was, and yet she didn't know exactly.

"Sakes alive, Pablo," Aunt Mat said when he brought in an armload of stovewood, "you look like you had lost your best friend."

A month later she set out with Tobe on a long-delayed visit to their daughter living on the Brazos River. They had not been gone three hours before Pablo was digging a hole at the spot selected by María.

"How deep you say it was?" he kept asking.

"More deep than you are tall," she would invariably reply. "Better make the hole wide."

Pablo dug one hole fairly deep, though not so deep as he was tall. Then he began shoveling up spadefuls of dirt at other places round about. He worked maybe two hours.

"We wait for signs," he explained to María.

"What signs?"

"Maybe the prickly pear will grow from where it is buried."

"Not if it is buried deep."

"Then a light will show at night. A light always plays in the dark over a place where gold is buried."

Pablo began to take walks at night out to a place where he could overlook the slope across which the great drouth crack had opened and revealed its hoard. He was happy again, like the other animals of the fruiting earth.

"The gold is not destined for us," he said to María.

"Thus it seems," she agreed.

When Aunt Mat and Tobe came back, Pablo told the story — María's story. Aunt Mat told other people.

"Jes' Meskin imagination," was Tobe's only comment when the matter was mentioned in his hearing.

"They're still looking for fox fire to show the right place," Aunt Mat would laugh.

Before long unknown diggers began making holes at one place and another in the Tobe Pickett field. That was back in the nineteenth century. Men, more of them Americans than Mexicans, are still digging holes and telling María's story. And now, whenever it gets dry enough on the old Pickett farm — long since passed into other hands — for the black land to crack, individuals not noted for industry may be seen peering into the seams.

The Mezcla Man

ELOJIO JUAREZ of the Rancho de Los Olmos and I were riding in the big pasture of open hills on the south side of the Nueces River. He knew all that country in the way the thousands of deer and javelinas knew the trails through their own thickets. Its traditions had come down to him through generations of vaquero people. He was quiet and had laughing eyes, and no better vaquero ever *pialed* (roped by the hind legs) in a blackbrush thicket with more gusto or more precision.

Fine September rains had fallen that year. Calves, tails stretched out, were running around their grazing mothers. Bulls had mats of mud on their heads from butting gully banks. Our horses seemed to feel as fresh and free as the white-tailed deer showing us their flags as they bounded into the mesquites. Elojio and I felt fresh and free too. When we came up on a high ridge where we looked across the San Casimero — twenty thousand acres in one pasture — to the Casa Blanca hills, towards San Diego, we stopped and got down on the green-turfed ground. Elojio rolled a shuck cigarette; I filled my pipe. We loosened girths, removed bridles, tied our ropes around the necks of the horses, and they went to chopping off mouthfuls of mesquite grass. How good it was to be free, to be masters of time, and to sit on grass gazing in repose *hasta la cola del mundo* — clear to the tail-end of the world!

"Know you," Elojio said, "that all this land down the Nueces and far to the south used to be in sheep?"

"I have heard so," I answered.

"There was the *brasada*," he went on, "but between the thickets was all prairie, where mustangs ran and the flocks of sheep moved slow and white, like clouds from the Gulf of Mexico with morning sunshine on them. It was the time of rich, rich *hacendados* and poor *pastores*" — the owners of haciendas and peonized sheepherders.

And then, for we were in no more of a hurry than the floating Gulf clouds, Elojio told this story:

There were no banks in the country then, and so when the rich ones sold their wool and sheep, they brought the money home. It was gold, with some silver. They had secret holes in the rock walls of their houses for hiding away the money. Often they buried it in the floor. The floors were of dirt cemented with bull blood to make it hard. They had secret places for gold under the fireplace rocks. Sometimes they put it in holes outside the houses, maybe close to the corrals. There were many places in which to hide the gold.

There were robbers, too, who came down from the north, and bandits who raided up from the other side of the Rio Grande. And always there were the Indians, the Comanches and the Lipans, but they were not after gold; they took horses and children and girls.

Now, one ranchero had more sheep and more wool and more

pastores and *vacieros* than any other. Each *vaciero* super-intended several shepherds and kept them supplied with food, for they could never leave their flocks. This old *rico* had more gold also than any other man, and he was very cunning. He lived in the high hills of the Casa Blanca country west of San Diego. His house was a kind of fort, with walls higher than the flat roof and with loopholes in the walls to shoot through. He kept a guard up there on the roof day and night, night and day, in heat and in cold, looking, listening always. What tiresome-ness!

One time after he had sold thousands of sheep and had con-ducted a caravan of carts loaded with wool to San Antonio, he brought home more gold than he had ever had before. But now instead of hiding it in his house, he carried it in secret to the highest hill on his ranch. It was not far from the big house. Peo-ple still call it Cerro del Rico — Hill of the Rich One. On the upper slopes of this hill and on top of it black chaparral and cat's-claw and other thorned brush grew so dense a javelina could hardly squeeze through it. The top of the hill was flat; perhaps it still is, and here in the middle of the thicket was a small natural clearing. The trail up to this clearing was very dim and thorny, for hardly anybody but the wildcats ever traveled it.

The cunning old *rico* knew it though. He went up alone with his gold. It must have been right after a rain, for he found mud. There in the middle of the clearing he made a great big man out of *mezcla* (a mixture of mud and straw or little sticks, the same as adobe). Big sticks supported the legs and neck and arms of the *mezcla* man. He was as big as a giant, and he was natural like a picture. His head was thrown back, and his mouth was wide open. He stood with arms stretched to the east and to the west, and across his chest was this writing:

DIG OUT TO THE EAST AND TO THE WEST
THE WAY MY HANDS ARE POINTING
AND YOU WILL FIND
THE GOLD

Oh, but this *mezcla* man was strange-looking, and his stomach was so big that anybody who looked at him would have to laugh. Perhaps Sancho Panza looked like him.

After the cunning old *rico* had finished making the *mezcla* man there in the middle of the thicket on top of the hill where nobody ever went, he kept on raising more sheep, and the shearers sheared more wool for him and he got more gold and hid it. All he paid out was coppers. He was like two millstones grinding out gold from the people under him and around him. They say that when he snored at night his snores said, "*Más oro, más oro, más oro.*"

Then one night while he was snoring for "more gold, more gold, more gold," the bandits came as quietly as the owl flies and choked the guards before they could shoot or cry out and then they went into the snoring room. They grasped the cunning old *rico* while he was still on his back.

"Your gold," the chief of the bandits said.

"There is none," the *rico* replied.

"You had better say." The *bandido* was not smiling.

"There is none," the *rico* repeated. That is all he would say.

"Hang him," the chief of the *bandidos* ordered.

The others tied his hands behind him and took a hair rope, so that it would not cut his skin too much, and noosed him by the neck. Then they drew the other end of the rope over a beam and pulled him up until his feet were kicking nothing but air. When he went to breathing like a lassoed wild horse choking down, they lowered him.

"What is the name of the dance you were doing for us?" one of the bandits laughed.

The *rico* said nothing.

"Now say where the gold is," the leader ordered.

"There is none."

"One more chance you have," the leader said.

"There is none."

"All right," the leader cried, "let him do the air dance once more."

Again he danced and again he strangled, but the dance was weaker and the sound of the little air passing through the tight noose was shriller. The bandits let him down again.

"For the last time," the chief said, "I ask where is the gold."

The *rico* was purple in the face and coughing, but once more he wheezed out, "There is none."

"May you go with God!" one bandit called as he tightened his hand on the rope to pull.

"And all you to the *infierno*," the *rico* gasped back.

"That's where you will snore for more gold tomorrow night," another bandit taunted.

After the *rico's* legs had made their last jerk, the taunter observed, "He loved his gold better than his life."

"It was his pride that he loved," the bandit chief said, "even better than the Holy Virgin."

Another said, "Our dancing master quit while telling a lie. Where will he go?"

"It's nothing," the chieftain snapped. "We have brief time for disproving that lie."

Then all went to searching. They looked in his bed and under his bed and turned all the other beds upside down, paying no attention to the crying women and children. They got bars and dug into the floors and pried up rocks of the fireplaces. They found the stores of candles and had the rooms all lit up while they tapped and hammered on the walls searching for secret little holes fitted with money boxes. They pried up the lid of the big leather chest. They looked everywhere there was to look inside the house and found not one piece of gold, but they knew plenty of it was somewhere.

When daylight came they went to digging holes at certain places under mesquite trees and around the big corral. They were many and well armed, and they impressed all the *peones* to dig for them. They were as cunning as the old *rico* himself, and some rode around looking for signs. One found the trail going up through the brush on that hill and followed it and came to the *mezcla* man. He could not read the writing on the *mezcla* man's breast, but he knew it meant something. He came back yelling, "Now it is found, now it is found."

All the bandits went up the hill. The leader read aloud the words on the *mezcla* man's breast: "Dig out to the east and to the west the way my hands are pointing and you will find the gold."

What joy they had! Quickly they dug under the hands of the *mezcla* man, but the packed earth had never been softened by digging. The directions did not say how far out to dig, and now the bandits ran east and ran west the way the hands pointed, looking for likely places to dig. Perhaps it is here, perhaps it is there, perhaps it is over yonder. They dug and they dug. They were in a hurry, not only from eagerness for the gold but from knowledge that before long honest people would find out about the murder of the *rico*, a very important man, and begin trailing them down.

With all the travel up and down the hill, from digging to water and food and from water and food to digging, the trail became as plain as the road to Laredo. On the afternoon of the second day the bandits heard horses galloping. They left the country.

When the ranchmen who were after the bandits came to the thicket and saw the strange *mezcla* man and read that writing on his breast, they forgot all about murder and justice. They thought only of finding the gold. Nobody was after them, and so they could dig as deep and as far out as they wanted to. They would sight along the *mezcla* man's shoulders and along his arms and out his forefinger and out his middle finger and out his little finger, trying, trying to locate the right place on the ground to dig for the gold. They even sighted out to a hill five miles away and dug a hole there. They cut paths through the brush east and west. But after they had dug and dug and found nothing, they became disgusted and quit.

Then the *pastores* began grazing their sheep up to the Cerro del Rico. Each had a shepherd dog with his flock. The way to train a dog to guard sheep is to take him away from his mother before he opens his eyes and let him suck a ewe. When he grows up, he thinks he is a sheep and will not let a coyote or anything else bother his kinspeople. These *pastores* would leave their dogs to care for the sheep and go up the hill and dig all day long. They dug new holes and they dug the old holes deeper. But they did not find anything, and after a while they became disgusted and quit coming.

Only one old *pastor* did not quit. He was more wise and had more knowledge than any of the other *pastores*. He knew what it meant when the bullbats were thick in the evening air. He knew what it meant when rattlesnakes crawled around in the middle of a summer's day instead of remaining asleep in the shade of bushes. He said that when a *paisano* (roadrunner) stopped suddenly while running down a trail, stood on one leg, and bowed his head, he was praying — praying for rain, perhaps. He could make better medicines than anybody else out of the leaves of the gray *cenizo* plant, the bark of the huisache tree, and the roots of the leather weed. He could read in the stars, and also, it was said, he could read an almanac. He was very astute, very sagacious.

So he kept on coming to that high hill and digging. Every morning he would put his gourd of water down at the *mezcla* man's feet, take his grubbing hoe and spade, and then for hours dig, dig, dig. He made some of the old holes deeper and he put down new holes. Meanwhile his shepherd dog kept the sheep out on the prairie.

One hot day after he had been working very hard and was very thirsty and tired, he came in from his digging to drink from the gourd. He took the stopper made of shucks from its mouth and, while his head was raised up to receive the water, his eyes fell again on the writing upon the *mezcla* man's breast. He had read it many times, but he read it again out loud: "Dig out to the east and to the west the way my hands are pointing and you will find the gold."

After he had done drinking, the *pastor* regarded the writing for a long time. He read it again, over and over. At last he said, speaking to the man of mud and sticks in front of him:

"Why, the robbers came here and found you and read what you say, and they dug out to the east and to the west, and they did not find any gold. Then all the rich and important rancheros in the country came. They had confidence in your word, and they dug east and they dug west, and they did not find gold. Then after they quit, the *pastores* still believed you, and they dug more holes and made the old holes deeper. But they did not find any gold. And I! Well, here I have been having confidence in your word and digging my arms off for over a year, and I have never found so much as a copper centavo.

"Why, you are just an old billy goat of a liar!" Then he slapped him on his big mouth.

The *pastor* was very indignant. "Shameless one," he said, "it is not with your mouth that you deceive. Right now your lying to honest people will end."

He seized his spade and hacked off the head of that *mezcla* man with his wide-open mouth. Then he chopped off the right arm, which pointed to the east, and then the left arm, which pointed to the west. And then, *wow!* he came with all his might down through the words on the *mezcla* man's breast and into his enormous stomach.

And when he did, gold coins and silver coins too just poured out on the ground. They were so heavy that the *pastor* could not carry them all. You see, the cunning old ranchero had built the man to hold plenty, and then he had fed him through his open mouth until he was full.

"Elojio," I asked when he thus ended his story, "what did the *pastor* do with so much money?"

"Oh, he gave his master some of it, and he kept the rest, and he never had to herd sheep any more. He went back on the other side of the river into his own country, and there he lived *muy contento* all the rest of his life."

And very contented I now rode on with Elojio.

The Rider of Loma Escondida

BOYS, ever' time I camp at this crossing I think of the way Jeff Cassidy got waylaid and murdered between here and Loma Escondida."

The speaker was Captain Crouch. He was with his outfit at the old Presidio Crossing on the Leona River near the border. Supper was over.

"Yes," Captain Crouch went on, "that was a long time ago, and tough hombres in this country were thicker'n preachers are now. Horse thieves was so bad that a man couldn't hardly keep a gentle saddle horse without hiding him in a thicket after dark and then sleeping by him. Money was safer'n horses, but a man riding a good horse and carrying gold in his belt had better be on the lookout."

When he got to talking about old times Captain Crouch inclined to lay it on a little thick.

"Now, about Jeff Cassidy. He represented the Seven D brand, a big outfit. One day he left San 'tonio for the old H-Triangle Ranch below here to receive a herd of steers and start 'em up the trail. As the custom was at the time, he carried money in his saddle pockets — hard money, of course — to pay for the stuff. He had five thousand pesos, gold, the balance to be paid when the cattle were sold in Kansas and the money brung back.

"The second night out Jeff slept in Friotown. He left there at daylight next morning, coming this way. He was alone, and was riding a little creamy dun pony that I'll tell you about d'reckly. He'd got into Friotown after dark and somehow had failed to learn that the sheriff was going down to inspect brands on the herd, or he might have had company. He left before daylight. The sheriff was late getting off. When he got about halfway between Loma Escondida and this crossing where we're camped, he found Jeff and his dun horse in the middle of the road, both deader 'n thunder.

"He hit the trail in a high lope, struck a couple of hands who joined him, and together they overtook the murderers somewhere this side of Eagle Pass. Everybody knowed them Newton boys wasn't no 'count and was rustling cattle, but nobody would have suspicioned them of killing a man in cold blood like they did Jeff Cassidy. The case was plain as daylight and the Newtons owned up. Still, they didn't have any of the gold with them, though the pockets had been stripped off Jeff's saddle. Furthermore, neither Jim nor Tom Newton could be forced to tell where the stuff was. They was hung, of course, and —"

But at this point the Captain's narrative was interrupted by an unceremonious announcement from the cook, Alfredo, that the camp was out of coffee.

Alfredo was a new *cocinero,* and in terms free but not fierce Captain Crouch expressed his opinion of a cook who would leave headquarters without enough coffee and not say anything about the shortage until it was nearly time to cook breakfast. The fact that Alfredo had carefully put his coffee in a big can and then loaded on in its place a similar can containing frijoles did not remedy the mistake.

"Well," concluded the Captain, "there ain't but one thing to do, and that's for somebody to ride to Charlie Trebes's commissary and get the coffee."

It was ten miles to the Trebes ranch. Twenty miles on horseback will not leave the rider much of a summer's night for sleeping. None of the hands said anything. It was not for them to say.

Otis Coggins, who had been working on the Crouch ranch since boyhood, was patching a stirrup-leather. He was a tall, swarthy man under thirty.

"Otis," the Captain went on, "I reckon you're the man to go for the coffee. You know old man Trebes better 'n anybody else, and if you get back here by breakfast time you can stay in camp and sleep all morning. Better get about ten pounds, I guess."

"All right," said Otis.

Then addressing a Mexican vaquero, he ordered, "Go get me that Trigeño horse. It's lucky I staked him."

"Guess I taught you never to be caught afoot, even if your back was broke and you couldn't fork a pillow," remarked Captain Crouch. "That reminds me —"

"But, Captain," Otis broke in, still mending on his saddle, "don't you reckon them Newton boys musta buried that gold around somewhere clost to where they killed Jeff Cassidy? They shore aimed to make use of it some day."

"Yes, I guess they did hide it somewhere," Captain Crouch agreed, his mind brought back to the story he was telling when the *cocinero* interrupted. "I don't know as anybody's ever looked for it much. There never was anything that hurt me more 'n Jeff's death. He and me had been side pardners — regular yoke mates, you might say — for years. I guess we broke enough horses together to furnish a dozen outfits going up the trail. There was still some mustangs in the country, and one day we laid into a little bunch that had their bellies too full of water to run much and roped one apiece. Mine was a purty black filly; I broke her neck a-trying to get the saddle on her. Jeff's was a creamy dun stallion with a black stripe down his back about the width of your hand — a *bayo coyote*. He was all life and bottom, and Jeff got so he didn't want to ride anything else. He was riding him when he was killed. I always figgered one of them Newton boys made a misshot and killed the horse accidentally. They'da' been mighty glad to take him as well as the gold."

By now the vaquero had led up Otis's brown horse. The saddle on him, a sack for the coffee was tied behind the cantle. It was a sack from Mexico, sewn together in the middle and open at each end, designed for horseback carrying. With an *adiós* the rider was off.

Otis Coggins was a silent kind of man. He liked to be alone. His route lay through a vast flat country, partly prairie but mostly pricky pear mixed with mesquite, cat's-claw, *guajillo,* *chapote,* and other kinds of brush common to southwest Texas. The only break on the plain that his brush-lined road traversed was the solitary hill known far and wide as Loma Escondida. It is *escondida* — hidden, the brush so high and thick around it that a rider cannot see it until he is almost upon it.

The moon was full; as usual the sky was flawlessly clean; one might have read ordinary book print in the moonlight. As he approached Loma Escondida, not a sound but the pad of his horse's hoofs and the squeak of saddle leather breaking the silence, Otis Coggins noticed an object, or rather, two objects, in the road some distance ahead of him. They were partly in the shadow of high brush, and at first he took them to be a cow and calf. Cattle in brush country often bed down in open roads. But presently Otis saw that the larger of the objects was a horse and that the lesser was a man apparently humped over on the ground. The man soon straightened, mounted, and started up the hill ahead of Otis.

Now, the road that Captain Crouch's most trusted hand was traveling was a private ranch road. It was his business to know who was riding around in his employer's pasture at night. He hailed the rider. There was no response. He set spurs to his horse to overtake the trespasser, and, without hard running, was soon close upon him. He saw — saw plainly — that the horse ahead was dun-colored with an extra wide black stripe down his back. "He's a *bayo coyote* striped like Jeff Cassidy's mustang," Otis reflected.

Near the top of the hill he was actually by the stranger's side; neither spoke a word, and Otis could not get a view of the rider's face. Then suddenly the stranger pulled out of the road into some half-open ground and headed straight for a stark, dead mesquite tree, the trunk of which was exceptionally large. Otis knew that tree; he recalled how one evening about dusk while he was driving a bunch of saddle horses over Loma Escondida, something — he did not see what — jumped out of this very tree and stampeded the *remuda* so that they ran two miles before he could get around them.

He saw something now that he did not believe. He saw horse and rider head into the tree — straight into it — and disappear. The ground beyond was open enough that anything traversing it would have been plainly visible.

He pulled up his horse and looked, just looked. Like most other range men, he had a prosaic head that refused to harbor ghosts and other such superstitions common among the Mexicans. He guessed maybe he had been half asleep and did not know it. Yet he could not have been mistaken about seeing the man down by his horse, back there in the road, the man mounting and riding off, the dun horse with a black stripe, extra black and extra wide down his back to the root of his tail. All the details were clear.

He rode on now to get the coffee, got it, answered a few questions about the cow work, and started back.

He rode absorbed in perplexity over the strange rider and horse. He determined to investigate the mesquite tree into which they had vanished. Once he turned in his saddle to look behind him, and down a straight stretch of the road saw a coyote following. Off in the brush he heard now and then the lonely wail of other coyotes; he liked to hear them.

True to its name, Loma Escondida did not reveal itself until he was at it, and then Otis saw something that made him know he had not dreamed the rider on the *bayo coyote*. There he was, trotting his horse leisurely up the hill, going in the opposite direction from what he had been going when seen earlier in the night. Otis reined up. He heard distinctly the sound of the dun's hoofs on the dry, hard ground. Those very material sounds made him realize that some trick had been played on him, and he resolved to end the mystery. He knew that his Trigeño could put up a hot race, even if the race led clear to camp on the Leona; and if it came to running in the brush, he wore his regular protection of ducking jacket and leather leggins and he considered himself second to no man in skill as a brush popper.

Vamonos! The stranger was a full hundred yards ahead, up the hill. For a minute he continued the leisurely trot, but when Otis had lessened the interval by half he saw the man ahead of him strike into a run. Now the squat top of the hill was reached; Otis was gaining. He was not more than twenty yards behind. They were coming to the half-opening into which the mysterious rider had before turned out of the road. Here he suddenly turned again. Otis was not surprised. In less time than it takes to draw a six-shooter he had the horn string around his rope loose and a loop shaken out.

"*Ahaha!*" he yelled. "Damn you, if I can't catch you, I'll rope you." But he was too late. Just as he prepared to cast his loop, the pursued rider and horse disappeared into the dead mesquite. There was no sound of impact. Otis himself dodged under a low-hanging limb of the old tree so as to be upon the tricky stranger on the other side. On the other side was nothing but bush, moonlight, vacancy, silence.

Otis got down and led his horse up to the old mesquite. The first episode had been a surprise. The second, with every sense of the observer alert and expectant, was overwhelming.

"Has somebody put peyote in my frijoles to make me see things?" Otis asked himself aloud, for he was determined not to be awed. Then he answered the question with "No, and I haven't been smoking marihuana either."

He determined to give the tree a thorough examination. First he bent over to look at the ground around it. The moon, still high, revealed nothing but his own horse's tracks. The tree itself, though dead, was far from rotten. However, his eye caught a long groove in it. He felt the groove with his hands. It had been made with an ax long ago.

With face averted he was slowly circling the old trunk when his boot caught on a flat rock. It was in shadow and he lit a match to examine more closely for other marks on that side of the tree. Glancing down, he noticed a dull glint of metal. He picked it up, lit another match; it was a twenty-dollar gold piece.

If there was one coin, there must be several. In order to clear the ground for closer inspection, Otis lifted the rock out of place. He hardly needed the light of a match to see what now lay exposed. It was a pair of old saddle pockets. They were so rotten that they almost fell apart when he picked them up. Several coins fell out.

"Jeff Cassidy's gold right where the Newton boys hid it!" Otis exclaimed aloud.

He was not excited. He never got excited. Calmly he went to his saddle, took down the sack, emptied all the coffee into one end of it, and then secured his find in the other end, having taken off his undershirt and wrapped it tight around the coins to prevent their jingling. Counting them could wait.

When he got into camp on the Leona, it still wasn't daylight, but Captain Crouch and the *cocinero* were up and a fire was going.

"I've shore been wanting that coffee," the Captain greeted him. "The water's been biling half an hour."

"Well, here it is," Otis spoke low, at the same time dismounting. Untying one end of the sack, he emptied the brown coffee beans into an empty lard can provided by the cook. "Coffee's already roasted," he said. "Hurry up, *cocinero,* and make music on that coffee grinder."

The Captain and the cook were too intent on coffee to notice what Otis did with the sack, which happened to be his own property.

General Mexhuira's Ghost

A FULL hour after our leisurely and rather late breakfast, Dr. Black and I walked to a certain number on the Avenida Cinco de Mayo. A *mozo* conducted us into one of those cavernous rooms of stateliness and perpetual discomfort that the hidalgos erected. Slinger, straight out of bed, met us in his pajamas. They were of the hue and texture of those blanket-sized red silk bandannas imported from the Orient, the design on them the Quetzalcoatl — the plumed serpent of the Aztecs — and as he moved, the serpents seemed to writhe. Thus appareled, wearing sandals of brilliant blue straw, in his mouth a freshly lighted black cigarette of opiate fumes, his scraggy eyebrows and tousled hair snow-white, he appeared as bizarre as his surroundings. I could not for some time concentrate my observation on either.

The enormous room, as cold as an underground cell, without stove, gas or fireplace, a huge old brass brazier by the writing table appearing to serve merely as another antiquity, was lined with rawhide-bound books that had been branded by monks of Spanish times and with bales of manuscripts, some of them parchment, that had been gathered from abandoned sacristies and uprooted *científico* libraries over half of Mexico. Some of the shelves were heaped with terra cotta heads and figures common to Aztec ruins; among them reposed stone gods of the same ancient people. Stone artifacts and figures cluttered the floor about the walls. One that drew my attention particularly was a jade-green stone shaped somewhat like a half-egg and carved with the ubiquitous Quetzalcoatl. In this room Slinger slept and sometimes ate as well as read. As Dr. Black and I shivered in our overcoats —in wintertime any spot of Mexico City out of the sun is as cold as a frozen eel — Slinger did not even bother to wrap himself in the Oaxaca blanket that lay ready on a chair beside his bed.

Something of an antiquarian by taste and a collector by virtue of the pack-rat instinct inherent in most men, he was a physician by profession and had spent thirty-five of his sixty-odd years practicing in "the Republic." It was through Black, who had been in medical school with him, that I received the invitation to inspect his collection. In particular I wanted to examine a manuscript said to be four centuries old and to contain a description of certain tombs and bones of giants exhumed by conquistadores while digging for Aztec gold.

I had heard of Dr. Slinger, one of the legendary oddities of Mexico. I had heard how for years before her death he never allowed his wife to come into the room he occupied — though the remainder of the house allowed her ample domain to wander through. I had heard people whose lives he had saved, so they said, swear by his skill and extol his kind heart. I had heard how at times he went off from a lucrative practice to live with Indians and absorb their herb lore. Members of the American colony in Mexico City generally had, it seemed, more opportunities to talk about him than to talk with him. Most of them agreed that he had become Mexicanized; upper-class Mexicans said that he was Indianized; the Indians didn't say.

And now as I tried to take in the contents of the room, my eyes were arrested by a single large photograph, framed in jet-black wood inlaid with bone, that sat on top of a cabinet. The eyes of the man in the photograph drew me towards them.

When I glanced at Dr. Slinger to make inquiry, his eyes were boring into me, but he waited for the question.

"That is General Mexhuira," he answered.

"I never heard of him," I said.

"Quite possible," he replied, "but, for all that, he was the gamest general of the revolution. He was the best friend I ever had. He died in my arms."

"Where was he from?"

"Oaxaca."

I knew that Slinger had practiced in Oaxaca before coming to Mexico City. It required little urging to learn more about General Mexhuira.

"He was in charge of the revolutionary forces of Oaxaca," Slinger went on. "Nobody else could have handled the Indians as he handled them. I was his chief surgeon. In fact, when the fighting was hottest I was his only surgeon. After one battle, in twenty-four hours' time, I operated on eight hundred men."

"But, Dr. Slinger," interposed his medical friend, "that sounds incredible, humanly impossible."

"Oh, I'll admit," Slinger laughed, "that some of the operations were hasty. A lot of the wounded would have died anyway. It was like administering extreme unction. I got so damned exhausted cutting and cutting that finally I had a *mozo* strap my body to his. He supported me and held me up while I went on using my arms to cut. I wouldn't have gone through what I did for anybody but Mexhuira.

"As everybody knows, when the Revolutionists finally won out, the country was still divided among local leaders. Villa was still out in the north; to the west the followers of murdered Zapata remained unreconciled; the oil companies around Tampico were paying another general to protect them; and Mexhuira held out too. But the fighting was mostly over. There wasn't enough money left in Oaxaca to support a doctor, and I withdrew from the army and came up to Mexico City and opened the office I have now. Everybody was watched in those days. For that matter, I am still watched. More than one Indian trying to smuggle a stone god or something like that in to me has been killed.

"Well, I had not been here long when a government agent called on me to use my influence to persuade Mexhuira to give up. I thought it was the best thing for him to do. I received absolute promises that he would be safe physically, and then I went down to see him. He was a little fellow, weighing less than a hundred pounds. The force in a man's veins, the energy of his spirit, the activity of his mind, the light in his eyes don't weigh on metal scales, you know. He embraced me, trusted my judgment, promised to come up to Mexico City right away and make his peace with the powers.

"He kept his promise. He was met at the station by a whole corps of staff officers, was conducted to the President's palace, served a banquet, and then for two weeks wined and dined like a visiting king — which he was. I saw him nearly every day, and I saw him going to pieces. He never had been a city man; he was man of the *campo*, a native of the wildest sierras. He was so aboriginal that when he started out he had the Mexican eagle on his flag clawing a plumed serpent instead of the rattlesnake. This Quetzalcoatl reached clear across the flag. Some Indian had worked it into the cloth for Mexhuira. It was like a sign in the sky for drawing his followers, and he himself had such a belief in it that he would not have gone into battle without it.

"One afternoon I was summoned to the hospital, and there I found Mexhuira in a paroxysm of pain. He was absolute master of himself, however. He told me he had been poisoned, and after examining him I had no doubt of the fact. I don't go around publishing this opinion. Such suffering as his could not last. When his pain was at its worst, I held him in my arms as I would hold a child, and thus he died.

"I saw attendants lay him out, and then I came home and came into this room to read and try to throw off my depression of spirit. I had lost, as I have already told you, the best friend of my life. For maybe an hour I had been trying to read — and I always use strong lights — when I heard a slight noise. Looking up, I saw Mexhuira.

" 'What are you doing here?' I said.

" 'I have come to say good-by and to make a request,' he answered.

"He was standing in front of me and I reached out to grasp his hand. I could not feel it. Then I passed my hand through his body without feeling it. Yet he looked natural and his voice sounded natural.

" 'No,' he said, 'you cannot feel my body. I am dead, nothing but a spirit. The request I make is this: that you educate my two sons and see that they get a square start in life; that you guard my daughter until she is married; and that you act as adviser to my wife. You will need money to fulfill such a guardianship.'

"Then he told me to go to a certain number on a certain street.

There I was to knock. An Aztec Indian would appear. This I wondered at, for Mexhuira was himself a Mixteco. Anyway, I was to give this Indian the password, a word in his tongue that you would not remember if I repeated it to you. 'Whatever money you require will be delivered to you,' Mexhuira said.

"I promised him on my soul to care for his wife and children. Then we talked for a long while about various matters. He told me that since dying he had learned the absolute facts about his poisoning, and he detailed the circumstances, not omitting names of politicians. A little before daybreak he said he must go. 'I have to be back with my body,' he explained. Then he came nearer and put his arms around me. Though I cannot swear that I felt them, I seemed to feel them. With a 'May God go with you,' he was gone.

"The newspapers had long accounts of the sudden death of General Mexhuira with the usual pictures of the corpse and with comments on his frail body. The President proclaimed national mourning and sent his condolences both to Mexhuira's family and his native state. After that he was buried with military pomp, as a national hero, here in the nation's capital.

"I had a good practice and was kept busy. Now and then I heard an echo of dissatisfaction from the south, where the Indians, it seemed, wanted their Mexhuira back. Then I read that the government had decided to take up the body and move it to Oaxaca. In all of this I was not consulted. I am getting ahead of the order of events, however.

"The day after I saw Mexhuira buried, I directed my chauffeur to drive me to the house where I was to get the money. The street was so little known that we had to go to police headquarters to learn its direction. It proved to be away out on the edge of town. I knocked at the number; it was over a closed door to a run-down adobe building. A blanketed Indian opened — old, silent, erect. Though polite in his salutation, he looked at me searchingly. I merely gave the password.

"'How much do you want?' he asked.

"'Five thousand in gold.'

"'Does it have to be all in gold?'

"'Yes,' I said, 'it needs to be all in gold.'

"'Very well,' he said, 'come back at the hour of the deer [dusk] and the gold will be ready.'

"I was back just as night was about to fall. The old Indian invited me in. The house was as bare as any Indian house. He closed the door. Then he delivered a heavy bag made of dressed pigskin.

"'There is one other thing you are to have,' he said. With that he indicated a jade-looking rock carved with the plumed serpent and shaped something like a half-egg."

At these words my eyes turned to the stone I had already noticed.

"Yes, that is it," Slinger said.

"Slinger," Dr. Black broke in, "I did not know that you drank those mezcal cocktails before breakfast."

"I don't," he answered vigorously. "You can smell my breath if you want to."

My companion not only smelt his breath but felt his pulse. He told me later that he could detect no evidence of alcohol.

"Go on," I said.

Slinger went on.

"The old Indian volunteered that the green rock had come out of the Buried City of Mexico — *La Ciudad Enterrada.* I suppose you have heard of it. All the natives in Mexico know about it, how it lies enchanted and how it holds more riches than Montezuma or Cortés ever dreamed of. The old Aztec knew somehow about my interest in antiquities, and he asked if I'd like to see the city. I did see it — but all that belongs at another place. I did not ask where the money came from. In utter darkness, not a light on the street, the Indian carried it and the stone to the car, where my chauffeur waited. I brought them both home, and at once began spending the money on Mexhuira's family.

"And now to get back to the removal of Mexhuira's body to Oaxaca. I read that there was to be a military escort. About twelve o'clock on the day that the body was to be conducted out of the city, I was performing a minor operation in a room adjoining my office. The window of this room, overlooking the Avenida Cinco de Mayo, was open. A nurse was assisting me. I had just given the patient, a man, a local anesthetic when, of a sudden, we all heard a blare of military music. Military bands and parades are far from uncommon in Mexico City, as you know, and it was only with a mild curiosity that I stepped to the window to look out.

"What was passing was the funeral cortege of General Mexhuira. The black coffin, draped with flags, was on a caisson. Then Mexhuira himself floated into the window. When he did, the nurse fainted and the man rolled off the operating table in a faint also. I am sure that I alone heard my friend's words.

" 'I know you were not expecting me,' he said, 'and I have only a minute to stay. They are taking me back home where I belong. There I'll be at rest. I have come to give the last farewell.' Then he thanked me for the way in which I was taking care of his family, told me again that when I needed money the old Indian would furnish it, gave me a final *abrazo*, and floated out the window. I saw him float over the crowds in the street, rest a moment on the caisson, wave me an *adiós*, and disappear into the coffin. You may think it strange, and I thought it damned strange, that while the nurse and the man to be operated on saw him, no one in the street seemed aware of his presence. After a bit the nurse came to, and with her help I finished with the patient. I could have cut his liver out, he was so thoroughly unconscious.

"That was the last I ever saw of Mexhuira. His boys I kept for several years at a school in Pennsylvania. With a suitable education each of them now has an excellent position. The girl I kept in a private school — not a damned convent oozing out superstitions — here in Mexico City, and she is well married. She has begun having babies and won't have time from now on to be unhappy. The widow lived well provided for until last year, when she died.

"No, I never took a centavo from the old Atzec that I did not spend on the family. I'll be honest and say I knew Mexhuira, both alive and dead, too well to misuse any of the money.

"And now," Slinger concluded in his hearty voice, "we'll examine that material on the ancient giants of Mexico. I am sorry that the room seems cold. After a man has run with the Indians down here as much as I have, his nerves and senses go to recording stimuli in a different way."

"Before we take up the giants, Dr. Slinger," I said, trying to keep my teeth from chattering, "I wish you'd finish what you started to say about that green rock."

"Oh, yes, that rock. Well, when I went back to have the old Aztec guide me to the Buried City of Mexico, he made me swear all kinds of oaths of secrecy. And don't imagine for a minute that the watch kept over a man after he has sworn an Indian oath and been made partner to an Indian secret is just fiction stuff. I know.

"I was blindfolded — even if that's fiction stuff also. All I know about the course we took is that we went out of the Aztec's house by the back door, which opens into a big walled-in yard. He seemed to lead me down a tunnel.

"When the blinds were taken off me, we were on the edge of a street paved with cobblestones and lined with squat rock houses. The fronts of these houses were so becarved with plumed serpents and other serpentined beasts and the light was pulsing in such a way that you might have imagined you were looking down on one of those conventions of rattlesnakes the Indians tell about. They say that sometimes hundreds and

hundreds and thousands of snakes come writhing and crawling together, usually in some canyon, and there twist into a solid mass that keeps on twisting. Those plumed serpents on the houses and temples of the Buried City had been fixed there, in stone, for thousands of years; yet somehow the light made them seem to be moving. I could not for the life of me make out where the light came from. It actually looked as if it were coming out of the eyes of the carved snakes. I saw hundreds of jade stones the size and shape of this, carved in the same way. This is the only proof I have of what I tell you. I used to think I'd like to possess some of the riches of that *Ciudad Enterrada,* and reveal its existence, after all these centuries still only legendary, to the world. Maybe it's having become an Indian myself that has killed such ambitions dead, maybe it's the years."

At this juncture a servant brought up Dr. Slinger's breakfast, which he at once set about prefacing with mezcal cocktails for the company as well as for himself.

"Maybe it's Mexhuira cocktails," Dr. Black suggested.

"They belong to the country," Slinger observed.

I did not learn a single fact from the manuscript about the giants of ancient Mexico. The Buried City of Enchantment never was supposed to be documented.

Midas on a Goatskin

H E'S the second sorriest white man in town," my host said.
"The sorriest white man keeps a Mexican woman without mar-
rying her, but Dee Davis lawfully wedded his. He's town scavenger, works at night, sleeps most of the day. He'll probably be
awake 'long about four o'clock this evening and more than ready
to tell you the kind of yarns you want to hear."

We found Dee Davis just waking from his siesta. He occupied
a one-room shack and sat on a goatskin in the door, on the shady
side of the house.

"I'm a great hand for goatskins," he said. "They make good
setting and they make good pallets."

I sat in a board-bottomed chair out on the hard, swept
ground, shaded by an umbrella-China tree as well as by the
wall. The shack was set back in a yard fenced with barbed wire.
Within the same enclosure but farther towards the front was a
little frame house occupied by Dee Davis's Mexican wife and
their four children. The yard, or patio, was gay with red and
orange zinnias and blue morning-glories. Out in a ramshackle
picket corral to the rear a boy was playing with a burro.

"No, mister," went on Dee Davis, who had got strung out in

no time, "I don't reckon anything ever would have come of my dad's picking up those silver bars if it hadn't of been for a surveyor over in Del Rio.

"You see, Pa and Uncle Ben were frontiersmen of the old style and while they'd had a lot of experiences — yes, mister, a lot of experiences — they didn't know a thing about minerals. Well, along back in the eighties they took up some state land on Mud Creek and begun trying to farm a little. Mud Creek's east of Del Rio. The old Spanish crossing on Mud was worn deep and washed bad, but it was still used a little. One day not long after an awful rain, a reg'lar gully-washer and fence-lifter, Pa and Uncle Ben started to town. They were going down into the creek when, by heifers, what should show up right square in the old trail but the corner of some sort of metal bar. They got down out of their buggy and pried the bar out and then three other bars. The stuff was so heavy that after they put it in the buggy they had to walk and lead the horse. Instead of going on into town with it, they went back home. They turned it over to Ma and then more or less forgot all about it, I guess — just went on struggling for a living.

"At that time I was still a kid and was away from home working for the San Antonio Land and Cattle Company, but I happened to ride in just a few days after the find. The old man and Uncle Ben never mentioned it, but Ma was so proud she was nearly busting, and as soon as I got inside the house she said she wanted to show me something. On a wide bed in one of the rooms was an old-timey covering that came down to the floor. She carried me to this bed, pulled up part of the cover, and told me to look. I looked, and, by heifers, there was bars as big as hogs. Yes, mister, as big as hogs.

"Nothing was done, however. We were a long ways from any kind of buying center and never saw anybody. As I said in the beginning, I don't know how long those bars might have stayed right there under that bed if it hadn't been for the surveyor. I won't call his name, because he's still alive and enjoying the fruits of his visit. Pa was a mighty interesting talker, and this surveyor used to come to see him just to hear him talk. Sometimes he got information on original survey lines. Pa had hunted mustang cattle over the whole country before there were any surveys. On one visit the surveyor stayed all night and slept on the bed that hid the bars. One of his shoes got under the bed, and the next morning in stooping down to get it he saw the bars. At least that's the explanation he gave. Then, of course, he got the whole story as to how the bars came to be there and where they were dug up.

" 'What you going to do with 'em?' he asked.

" 'Oh, I don't know,' Pa says. 'Nothing much, I guess. Ma here figgers the stuff might be silver, but I don't know what it is. More'n likely it's not anything worth having.'

" 'Well,' says the surveyor, 'you'd better let me get it assayed. I'm going down to Piedras Negras in my waggin next week and can take it along as well as not.'

"The upshot was that he took all the bars. Two or three months later when Pa saw him and asked him how the assay turned out, he kinder laughed and says, 'Aw pshaw, 'twan't nothing but babbitting.' Then he went on to explain how he'd left the whole caboodle down there to Piedras Negras because it wasn't worth hauling back.

"Well, it wasn't but a short time before we noticed this surveyor, who had been dog poor, was building a good house and buying land. He always seemed to have money and went right up. Also, he quit coming round to visit his old friend. Yes, mister, quit coming round.

"Some years went by and Pa died. The country had been

consider'bly fenced up, though it's nothing but a ranch country yet, and the roads were changed. I was still follering cows, over in Old Mexico a good part of the time. Nobody was left out on Mud Creek. Uncle Ben had moved to Del Rio. One day when I was in there I asked him if he could go back to the old trail crossing on Mud. The idea of them bars and of there being more where they come from seemed to stick in my head.

" 'Sure, I can go to the crossing,' says Uncle Ben. 'It's right on the old Spanish Trail. Furthermore, it's plainly marked by the ruins of an old house on the east bank.'

" 'Well,' says I, 'we'll go over there sometime when we have a day to spare.'

"Finally, two or three years later, we got off. First we went up to the ruins of the house. About all left of it was a tumble-down stick-and-mud chimney.

"Uncle Ben and Pa, you understand, found the bars right down the bank from this place. Just across the creek, on the side next to Del Rio, was a motte of *palo blanco* (hackberry) trees. The day was awfully hot and we crossed back over there to eat our dinner under the shade and rest up a little before we dug any. About the time we got out horses staked, I noticed a little cloud in the northwest. In less than an hour it was raining pitchforks and bobtailed heifer yearlings, and Mud Creek was tearing down with enough water to swim a steamboat. There was nothing for us to do but go back to Del Rio.

"I've never been back to hunt those bars since. That was close to forty year ago. A good part of that time I've been raising a family, but my youngest boy — the one out there fooling with the burro — is nine years old now. As soon as he's twelve and able to root for himself a little, I'm going back into that country and make several investigations."

Dee Davis shifted his position on the goatskin.

"My eyes won't stand much light," he explained. "I've worked so long at night that I can see better in the darkness than in sunlight."

I noticed that his eyes were weak, but they had a strange light in them. It was very pleasant as we sat there in the shade, by the bright zinnias and the soft morning-glories. Pretty soon Dee Davis would have to milk his cow and then in the dark do his work as scavenger for the town. Still there was no hurry. Dee Davis's mind was far away from scavenger filth. He went on.

"You see, the old Spanish trail crossed over into Texas from Mexico at the mouth of the Pecos River, came on east, circling Seminole Hill just west of Devil's River, on across Mud Creek, and then finally to San Antonio. From there it went to New Orleans. It was the route used by the *antiguos* for carrying their gold and silver out of Mexico to New Orleans. The country was full of Indians; it's still full of dead Spaniards and of bullion and bags of money that the Indians captured and buried or caused the original owners to bury.

"Seminole Hill hides a lot of that treasure. They say that a big jag of Quantrill's loot is located about Seminole too, but I never took much stock in this guerrilla treasure. But listen, mister, and I'll tell you about something I do take consider'ble stock in.

"Last winter an old Mexican *pastor* named Santiago was staying here in town with some of his *parientes*. He's a little bit kin to my wife. Now, about nine tenths of the time a sheepherder don't have a thing to do but explore every cave and examine every rock his sheep get close to. Santiago had a dog that did most of the actual herding. Well, two years ago this fall he was herding sheep about Seminole Hill.

"According to his story — and I don't doubt his word — he

went pirooting into a cave one day and stepped right on top of more money than he'd ever seen before all put together. It was just laying there on the floor, some of it stacked up and some of it scattered around every which way. He begun to gather some of it up and had put three pieces in his *hato* — a kind of wallet, you know, that *pastores* carry their provisions in — when he heard the terriblest noise behind him he had ever heard in all his born days. He said it was like the sounds of trace-chains rattling, and dried cowhides being drug at the end of a rope, and panther yells, and the groans of a dying man all mixed up. He was scared half out of his skin. He got out of the cave as fast as his legs would carry him.

"An hour or so later, when he'd kinder collected his wits, he discovered three of the coins still in his *hato*. They were old square 'dobe dollars like the Spanish used to make. As soon as he got a chance, he took them to Villa Acuña across the river from Del Rio, and there a barkeeper traded him three bottles of beer and three silver dollars, American, for them.

"Well, you know how superstitious Mexicans are. Wild horses couldn't drag old Santiago back inside that cave, but he promised to take me out there and show me the mouth of it. We were just waiting for milder weather when somebody sent in here and got him to herd sheep. Maybe he'll be back this winter. If he is, we'll go out to the cave. It won't take but a day."

Dee Davis rolled another cigarette from his supply of Black Horse leaf tobacco and corn shucks. His Mexican wife, plump and easygoing, came out into the yard and began watering the flowers from a tin can. He hardly noticed her, though as he glanced in her direction he seemed to inhale his smoke with a trifle more of deliberation. He was a spare man, and gray mustaches that drooped in Western sheriff style hid only partly a certain nervousness of the facial muscles; yet his few gestures and low voice were as deliberate — and as natural — as the flop of a burro's ears.

"What I'd rather get at than Santiago's cave," he resumed, "is that old smelter across the Rio Grande in Mexico just below the mouth of the Pecos. That smelter wasn't put there to grind corn on, or to boil frijoles in, or to roast goat ribs over, or anything like that. No, mister, not for anything like that.

"It's kinder under a bluff that fronts the river. I know one ranchman who had an expert mining engineer with him, and they spent a whole week exploring up and down the bluff and back in the mountains. I could of told them in a minute that the mine was not above the mouth of the Pecos. If it had of been above, the trails made by miners carrying *parihuelas* could still be seen. I've peered over every foot of that ground and not a *parihuela* trace is there. You don't know what a *parihuela* is? Well, it's a kind of hod, shaped like a stretcher, with a pair of handles in front and a pair behind so two men can carry it. That's what the slave Indians carried ore on.

"No, sir, the mine that supplied that smelter — and it was a big mine — was below the mouth of the Pecos. It's covered up now by a bed of gravel that has probably washed in there during the last eighty or ninety years. All a man has to do to uncover the shaft is to take a few teams and scrapers and clear out the gravel. The mouth of the shaft will then be as plain as daylight. That will take a little capital. You ought to do this. I wish you would. All I want is a third for my information.

"Now, there is an old lost mine away back in the Santa Rosa Mountains that the Mexicans called El Lipano. The story goes that the Lipan Indians used to work it. It was gold and as rich as twenty-dollar gold pieces. El Lipano didn't have no smelter. The Lipans didn't need one.

"And I want to tell you that those Lipan Indians could smell gold as far as a hungry coyote can smell fresh liver. Yes, mister, they could smell it. One time out there in the Big Bend an old-timey Lipan came to D. C. Bourland's ranch and says to him, 'Show me the *tinaja* I'm looking for and I'll show you the gold.' He got down on his hands and knees and showed how his people used to pound out gold ornaments in the rock *tinajas* across the Rio Grande from Reagan Canyon. Of course the holes in the rock had to be dry for that; it's not often in that part of the country they ain't dry.

"Now that long bluff overlooking the lost mine in the gravel I was just speaking about hides something worth while. I guess maybe you never met old Uncle Dick Sanders. I met him the first time while I was driving through the Indian Territory up the trail to Dodge. He was government interpreter for the Comanche Indians at Fort Sill and was a great hombre among them.

"Well, several years ago an old, old Comanche who was dying sent for Uncle Dick.

" 'I'm dying,' the Comanche says. 'I want nothing more on this earth. You can do nothing for me. But you have been a true friend to me and my people. Before I leave, I want to do you a favor.'

"Then the old Indian, as Uncle Dick Sanders reported the facts to me, went on to tell how when he was a young buck he was with a party raiding horses below the Rio Grande. They raided regularly, claimed they let the rancheros down there live to raise horses for them. He said that while they were on a long bluff just south of the river they saw a Spanish cart train winding among the mountains. The soldiers to guard it were riding ahead, and while they were going down into a canyon out of sight, the Comanches made a dash, cut off three *carretas*, and killed the drivers.

"There wasn't a thing in the *carretas* but rawhide bags full of gold and silver coins. Well, this disgusted the Comanches mightily. Yes, mister, disgusted them. They might make an ornament out of a coin now and then, but they didn't know how to trade with money. They traded with buffalo robes and horses.

"So what they did now with the rawhide sacks was to cut them open and pour the gold and silver into some deep cracks they happened to notice in the long bluff. Two or three of the sacks, though, they brought over to this side of the Rio Grande and hid in a hole. Then they piled rocks over the hole. This place was between two forks, the old Comanche said, one a running river walled with rock and the other a deep, dry canyon. Not far below where the canyon emptied into the river, the river itself emptied into the Rio Grande. Now rivers in this country, as you know, are about as scarce as bankers in heaven. Yes, mister, as bankers in heaven.

"After the Comanche got through explaining to Uncle Dick Sanders, he asked for a lump of charcoal and a dressed deerskin. Then he drew on the skin a sketch of the Rio Grande, the bluffs to the south, a stream with a west prong coming in from the north, and the place of the buried coins. Of course he didn't put names on the map. The only name he knew was Rio Grande del Norte. When Sanders came down here looking for the Comanche stuff, of course he brought the map with him and he showed it to me. The charcoal lines had splotched until you could hardly trace them, but Uncle Dick Sanders had got an Indian to trace them over with a kind of greenish paint.

"He had some sort of theory that the Comanche had mistook the Frio River for the Rio Grande. Naturally he hadn't got very far in locating the ground, much less money. He was disgusted with the whole business. Told me I could use his information and have whatever I found. I'm satisfied that Devil's River and Painted Cave Canyon are the forks that the Indians hid the *maletas* of money between, and the long bluff on the south side of the Rio Grande where they poured coins into the chinks is the same bluff I've been talking about."

Dee Davis got up, reached for a stick, squatted on the ground, and outlined the deerskin map that Uncle Dick Sanders had shown him. Then he sat down again on the goatskin and contemplated the map in silence. To him it was one of the indelible realities of life — far more real than his scavenger cart, or the one banker in town, or the several preachers.

It was wonderfully pleasant sitting there in the shade, the shadows growing longer and the evening growing cooler, listening — whether to Dee Davis or to a hummingbird in the morning-glories. I did not want the tales to stop. I remarked that I had just been out in the Big Bend country and had camped on Reagan Canyon, trailing down a story on the Lost Nigger Mine. I didn't add that I never looked for gold itself, only gold stories. I expected that Dee Davis would know something about the famous lode of the Big Bend.

"Now listen," he interposed in his soft voice, "I don't expect you to tell me all you know about the Lost Nigger Mine, and I know some things I can't tell you. You'll understand that. You see I was *vaciero* for a string of *pastores* in that very country and got a good deal farther into the mountains, I guess, than any of the Reagans ever got. You may not believe me, but I'll swear on a stack of Bibles as high as your head that I can lead you straight to the Seminole who found the mine. Of course I can't tell you where he is. You'll understand that. It was this away.

"One morning the Reagans sent Bill Kelley — that's the nigger's name — to hunt a horse that had got away with the saddle on. A few hours later Jim Reagan rode up on the nigger and asked him if he had found the horse.

" 'No, sah,' he says, 'but jes' looky here, Mister Jim, I'se foun' a gold mine.'

" 'Damn your soul,' says Jim Reagan, 'we're not paying you to hunt gold mines. Pull your freight and bring in that horse.'

"Yes, mister, that's the way Jim Reagan took the news of the greatest gold mine that's ever been found in the Southwest — but he repented a million times afterwards.

"I've knowed a lot of men who looked for the Lost Nigger Mine. Not one of them has gone to the right place. One other thing I will tell you. Go to that round mountain down in the *vegas* on the Mexican side just opposite the old Reagan camp. They call this mountain El Diablo, also Niggerhead; some call it El Capitan. Well, about halfway up it is a kind of shelf, or mesa, maybe two acres wide. On this shelf close back against the mountain wall is a *chapote* bush. Look under that *chapote* and you'll see a hole about the size of an old-timey dug well. Look down this hole and you'll see an old ladder — the kind made without nails, rungs tied on the poles with rawhide and the fiber of Spanish dagger. Well, right by that hole, back a little and sorter hid behind the *chapote,* I once upon a time found a *macapal.* I guess you want me to tell you what that is. It's a kind of basket Mexican miners used to carry up their ore. It's fastened on the head and shoulders.

"Now, I never heard of a *macapal* being used to haul water up in. And I didn't see any water in that hole. No, mister, I didn't see any water.

"As I said, as soon as my boy gets to be twelve years old — he's nine now — I'm going out in that country and use some of the knowledge I've been accumulating."

Dee Davis leaned over and began lacing the brogan shoes on his stockingless feet. It was about time for him to begin work. But I was loath to leave. How pleasant it was there! "The second sorriest white man in town?" It seemed to me then, and it seems to me still, that there are many ways of living worse than the way of this village scavenger with a soft goatskin to sit on, and aromatic Black Horse tobacco to inhale leisurely through a clean white shuck, and bright zinnias and blue morning-glories in the dooryard, and long siestas while the shadows of evening lengthen to soften the light of day, and an easygoing Mexican wife, and playing around a patient burro out in the corral, an urchin who will be twelve *mañana*, as it were, and then . . . Then silver bars out of Mud Creek as big as hogs — and heaps of old square 'dobe dollars in Santiago's cave on Seminole Hill — and Uncle Dick Sanders's gold in the chinks of the long bluff across the Rio Grande — and somewhere in the gravel down under the bluff a rich mine that a few mules and scrapers might uncover in a day — and, maybe so, the golden Lipano out in the Santa Rosas beyond — and, certainly and above all, the great Lost Nigger Mine of free gold far up the Rio Bravo in the solitude of the Big Bend.

Ironies

A Machete with a History

THIS was not the kind of cow camp familiar in the States. No chuck wagon or pack mules carried bedding, cooking utensils, provisions. Probably not one of the vaqueros had ever been in a tent. Unhampered by things, each could tie blanket on saddle, stuff scant rations and cup into his *morral* — the fiber bag carried at the saddle horn — and be off instantly. Their horses were trained to whirl inward the moment the rider lifted foot for the stirrup and to leave in a rush: there may be times when a rider in wild country needs to get away quick.

These men — always eager for company from beyond — were butchering a brindle bull when I rode up. I needed no urging to camp with them. While we ate ribs roasted on fresh-cut spits stuck slantwise into the ground against the fire, coals were heating a hole that had been dug in the earth. After it was well heated, the head of the brindle bull, hide still covering it, wrapped in long grass bound with Spanish dagger fiber, was placed in the homemade fireless cooker and covered with hot earth, over which coals were placed.

During supper nobody said much, but I had already singled out the aging vaquero whom the younger ones called Don Inocencio. Him I was to come to know better than I know most men. In certain ways he justified his name. In other ways he was more sophisticated than innocent. He never admitted to me that he could not read; even if he could not, he knew more about his world than most university professors know about theirs, and his knowledge was always refreshing. Early in life he had been a muleteer, but most of his years he had been a vaquero. For three of them he had been with the *rurales* — the mounted police of Mexico organized under President Díaz — and this experience accounted not only for his wide knowledge of trails and ranches in the whole north country but also, in part, for his conservatism. In walking he appeared lame in both legs, but he was merely stiff. He wore thigh-high leggins, whereas most of the other vaqueros wore leather or rawhide *chivarras* coming to the waist and supported by a belt. His voice was very soft and his eye as clear as a child's.

After he had eaten, he pulled from its long scabbard the knife with which he had stabbed the bull and began whetting it on a stone evidently carried for the purpose. The knife-handle was of horn carved into the neck and head of an eagle.

"A potent knife," I remarked.

"Yes, *señor*," one of the vaqueros spoke out, "and it has a name and it has a history."

"What is its name?" I addressed the question to the man who had given me an opportunity to ask it.

"The Faithful Lover," he answered with a laugh. "Read what it says for itself."

The speaker chunked the fire into a blaze and very modestly Inocencio allowed me to turn the blade so that the inscriptions upon it could be deciphered. They were stamped in crudely but plainly: on one side, *"Yo te amo"* (I love you); on the other,

"A quien pica esta víbora
No hay remedio en la botica."
(For whomsoever this snake bites
There is no remedy in the shop.)

Now it happened that I carried in a scabbard on my saddle a machete I had procured in Oaxaca, where inheritors of the three-hundred-years-old secret of Toledo steel forge the best blades in the three Americas. Knowing how pleased nearly all human beings, and especially vaqueros, are with some novel object, particularly if it connects with their life, I went to my saddle and brought the beautiful machete.

Every individual in the group handled it admiringly, and two spelled out aloud the mottoes embossing the steel: *"To conquer me you need what the bamboo lacks," "Don't flock together, little doves, for here comes your hawk."*

"A certain *señor* presented Pancho Villa with a machete maintaining mottoes more *bravos* than these," said one.

"How?"

" *'I am the friend of guts'* and *'Get ready, lice, for the comb.'* "

"Before robbers of the Villa party took it away," Don Inocencio said, "there was a machete at the Hacienda of the Five Wounds bearing this, *'Now is when the mint is about to season the soup.'* "

"Oh," exclaimed another vaquero, "the sayings on blades are as many as the stars that light up San Pedro's Road." (The Milky Way.)

"Tell some saying you like," I suggested.

"Come on, bedbug, to the bite." There was a laugh at this countryism and the giver of it added, *"Saco tripas"* (I get the guts).

" 'Give me the kiss of love,' " put in another vaquero without explanation. Then, stimulated by attention, he called out, " 'I am the cock that sings with joy when he gets up.' 'Don't wrinkle yourself, old hide: I want you for a drum.' "

"Now this machete of mine," I said, "is a virgin without a name and it has no history. I am waiting for that of the Faithful Lover."

"The matter is not personal with Don Inocencio," spoke the vaquero who had introduced the older man's knife.

"No, it is not personal," Inocencio answered. "I will speak. During the times of revolution, Destiny took me above the mouth of the Río Soto la Marina, there in the Huasteca. For a while we kept camp in a pueblo where the men fished and where there was a priest. He was a good man but he always went by rules in books. He was an *Italiano*.

"One day while some women were washing clothes at the edge of the water, a boy waded out to catch a horse-of-the-devil with red wings. The creature skimmed farther out and the boy followed. He was just playing. All this the mother later told. She heard a scream and saw a shark cutting him in two. She rushed to the rescue, but all she got was the legs and part of the trunk of the child. Poor little one! Poor little mother! Poor little father!"

"*Pobrecitos!*" came voices of other vaqueros out of a silence as profound as the night.

"The father," Inocencio continued, "was in his house a little way off. I was talking to him at the very moment when the cries of the women came to us. He grabbed his machete. It was always at his hand. When he got to the water and saw what was left of the boy, he ran for the priest.

"The priest came at once. He was not fat. He had no smile. He was straight, straight, like a pine tree, no bend in his body.

He looked at the pieces of the child. 'It is not possible,' he said, 'for the church to perform rites over this. The head is gone, the heart is gone. The home of the soul is not here, and it is for the soul that the church acts.'

" 'Oh, *padre*,' the father of the boy said, 'I will pay all I have, my burro, my house, my skiff, and hooks.'

" 'No, it is not possible.'

"Then this father turned to the mother. 'Show me exactly where the shark was.' She pointed and threw a rock to indicate. He did not say a word. He first pulled off his shirt. He wore no shoes. The *calzones* were all he had on. Then with his knife he cut off a leg from the corpse and threw it into the water at the spot where the rock had fallen. He knew that the shark, hungry for more, was hunting, waiting.

"As he cast the bait, he began walking toward it, his eyes searching, his machete arm ready. He was not disappointed. The shallow water compelled the shark to show part of his body as he grabbed the leg. The man with the machete was against him. I could not say how long the two fought. I was without power to help. Every person there looking stood like a stone. It was naked knife against naked teeth. The water showed streaks of blood, but in the end the shark was dead. The man hauled him to the bank and slashed his belly open. There the head and heart of the boy showed themselves. They were white and partly gone but they were plain.

"The straight priest had not said a word during all this time, not one little word. Now he said, 'The church will bury the child.'

" 'Thanks be to God,' the father said.

"But that was not all," Inocencio concluded. "Those people of the Huasteca are not like us. A long time ago they prayed to the Shark God. That night the shark eater of *cristianos* was stretched out on rocks and wood was placed all over him. Then while the fire burned, the people danced around and around the carcass, one old man beating a drum and all of them singing strange words."

"And so this is the knife that killed the shark?" I asked.

"Sí, señor. For a favor the slayer gave it to me."

This favor, I judged, was a matter "personal" to the narrator.

When I lay down on my pallet, the vaqueros about the low fire were still talking, their habitually low voices diffusing into night's stillness. While early next morning, having, in Parkman's phrase, "performed my ablutions," I was walking towards the fire, Inocencio met me with a tin plate bearing, along with some of the brains, the choicest morsel of the bull's head — the eyes.

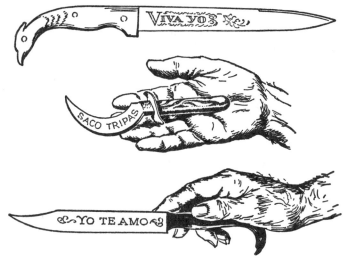

"Have you ever eaten such?" he asked.

"No," I said, for I did not want to deprive him of his triumph.

"Ah," he exclaimed, his own eyes kindling with the pleasure of one who luxuriates in pleasing, "they eat divinely well. Thus we people of the ranches are like the *zopilotes* (buzzards), which consider the eye the greatest delicacy in a carcass and always eat it first."

Godmother Death and the Herb of Life

T H E one symbol of vanished power, property, importance, of principality itself, that the ruined inhabiter of the ruined hacienda retained was the maker of his personal cigarettes. She was old, old, more than a hundred years old, "older than fire itself," it was said, and here at the Hacienda of the Five Wounds her cigarettes marked the passing of time as softly as any sundial numbering only the hours that are serene ever marked them in some old-world garden of flowers and sunshine.

Before the little old woman's cigarettes were ready for her *patrón* to inhale, the black leaf tobacco and the corn shucks in which it was rolled had been curing for two years. A year more or less meant nothing to her — or to him. She seemed to take more care with the shucks than with the tobacco. They were home-raised, not imported from Portugal as certain *hacendados* of the swelling times of Don Porfirio Díaz used to import them. The ancient *cigarrera* would pick the shucks for soft grain, pliability, whiteness; she would moisten them with water and dry them in the shade; she would scrape them, and then with brandy moisten and remoisten them, turning them every so of-

ten, until at last they were cured to suit her. The process was a
ritual.

She delivered the cigarettes in little round bundles, each tied
with shuck string, every *cigarro* tightly rolled, the shuck twisted
into a point at one end and doubled back at the other. It was a
formula with Don Marcelo to bite off the doubled end, unroll
the shuck very, very slowly, and reroll it. He was generous to his
friends, and one of them now asserts that no manufactured paper adds to the flavor of tobacco as does a well-selected, well-
cured shuck.

The most ardently pious of all pious — ritually, at least —
people on the hacienda was the old cigarette woman. She was
quixotically religious, always saluting in the antique manner, instead of saying simply *"buenos días"* invariably using the cere-
monious "May God give you a good day," and so on. On account
of her extreme age, she was popularly regarded as being a
miramuerte, one who sees death (*muerte*) coming from afar.

The room in which she ate, slept, and made cigarettes was a
cavern-like corner of what was once a monastery but long before
Mexico separated from Spain had been turned into a stable.
Once when by accident I learned how she craved a little sugar
I gave her a twenty-centavo piece. That was the first time she
prayed for me the "Prayer to the Just Judge." She had strong
dislikes, strongest of all against an herbwoman of the hacienda.

"Only fools who are the sons of fools," she shrilled one day,
"could imagine that this old witch of a *curandera,* this ungraced
one, with her herbs, her burnt bones, her dried cow dung and
the like can cheat Death. Not even the godson of Death could
cheat her."

"I did not know that Death ever had a godson," I said.

"Why not?" The beldame's voice sank downward toward the

level of memories. "It is a *cuento* come down from the ones who have passed."

It proved to be not a very long *cuento*, but the palsy-voiced *cigarrera* took, it seemed to me, nearly as long to tell it as it takes for a young man in love with life to learn that he himself is not immortal. It seemed to me that she might be Death herself talking. I remember that after she had done and I had been silent a long time, I said, "This seems impossible."

"*No es imposible,*" she answered. "The Devil knows a great deal because he is the Devil but more because he is old."

The thing she told has mulled in me so long and has become so much a part of my own imagination that I should be dishonest did I claim that what I now put down is exactly what I heard. Nevertheless this story of Godmother Death is a true chapter, a chapter of reality, out of the pages of the long, long storybook — with "pictures and conversations" — that I turned through before I rode away from the Hacienda of the Five Wounds forever:

The single-roomed *jacal* in which Pablo, his wife, and four children ate and slept was under the mountain far out from the city. They did not eat much, often not even tortillas, and Pablo ate least of all. Had any man hired Pablo he would have been obliged to feed him for a week in order to produce strength for a day's work. But he neither sought the wage of bread nor was sought by it; and as day by day, in sunshine and in shadow, he crouched with sombrero on head and head on knees, the life-sense pulsed on in him.

Now it was the Day of the Dead — that day when all of Mexico toasts Death herself and, familiarly, without fear, because she is seen so often, makes her a comrade. In pul-

que shops men were drinking out of goblets shaped like skulls;
in humble homes women were setting out, for those who have
"ceased to be," the big-loafed "bread of the dead"; in the market
booths vendors were eagerly offering toy hearses, jumping-jack
skeletons, and doll corpses that leaped out of coffins at the pull
of a string. Into the graveyards throngs were carrying the yellow
"flower of the dead," there to spend the day burning candles
and drinking wine in honor of the silent host beneath the sod,
spreading over tombs picnic lunches from which the children
would merrily devour sweets cut in the forms of urns, cross-
bones, and death's-heads, while balladists sang and peddled
broadsides displaying the skull as both clown and king.

And on this morning of the Festival of the Dead, Pablo and
his wife Concha found themselves the parents of another child.
It was their tenth, but five of them were in the *campo santo* —
and did not have to be fed. The father and the mother took
counsel as to who should be the new one's godmother. It was a
boy. They spoke of this woman and of that woman, but neither
could arrive at a decision with himself or herself, much less with
the other. Only they were agreed that the *madrina* chosen must
be just and merciful and, if God were willing, potent.

Then Pablo said: "This day the whole world is astir to do
honor to Death. I will go out upon the road towards the city
and find a *madrina*."

"Yes, go," Concha said, "and remember that it is a boy.
Choose well for justice and mercy and power to help. Perhaps,
too, you may find some crumbs of the *pan para los muertos*
that I may eat and give milk."

So Pablo went out. He had not traveled far before he was
overtaken by a carriage carrying, as he recognized, the wife of
the owner of the hacienda on which by sufferance his hut stood.
The woman was beautifully dressed, and this morning she

shone with the light of charity. She bade her driver halt the carriage.

"Good morning, *señor*," she said in politeness. "Who are you?"

"*Buenos días, señora*," he answered, his hat off. "I am the father of a newborn child, a male."

"Then you are seeking a *madrina*?"

"Yes," he answered, "I am looking for a godmother."

"I will act as *madrina* for your child."

For a moment Pablo hesitated, while the memories of generations went through his mind. Then, "No," he answered, "you have so much that you will not care for more. You are like God. You give to those who already have much; from those who have nothing you take away. While it is in your power to be just, you idly watch the poor man slave all his life, his family starving and the rich oppressor growing richer. No, I thank you, *señora*, but I cannot choose you for a godmother."

The rich woman drove proudly on and Pablo followed in the dust. A long way down the road by a scummy hole of water in a solitary place of rocks he saw another woman, afoot as he was, dressed in dirty rags as he was dressed. While he paused to drink, she arose from her knees, on which she had bent to lap the water.

"*Buenos días, señora*," he said.

"Good morning, *señor*," she responded. "Ave María Purisima of the Refuge."

It was evident that she was the most humble of the folk who call themselves *humilde*, and when she gave the salutation of the Virgin Mary, Pablo gravely gave back "In grace conceived without original sin."

"And who are you?" she asked.

"I am the poor father of a newborn and am seeking for him a godmother."

"Oh," she said, "I am but a beggar woman, but I have eaten of the bread that brings to Christian souls pity and charity. My soul glorifies the Savior. I will stand as *madrina* for your little boy."

Pablo's heart was touched; yet again he hesitated. "But, no," he slowly answered. "You are merciful and you would do what you could, but as this world goes there is no potency in lowliness and poverty. I seek for my son's future and I cannot choose you. My heart gives thanks. Now go with God."

So the two parted. Then coming into a heavy wood, Pablo encountered a third person. She was all wrapped so that not even her lips could be seen, and she moved evenly as if she were used to going where she willed.

"Buenos días, señora," he said.

"Good morning, *señor,*" she responded. *"Soy la Muerte.* I am Death, and you are a poor man looking for a godmother to your son. I will be his godmother."

"Dark One," he answered, "I thought I should encounter you on this Day of the Dead. Yet every day is your day. I know you well and you I accept for my son's godmother. I accept because you alone are impartial and treat all equally, the rich and the poor, the young and the old, the high and the low, the ugly and the beautiful, the valiant and the cowardly, the weak and the strong. You take them all with you. When there is no other to relieve wretchedness, you end it. You grant to toiling slaves release and rest. You dry tears and stop hunger. In your ways of justice and mercy you are the only friend of the poor, and you are most powerful of all powers. You, then, I choose as *madrina* for my child."

"Go in peace," Death said. "In season I will come to perform my duties."

Then Pablo went home and told his wife Concha how he had found a godmother just and merciful and potent, and how in season she would come to help them. Then, if not in happiness, in something like peace Concha slept.

True to her promise, the *madrina* came one day to the little *jacal* to visit her *compadres* and take counsel with them concerning her godchild. In his thin face he had shining eyes. His name was Favián. When the *madrina* looked upon him, she said, "With permission I will take this child into the *campo*. I will keep him and care for him and teach him to be a healer. I will instruct him in the ways of life and death."

So the *madrina* took Favián out into the countryside. Under her care he throve and grew. Very early she began teaching him the secrets of all the herbs of the *campo* so that by the time he was of age he knew every *remedio* the land afforded.

When he was eighteen years old, she said to him, "I have taught you the uses of all the plants of the *campo*; no other *curandera* of the land knows so much. Now I am going to make you a gift. Look! This herb is called *la Yerba de la Vida* — the Herb of Life. Only I know where it grows. All the other herbs you can gather for yourself, but only from me can you procure this. If you are obedient and use it according to my instructions, you will be happy. With it you will be able to cure all kinds of sickness in all kinds of people. It will not fail. Yet you must reserve it for extreme cases and often withhold it for the sake of charity. Also this one thing you must always remember. When you see me at the foot of the bed, do not offer *la Yerba de la Vida,* for when I stand thus, I have come to claim my own. Only your bright eyes and the dimming eyes of the one I have come to take will see me, but to you both I will be plain. Now my care as *madrina* is ended. Go your way."

It was destiny that a strong and comely young man so sage as Favián should soon be in great repute. He went by day and by night into hovels; he answered calls from big houses far distant. When he could not go, patients were brought to him. Always he used the Herb of Life with discretion. He was not mercenary and he was happy in doing good. To the people he was Favián de los Remedios.

Then one day a runner came saying that the Great Cacique of the land lay dying, that none of the court doctors could benefit him, and that Favián was called. The messenger added that the desire of the Great Cacique for life was so intense that he had promised the hand of the princess to whoever should heal him.

Favián went at once. In the outer court of the palace he saw only anxiety and grief. The Great Cacique was a good ruler and just. He was sinking fast. Favián was the last hope.

As he was rushing on through the long corridor leading to the dying king's chamber, he met the princess. He did not have to be told who she was; she did not have to be told who he was. She was beautiful like the sky, like flowers after a rain; her skin was as smooth as the grass under sunshine when seen far away, the curves of her body blended softness into firmness like the swell of waters drawn by an even tide. He was strong and straight, both kindness and power in his features, the lush vigor of youth in every motion of his body.

"Oh, save him for me," she said, the tones of life-giving and of life-hungering in her voice.

"I will save him for myself," Favián said, and he strode on feeling that he could tread down legions.

It was a case for no common herb. As Favián neared the bed, he drew from his wallet the bottle containing the elixir of the Herb of Life.

"A cup," he said to an attendant.

At that instant his eye fell upon the shrouded figure he knew so well standing at the foot of the bed, invisible to others but in silent eloquence looming before him as vivid as the flaming torch of an Indian running in dark night. Only for an instant did Favián pause.

"The air, the air!" he cried. "The Great Cacique is suffocating! Ventilation! Turn the bed around so that the royal one's head will be at the window!"

As quick as the command, the bed was turned — and La Muerte no longer stood at its foot. Death was cheated. The Herb of Life brought recovery.

That evening Godmother Death appeared to Favián, just for a minute. "You have disobeyed me," she said. "The next time the bed will not turn from me. Remember." Then she was gone.

Immediately the Great Cacique prepared to keep his word, and the palace was gay with preparations for the wedding of the princess to the savior of her father.

Now Favián no longer went like a benediction with his *remedios* into the hovels of suffering. The court in which he moved was for the time free from pain and sickness. The realm in which he was burgeoning rapt him beyond all things, all thoughts mundane. He had touched the hand of the princess and grown faint, and once when the softness of her breast brushed his arm he was dissolved into ecstasy. He had scented the aroma of her hair, the perfume of her breath. In what must have been but a dream his own lips on her ripe lips tasted the nectar of life that makes youth burst to pour out life itself.

In the way of lovers they gave each other special names. Out of his knowledge and experience he made one for her — Flower of Life, for the plant exists for the flower and the flower is the quintessence of the herb. And because, as she said, he had made her radiant and because he was the restorer, she called him simply Life.

He needed no sleep. For him all food was dross. He was more exuberant than the white-winged *zenzontle* that in the dawning darts straight up from the highest twig of the highest tree and then pitches straight down, singing, singing, singing. When he walked, his feet hungered to press against the juices of spring grasses and wild red begonias. He gathered petals of roses to strew for her to step upon, and for him the lightest print of her foot in the sand was too lovely for the elements ever to obliterate. He owned the whole world, but all the roses and jewels and beautiful things in it were not enough for one small gift to her who was above heaven and earth. With a prodigality as easy as an actor's gesture he would have flung away his own life for her; without a qualm he would have crucified all mankind in order to remain alive to love her. Death might beleaguer the world — a world as unreal and as far away as prenatal existence — but without thinking of the matter at all he was conscious of being immortal.

And so for Favián, no longer of the Remedios, the days approaching the bridal morning were flying by. And then without warning, without reason, the sun stood still, the earth ceased to revolve, the air that all human beings must breathe withdrew. The princess was sick, sick unto death.

Not even a horse ever forgets what he has learned. Favián the lover remembered Favián of the Remedies, remembered Godmother Death and her gift.

As he came into the sick room, the face on the pillow lighted. He knelt and took her hand. It was cold.

"Flower of my Life, I will make you well and you will yet be mine."

"Oh, Life," she faltered, her smile still gallant, "but your hand is warm."

There may have been other people in the room, but neither saw them. Then, the mist over his eyes, Favián arose and drew the bottle containing the elixir of the Herb of Life. It had never failed and there was the promise of the Power of Powers that it would never fail.

At this instant Favián heard a gasp. The imploring eyes of the princess were fixed on him, but one finger of her right hand pointed towards the foot of the bed.

La Muerte stood immobile. Only as if to enjoin silence, and at the same time to enforce a finality against all appeal, whether of man or the combined forces of eternity, she slowly raised her hand with the palm held open in front.

But Favián would not be silent. "*La Yerba de la Vida!*" he cried. "Oh, Flower of Life, drink quick!"

Quicker than his cry he had jerked the stopper from the bottle and was thrusting it forward. Then as if wrenched by some unseen force, it slid from his grasp and dashed to a thousand pieces on the tiled floor. When he looked up, the shrouded figure had vanished, and with her all the flowers that had ever blossomed in the world for Favián.

No Blue Bowl for Panchito

T H E S E two *compadres,* each godfather to the other's son, were burro drivers, making their living bringing down wood from the mountain to sell in town. Their lives were not marred by envy or ambition. One day Pedro came to his *compadre's* house to find him beating Panchito, his little godson.

"But, *compadre,*" he called out, "why are you thus without mercy lashing our Panchito?"

"I'll tell you why," replied the burro driver. "Here I have been making plans for the time when I am rich. I will have a cow. She will give so much milk that we will have all we can drink and all the cheese we can eat. Besides that, we will have cheese to sell. We will have money to throw away like rocks. One thing I will buy will be a blue bowl. It will be a beautiful bowl, as blue as the sky, with little painted figures on it coming up to the rim so that they can look over inside at the beautiful white milk.

"And here, *compadre,* I have been telling my sons how the beautiful blue bowl full of milk will be set on the board with Panchito on one side of it and Juanito on the other side of it. Panchito can drink out of his side of the blue bowl and Juanito can drink out of his side. But listen! This burro of a Pancho, so heady he is, stands braced like a bull calf against drinking out of the blue bowl with his brother. No, he will not drink. He does not like the blue bowl. Now, *compadre,* you comprehend with what reason I beat him."

Whence These Tales Have Come

UNLESS otherwise noted, the narratives composing the present volume are from my books published by Little, Brown and Company of Boston — for this writer, at least, the most generous and genial publishers in the world.

Everything in the first section, The Longhorn Breed, is from *The Longhorns* (1941), except the final Tom O'Connor episode, which is from an essay entitled "The Writer and His Region" published by *The Southwest Review* in 1950.

The second section, Mustangs and Mustangers, is derived from *The Mustangs* (1952) with the exception of "The Headless Horseman of the Mustangs" out of *Tales of Old-Time Texas* (1955).

In the third section, The Saga of the Saddle, "The Marqués de Aguayo's Vengeance" comes from *Tongues of the Monte* (1935); the other stories are from *The Mustangs*.

"Tom Gilroy's Fiddler" was printed for their 1958 Christmas greeting by Bertha and Frank Dobie. The Wilbarger, Bigfoot Wallace, Sam Bass, and "Yaller Bread" stories in this section, Characters and Happenings of Long Ago, are from *Tales of Old-Time Texas*, with two brief additions from Frank Dobie's

Sunday column that has been appearing since September, 1939, in several Texas newspapers. Isom Like's "taller" prescription for longevity and Rufus Byler's explanation of his bald head are out of *The Longhorns*. The drouth anecdotes are from *Tales of Old-Time Texas*. "Esau the Hunter" is from *The Ben Lilly Legend* (1950).

The coyote stories in the section, Animals of the Wild, are from *The Voice of the Coyote* (1949). "The Panther's Scream" and "Baby-Hungry" are from *Tales of Old-Time Texas*, while "Befriended by a Panther" and "Bear Nights in Mexico" are from *Tongues of the Monte*; "Pablo Romero Roped a Bear," "The Bear Who Fattened His Own Pork," and "Diamond Bill, Confederate Ally" are from *Tales of Old-Time Texas*.

In the section, In Realms of Gold, "The Broken Metate," "The Rider of Loma Escondida," and "Midas on a Goatskin" are from *Coronado's Children* (1930); "In a Drouth Crack" and "The Mezcala Man" are from *Tales of Old-Time Texas*; "Where the Gleam Led Captain Cooney," "Pedro Loco," and "General Mexhuira's Ghost" are from *Apache Gold and Yaqui Silver* (1939).

In Ironies, "A Machete with a History" and "Godmother Death and the Herb of Life" are from *Tongues of the Monte*. "No Blue Bowl for Panchito" is from "Charm in Mexican Folk Tales," in *Publications*, XXIV (1951), of the Texas Folklore Society.

Glossary of Spanish-Mexican Words

Glossary of Spanish-Mexican Words

abrazo an embrace
antiguos the ancients
arriero muleteer
asadero a soft cheese, shaped like a pancake
barbaridad, qué barbaridad! what a barbarity! what outlandishness!
bayo coyote dun with a dark stripe down the back (horse color)
brasada brush land
buenos días good morning
caballada band of horses (see *remuda*)
cabestro rope woven of horsehair (mane or tail or both) used to stake
    (tether) horses on prairie
calabaza cushaw
calzones breeches
camino real royal road, public road
campo country
campo santo graveyard
canicula dog days
carreta cart
cenizo an ash-colored bush
centavo cent, penny

chapote Mexican persimmon

chiltipiquín wild Mexican pepper

chivarras leather leggins, chaps

cholla a species of cactus

científico literally, scientific, but the word denotes an intellectual

cigarrera cigarette maker

cigarro cigarette

cocinero cook

compadre close friend; godfather

con permiso with permission

contento contented

cristiano Christian; the word sometimes denotes human in contrast to animal

cuento story

curandera herbwoman, a curer

derrotero chart, waybill

diablo devil

frijoles beans

golondrino swallow

granjeno species of brush

grullo sandhill crane; crane-colored horse

guajillo a bush acacia

guayule wild rubber plant

hacendado owner of a hacienda, ranch, plantation

hato wallet

hombre man; as exclamation, "man alive!"

humilde humble, humble one

infierno hell

jacal hut, cabin

javelina peccary

ladino wild; an outlaw animal

lechuguilla a low-growing agave

león lion; in Spanish-America, the puma, panther, also called Mexican lion

macapal basket or bag carried from forehead

madrina godmother

maleta bag, valise

manada band of mares and colts dominated by one stallion; the social unit among mustangs, also of early day horse-raisers in Mexico and the Southwest

mas allá farther on

mesteña, mesteño mustang

metate stone (usually of lava) on which corn is ground with a *mano* (stone) into *masa* (dough) for the making of tortillas

mezcal alcoholic drink made from either maguey or the mezcal plant (kin to each other)

mezcla mixture of mud and straw

morral nose bag, often used for carrying things, the strings looped over the saddle horn

mozo servant; also, at times, guide

oidor literally, one who hears; a judge

pan para los muertos bread for the dead

parientes kinspeople

parihuela hod

pastor shepherd

patrón patron, protector, employer-protector

pial to rope by the hind feet or legs

por Dios a mild oath

posta place for changing horses, relay station

pulque an undistilled alcoholic drink made from sap of the maguey plant

ramada shed

remedio remedy

ratón rat

remuda unit of saddle, or cow, horses

remudero man in charge of a remuda; horse-wrangler

rico rich one

rural mounted police of Mexican frontiers

sotolero cutter of sotol, a yucca, used to feed cattle, also for fiber as well as to make the liquor called sotol

tinaja rock waterhole, a hole in rock, a water jar

tortilla a flat, thin pancake of unleavened ground-up corn

triste sad, lonesome, down-spirited

vaciero overseer and supplier of several shepherds

vamos, vamonos let us go

vaquero cowboy

vega flat, meadow

zenzontle mockingbird

zopilote buzzard

zurron rawhide bag, suspended from forehead, for carrying ore and other material